The Vine Remembers
French Vignerons Recall Their Past

SUNY SERIES IN MODERN EUROPEAN SOCIAL HISTORY
Leo A. Loubère, Editor

The Vine Remembers

FRENCH VIGNERONS RECALL THEIR PAST

Interviews undertaken by

Leo A. Loubère

Jean Sagnes   *Laura Frader*

Rémy Pech

State University of New York Press

ALBANY

Published by
State University of New York Press, Albany

© 1985 State University of New York

All rights reserved

Printed in the United States of America

No part of this book may be used or reproduced
in any manner whatsoever without written permission
except in the case of brief quotations embodied in
critical articles and reviews.

For information, address State University of New York
Press, State University Plaza, Albany, N.Y., 12246

Library of Congress Cataloging in Publication Data

Main entry under title:

The Vine Remembers

(SUNY series in European social history)
Bibliography: p.
Includes index.
1. Vineyard laborers—France—Interviews. 2. Wine industry—France—History—20th
century. 3. France—Rural conditions. I. Loubère, Leo A. II. Series: SUNY series on
European social history.
HD8039.V52F88   1984   305'.9634   84-49
ISBN 0-87395-914-0 (pbk.)
ISBN 0-87395-913-2

10   9   8   7   6   5   4   3   2   1

Contents

ONE HECTARE	=	2.47 ACRES
ONE LITER	=	1.05 QUARTS
ONE HECTOLITER	=	100 LITERS (26.4 GALLONS)
ONE FRANC	=	100 CENTIMES

List of Illustrations

INTERVIEW LOCATIONS

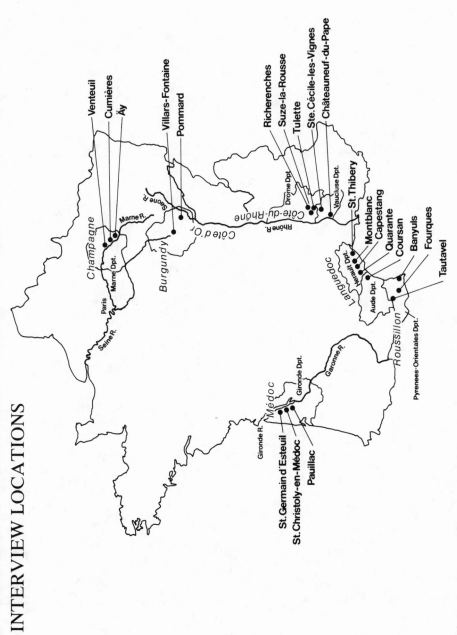

The interviews in this book took place in the above locations.

Introduction

SCHOLARS who study individuals in the past often wish it were possible to go back in time in order to discover what they were really like, especially ordinary people. Although government reports and vital statistics, newspaper accounts, and political sources are abundant for nineteenth and twentieth-century France, most ordinary people did not leave behind narrative descriptions of their daily lives and of the forces which shaped them. Those who have studied the people of the vine, the society and culture of winegrowing communities, are only too aware of this lack even for the more recent past.

Since the beginning of recorded history, men and women have celebrated victories ar drowned their sorrows with the fruits of the vine. Each year, millions of francs are spent on this salubrious beverage, prices at auctions of rare Bordeaux sometimes reaching thousands for merely one bottle of a rare old vintage. Yet what of the people who grew and produced it? Who were they? The *vignerons* or grape growers and workers of the nineteenth century have, of course, long since passed away. Their progeny, who are now in their old age, are also passing away, and thus far little attention has been paid to them. Indeed, neither historians nor sociologists have undertaken systematic studies of grape growers as people with a specific culture of their own. It is to fill this gap that we have turned to the individuals themselves, to hear their stories and understand their struggles, in their own words.

The interviews in this collection provide striking testimony of the variety of conditions among wineproducers and vineyard workers of the different wine regions of France. This marked variety is not a recent phenomenon but a result of historical developments that go back at least to the French Revolution of 1789, when a combination of geographic factors and human choices shaped the particular character of each region. In Burgundy, for example, certain landowners came to perceive their vineyards as symbolic extensions of their nobility and lofty aims; concentrating their investments on small properties along the Côte d'Or, they created wines whose high quality matched their own self-image. Their vineyards were small, rarely enclosing more than 4 hectares and sometimes less than one. Favored by Louis XIV, their wines had a reputation that grew until the name Burgundy became identified with exellence. In Champagne, the cultivation of fine grapes resulted primarily from the efforts of monks who owned large estates (as

1

they did also in Burgundy with the Clos de Vougeot) and of small, family growers. Property there has been highly divided until recently because the champagne firms that appeared in the eighteenth and nineteenth centuries bought grapes and made sparkling wine which they then marketed under their own labels. Both the large and small holdings acquired great value in time. During the French revolution of 1789, many of the larger estates were confiscated; enough land was put up for sale in both Burgundy and Champagne so that small farmers could acquire tiny plots, plots that in some cases became the focus of family ambition and were enlarged by the acquisitions of later generations. Several of our interviewees represent these later generations.

The wine of Bordeaux, or claret as the English call it, has also acquired a world reputation for quality, but its social history is different from that of either Burgundy or Champagne. In the Bordeaux region in the eighteenth and nineteenth centuries wealthy noble families, with large estates, improved the wine and then enhanced its reputation by making it a part of their *vie galante*. Those who wintered in Paris also served it as a suitable accompaniment to their gastronomic dinners. Small vineyards, of course, are numerous in the region, but the reputation of claret was made by and still depends on estates of considerable size, from fifty to one hundred and fifty hectares. Owners have only rarely resided on these properties, leaving management in the hands of experienced men like our interviewees.

Burgundy, Bordeaux, and Champagne have produced wines for the rich. For others, there are imitations of these wines, bottles wearing lables suggesting

Fig. 1 The best wine is aged in wood for one or more years, preferably oak as shown here in Châteauneuf-du-Pape. Courtesy of Photothèque ITV-M. Mackiewicz.

geographic parentage with the great, a device used by generations of lesser growers who have benefited from identification with the regions of the *grands crus*. Their marketing strategy has been remarkably successful and, despite the production of sizable amounts of mediocre wine alongside the finer wines, most of these growers have suffered fewer economic setbacks and enjoyed higher prices for lower quality produce. We are not suggesting that they are dishonest; rather that they have been resourceful. As a group they are serious people, knowlegable in the ways of production and markets, possessed of a keen sense of taste, a feeling of self-esteem that they earnestly project upon consumers, and a willingness to regulate and police themselves in order to create wines fit for kings.[1] Or at least kinglets. Although, on the whole, these growers have been prosperous, they are part of the national wine industry and are not immune to the weaknesses and crises of other sectors.

For the poor, there have been beverages of common quality, without any regional pretention save wholesomeness. Their history is part of that of the Mediterranean south, especially Languedoc and Roussillon, regions which more recently have begun to produce respectable wines of good quality, such as Fitou or Côtes du Roussillon. About 130 years ago, the peasants gradually abandoned the multiplicity of crops which had characterized their agriculture and concentrated all energies on the production of ordinary wines, or as it is put euphemistically, wines for immediate consumption. The building of railroads in the 1850s opened the huge markets of northern cities where numerous blue and white collar workers were able to afford this inexpensive drink with their meals.

To supply this market, both large and small growers planted extensive vineyards in the rich, fertile soil of the coastal plains, and for a few short years prosperity reigned. But a series of crises soon struck southern viticulture and plunged it into an economic turmoil from which it has yet to recover. Beginning in 1869, for almost two decades the phylloxera, a tiny root-sucking aphid, destroyed most of the southern vineyard until, in the 1880s, native vines were grafted onto American rootstock capable of resisting the aphids. With a wine-consuming public that was growing as industry expanded, the southern vignerons resorted to both mass production techniques and grape varieties capable of high yields, such as the Aramon.[2]

However, the population of France did not continue to grow, and its move to cities went on at a relatively slow pace. Consequently, southern wine was dependent upon a market that had reached its capacity as the century turned, and seven years later southern vignerons found themselves plunged into yet another crisis as a result of a glutted market and depressed prices. This time (1907) they took to rioting in the streets and organizing huge demonstrations in the large towns and cities of southern France. They were convinced that "false" wine made chiefly of raisins, chemicals, and water had flooded the market and brought prices down. By this time there was also a growing Algerian wine industry which had developed in the wake of the phylloxera and which had free access to metropolitan France.

Indeed, a wine crisis of massive proportions occurred everywhere because production of *vin ordinaire* had also begun to expand in regions renowned for

Fig. 2 A vine pruned as a goblet *(gobelet)*. Courtesy of Photothèque ITV-M. Mackiewicz.

better quality wines. In fact, great amounts of ordinary wine have always been produced in Bordeaux and Burgundy, two names that have come to symbolize vinicultural excellence; as their production increased, they so inundated the market that even their finer cousins, the great growths, felt the effects of lower prices. The plight of all growers was worsened by what economic historians refer to as the scissors effect: falling prices, on the one hand, and rising costs on the other. Vineyard expenses increased drastically as a result of grafting and the spread of various moulds, fungi, and diseases that attack European vines. To prevent their propagation, vineyards now required a regular schedule of powdering with sulphur and spraying with copper sulphate. Moreover, with their pursuit of high yields, growers shortened the life-span of their vines. Old vines give fewer grapes, even though their fruit makes better wine, but old stock was uprooted and replaced by new. In consequence the heavy cost of replanting faced each new generation.

   Growers of the Rhône River valley were by no means immune from these problems and had no clear ideas for their solution. Unfortunately we know very little about the conditions of life among growers in the Côtes-du-Rhône region, save that they were remarkably resourceful. They, like growers in Bordeaux,

Burgundy, and Champagne, were subject to periods of low prices and falling sales, but they seem to have been somewhat less harmed than the Mediterranean growers, perhaps because they did not turn to vineyard monoculture. Although grapes and wine constituted their cash crops, they also cultivated fruits as well as grains, excellent vegetables, and legumes. The soil on the valley floor is prime farm land and too rich for vines, which are located along slopes chiefly on the east bank and several miles from the river. Moreover, as family growers, their labor costs were minimal, and they were able to tighten their belts by spraying and cultivating their vines less aggressively than the coastal vignerons. This was equally true in other viticultural regions, such as Burgundy and Champagne, where small holdings predominated.

The mass production vineyards on the Mediterranean, however, left little land for other crops and required an extensive labor force to cultivate the sizable number of medium and large estates.[3] Several of our interviewees were part of the viticultural working class that characterized the lower south. Here, before the mechanization of viticulture, large land-owners, often absentee, resorted to wage workers on a far larger scale than was common in the smaller vineyards of Burgundy. In Bordeaux, large and medium owners also employed wage labor, on the basis of either crop-sharing, contractual arrangements for specific jobs, or an hourly wage system. Workers in all the finer vineyards enjoyed a more secure existence than those of employers bent on mass production for an uncertain market. The large-scale industrial viticulture of the lower south created and depended upon a rural proletariat that could be hired and fired as market conditions dictated. We shall see that some large owners, even absentees, were not indifferent to conditions among their workers, but the position of wage workers in the vineyard economy has changed over the years. Since World War II mechanization has spread rapidly everywhere, both on the large domains and on smaller family holdings; consequently the demand for wage labor has declined. In addition, on the large domains of the south, help is increasingly recruited from neighboring foreign countries rather than from the natives of France; Spanish, Portuguese and Italians as well as North Africans make up growing numbers of the labor force.

The mechanization which has made its way into the vineyards has not always done so without some ambivalence on the part of vignerons. Some of them have maintained, well into the present day, that no machine can perform as well as the human worker. Furthermore, on family holdings, the purchase of a tractor plus the equipment it requires greatly burdens a small budget. It is nonetheless true that whereas the older generation deplored having to resort to credit, the younger generation does so more willingly, sometimes wisely, sometimes foolishly. Typically, a father consents to the machine as one means of retaining a son on the land; he consents even to modernizing the cellar and house so as to attract a bride for his son, because departures from the land have been common among young women who are unwilling to face primitive living conditions and a life of economic uncertainty.[4] Abandonment of the family land, however, has not been effectively checked even by these changes, a point bemoaned by some of our elderly interviewees.

Fig. 3 Vines trained for mechanical picking. Courtesy of Photothèque ITV-M. Mackiewicz.

Young vignerons fled the land for the same reasons that polycultural peasants fled it: the low level of net income after years of labor, the hope that faded, and the terrible insecurity that constantly menaced every tiller of the soil. New cultural techniques, including the grafting of vines, have overcome some of the deficiencies of early viticulture; yields have risen, indeed have nearly doubled, from about twenty hectoliters per hectare to over forty as a national average by the eve of World War II. But, unlike cereals, yields of vines beyond a fixed level bring a decline in quality and, ineluctably, a decline of prices. This decline is aggravated by the rise of costs that are required to achieve higher yields. Such has been the growers' dilemma. Bearing this in mind, the reservations of some small growers about the immense purchase price and maintenance expenses of equipment such as a tractor become understandable. And they are all the more understandable when we remember that so many decisions to mechanize both in the vineyard and in the wine cellar had to be made by older men who had spent most of their lives behind a horse-drawn plow, with a reassuringly great muscular rump before their eyes, and that their hands had grown calloused from handling the vigneron's hoe. Their decision was their gift to the next generation.

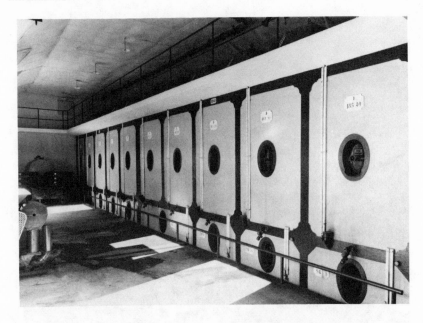

Fig. 4 Fermenting vats made of concrete with glass-lined interiors; a winery in Saint-Emilion. Courtesy of Photothèque ITV-M. Mackiewicz.

The persons whose remembrances make up this volume belong to three generations: that of 1910–14, that of 1940–45, and finally, that of 1975–80. The first generation, coming of age on the eve of World War I, was the progeny of those men and women who had suffered through the invasion of the phylloxera; it was also the generation that had witnessed the wine crisis resulting from low prices, overproduction and closed markets, whose intensity had aroused the Mediterranean south to riots of massive proportions, and although less painful elsewhere, left bankruptcies and frustration as part of the grapegrowers' heritage. Finally, it was the generation that turned over their recuperating vineyards to old men and to their wives and daughters, in order to fight in the blood-soaked trenches of the northeast in 1914. The Germans, in their mad advance, penetrated the magnificent vineyards of Champagne where artillery duels obliterated most of the recently planted vines, a full generation of labor blasted into heaps of ruin and death.[5] This was the generation, fewer in numbers, that came back to discover their vines half destroyed, as those who had been left behind to cultivate the soil lacked horses to draw plows and chemicals to protect the vines against the myriad insects that devoured their foliage and attacked their roots. Those who returned now had to replant large sectors of their land and, in Champagne, to fill in the bomb craters and level the surface as well.

After a brief interval of prosperity came the depression of the 1930s when massive harvests created such an excess of wine in an impoverished market that prices plummeted and there was a repeat of the crisis of 1900–1907. This time the government, driven by the initiative of a southern deputy, Edouard Barthe

Fig. 5 Pruning is winter work and the most delicate operation in vine culture. Courtesy of Photothèque ITV-M. Mackiewicz.

(1882–1949), responded with laws that forever put an end to the laissez-faire regime as regards grape cultivation and wine production. Legislation, such as the Statut de la Viticulture and the Code du Vin, now sought to limit the planting of new vineyards, to force distillation of excess wine, and to limit the quantity of wine available for wholesalers at any one time by spacing its release from producers' cellars in accordance with market needs.[6] From the most individualist to the most corporatist, such was the road along which necessity to survive was leading the vignerons and their political spokesmen.

This was also the generation that turned to cooperative wine-making, most intensively in areas which produce common table wine and to a much lesser degree, in areas of fine wine. We shall look at this phenomenon more closely in Chapter Five. Still, a combination of restrictive legislation and cooperation did not end the almost permanent crisis of the ordinary wine industry.

Crisis was the legacy of the second generation that came of age just before the German invasion of 1940. Once more, although they suffered less physical destruction than during World War I, French vineyards steadily deteriorated during

Fig. 6   Nearly all native European vines are grafted onto American root-stock. Here a
specialized team plants vines that have been grafted in hot-houses or nurseries.
Courtesy of Photothèque ITV-M. Mackiewicz.

the course of the war, because of insufficient tractive power, pesticides, and labor.
After the armistice, young vignerons bent their backs to replanting. Unfortunately,
in the south, they resorted to the same high-yield varieties, as well as hybrids,
and mass production strategies that had created the pre-war excesses. This behavior
led directly to the overproduction crisis of 1950-1955.[7]

Once more, growers appealed to the government for aid. It responded rapidly,
in 1953, with a new Code du Vin which encouraged uprooting vineyards, attempted
to raise the quality of wine by subsidizing the planting of superior grape varieties,
forced the distillation of excess production, and attempted to control the periodic
release of wine into the market. Like a bride's attire, there was something old
and something new. Producers of fine wines have benefited from legislation that
more or less controls the production of fraudulent wine, and from the ever rising
prices of their *grands crus*. The vignerons of Champagne have profited the most
from laws and professional arrangements that provide for quality control, price-
fixing for grapes, and guaranteed sale of grapes. With a hectare of prime vineland
selling for 800,000 francs ($145,000 before the 1981 devaluation by President
Mitterrand), family growers owning four or five hectares have become wealthy.
Those in Burgundy, Bordeaux and Châteauneuf-du-Pape are also well-to-do, while
the remainder of the Côtes-du-Rhône, where cooperation has spread, are only now
witnessing a rise in prices which surpasses their increasing costs of production.
At least their future looks bright for the youngest generation, whose style of life
rivals that of middle class urban youth.

Fig. 7   The vineyards of Champagne, Côte des Blancs.

For southern vignerons, however, the situation has been different. The loss of Algeria in 1962 was certainly a favorable step; for more than a century, Algerian wine had competed with southern wine on the French domestic market. The North Africans, who are forbidden wine by the Koran, replaced many of the massive vineyards that Frenchmen owned with the wheat fields they needed to improve their diet, and the flood of Algerian wine entering duty-free into France was reduced. This development, however, did not actually diminish the woes of southern vignerons.

Since the late 1960s, when France came under the Common Agricultural Policy of the European Economic Community, wines from southern Italy have entered the French market in even greater quantity than those from Algeria and now compete with French ordinary vintages. This competition and the southern French reactions to it have been the cause of almost yearly violent protests and demonstrations in the south, one of the most violent ending in the death of a police officer and a vigneron in Lower Languedoc in 1976.

These protests have blended with an awakened regionalism among the new generation. This indicates an upsurge of Occitanian consciousness among the thirty-one departments from Bordeaux to Nice where the Occitanian language has prevailed.[8] Occitania is a broad area comprising Languedoc as well as Provence, in fact much of France south of the Loire river. These authentic regionalists, many of whom are younger vignerons in the lower Midi, see in the government's policy of uprooting vines an effort to get rid not only of vines but of people who are themselves deeply rooted in the sun-scorched earth, and their rhetoric of protest reflects their love for their region and their desire to continue the life of the vine as their parents and grandparents have done.[9] *"Volem viure al pais!"* is their slogan in the *langue d'Oc* and means "We want to live in our region!" To be sure, this revolt of the South must be seen as an early development of a larger "rural revolution." [10] For farmers of all types have been seeking greater recognition of their needs since the 1930s. It is noteworthy, however, that vignerons, chiefly southerners, were the initiators of this movement.

The current dilemma of southern vignerons reflects the fact that since the mid-nineteenth century all vignerons have been less isolated than other French peasants; they have been well-integrated into the national market and consequently subject to the influence of national and international trade. As producers of a commodity sold chiefly in urban markets, they live close to arteries of commerce and are forced to look beyond their narrow environs. Even if they communicate among themselves in their native regional languages, French has long been the medium of their profession, and their major problem has continued to be one of resolving national policies in accordance with regional needs and concerns. About these they have much to say.

*

The present collection is squarely in the tradition of "oral history," a term that we use even though it is somewhat misleading. By the term we mean narrative and analytical writings based heavily if not exclusively on evidence gathered through interviews and conversations with persons who experienced the events or outlooks they are describing. This kind of written history, often looked upon by our colleagues with suspicion if not rejected outright, goes back to Herodotus, Thucydides, and Bede, and enjoys a noble lineage including Jules Michelet and H. H. Bancroft. This ancient tradition nonwithstanding, most historians remain attached to the dictum of C. V. Langlois and Charles Seignobos, in their *Introduction to the Study of History*, that the historian works with written documents, that without documents there can be no history.[11] History as it has been written until recent times has been narrowly conceived because the documents available have elucidated the political and religious affairs of illustrious men. We know little about the living and working conditions of grape growers, about their states of mind, precisely because the written evidence largely ignored them. Our colleagues of the future will have far richer sources, chiefly oral; indeed, given the growing number of interview projects, they may encounter the serious problem of an excess of data. They most certainly will if tape recordings are not transcribed and edited; it takes far more time to listen to a document then it does to read it. On the other hand, hearing the true voice of the individual often provides information that is lost in transcription, such as local accent, inflection, and the emphasis which denotes intent. At any rate, historians of the recent past must recognize that the age of the telephone and tape recorder has arrived and "a change in methods of communication . . . will in time bring about as important an alteration to the character of history as the manuscript, the printing press, and the archive have in the past.[12]

In recognition of this change, our collection offers the data that will be required for anyone interested in rural life. It is neither a narrative history nor a simple compilation of recalled events, raw and untouched. It has been edited to eliminate repetition and trivia and is organized thematically. Each chapter tells a story, or rather lets the growers tell their own story.

Its value is two-fold. First it provides sources of information that differ from those found in written or printed documents produced by functionaries in their official duties to investigate, to assess, to report. Interviews are truly personal sources and, as such, are more or less subjective, depending on the information and memory of the person. They are bits of autobiography, narratives of events that affected one or a few persons' lives, and provide information about impressions that remain in the mind. These recollections create sources that historians require to probe more deeply into the past.

Second, the personal interviews, as part of a large number that have been selected and organized thematically, provide a broad revelation of conditions and sensitivities, raising the personal *mémoire* to the level of the general. What appears unique in one grower's experience becomes part of the pattern of the outlook and actions of a broad social group. This has been our goal in this book, and we believe that its importance lies precisely in the multiplicity of outlooks. This is a method widely used in oral history.[13] Another method, no less important, concentrates on the recollections of one person.[14] It provides a richness of detailed personal experience that is not present in our collection. On the other hand, our larger representation adds to its value. The two really complement each other advantageously. Our work brings out the fact that there were several viticultural societies: that of great wines, that of lesser wines, and that of the in-between. The small grower in Champagne or Côte-d'Or, who may drive to his vines in a Mercedes, lives in a world notably different from that of a southern grower who lives from one crisis to the next. The need to gather this information became obvious to us when we were carrying out research on vignerons of the nineteenth century. They, of course, have all gone to their vineyards in the sky, and the information about their ways of life is far too scarce to give us their intimate portraits. Their progeny, who are now in their old age, are also passing away, and so far, little attention has been paid to them. Indeed, neither historians nor sociologists have undertaken systematic studies of grape growers as living beings with a culture of their own. Given the fact that this culture is changing, the living records of its earlier aspects are disappearing either through death or the weakening of memory.[15]

Our interviews were carried out mainly during 1978–1979; a few in 1973. Their purpose was clear from the beginning: to acquire first-hand information about the lives of grape and wine growers, chiefly older ones whose professional experiences covered three or more decades. This span of time seemed necessary in order to discover the changing conditions of life. For the young boy who began work at twelve or thirteen years of age during the 1920s or '30s, the transformations that followed World War II were full both of fright and of challenge. Reactions and styles of life evolved at unprecedented rates. The only comparable period was that of the phylloxera invasion from the 1870s to the 1890s. But that was a time of catastrophe. The more recent modifications have brought, at least for the successful growers, relief from back-breaking labor and a rising standard of living.

The choice of individuals to interview was in part the result of acquaintances made among vignerons after years of living in France. We are all students of French viticulture, wine economics, and politics in all their forms. Jean Sagnes and Rémy Pech both live in southern France and teach at the Université de Perpignan and the Université de Toulouse respectively. Both have studied seriously the development of viticultural capitalism and the workers' movements associated with it; both were indeed born into families of vignerons. Laura Levine Frader teaches history at Northeastern University in Boston. She has studied the village of Coursan in the Aude and has been particularly interested in the labor militancy of vineyard workers in the Aude, and in the women of the vine, their collective action and work. Leo Loubère has lived off and on in France and has spent many pleasant months traveling the wine roads and talking to winemen. In several cases he extended his acquaintances through the intermediary of regional societies of wine producers and merchants, the *comités interprofessionels.* He is particularly grateful to those of Champagne, Burgundy and Châteauneuf-du-Pape, who made special efforts to locate elderly growers famous for their long memories and who were active in viticultural organizations. He also owes a special debt to J. Mesnier of the Université du Vin at Suze-la-Rousse in Côtes-du-Rhône, and to Jean Nollevalle, former director of the Syndicat Général des Vignerons de Champagne. He is especially grateful to Irene and Arnold Meckel, who patiently transcribed two of the most difficult of the interviews and whose unstinting hospitality was invaluable for the completion of his part of this work. We should all like to name everyone who was helpful in this enterprise, but such a list would run to pages; therefore we limit ourselves to a general recognition of the aid and hospitality of those who have permitted us to share in their memories of viticultural life.

One further notice: the territories we covered do not include all the wine regions of France, but certainly the most important. From Médoc in the Bordelais, our paths covered Languedoc-Roussillon, the Côtes-du-Rhône, Burgundy, and Champagne. Since about eighty-five percent of all vignerons live in these regions, our sample is more than representative.

The present compendium of memoirs is a selection from a much larger tape library of several hundred hours. The tapes are presently located in the office of Leo Loubère, who is presently using them as sources for a narrative history of wine growing since 1914. They will eventually be placed in the archives of the State University of New York at Buffalo. For this book, we have chosen the most informative and most credible of them. A grant from the American Council of Learned Societies paid the costs of transcription, and we are grateful to Ms. Marie-Jose Perrot and Marie-France Carrera, whose abilities to deal with numerous and various accents in the course of transcribing interviews were invaluable.

1. For Bordeaux see Edmund Penning-Rowsell, *The Wine of Bordeaux* (New York, 1970); Charles Higounet, et al., *La Seigneurie et le vignoble de Château Latour* (Bordeaux, 1974), 2 vols.; René Pijassou, *Un Grand vignoble de qualité; Le Médoc* (Paris, 1981), 2 vols. For Burgundy see, Rolande Gadille, *Le Vignoble de la Côte Bourguignonne* (Paris, 1967); Robert Laurent, *Les Vignerons de la Côte-d'Or au XIXe siècle* (Dijon, 1958), 2 vols.; H. W. Yoxall, *The Wines of Burgundy* (New York, 1968). For the Beaujolais, Gilbert Garrier, *Paysans du Beaujolais et du Lyonnais, 1800-1970* (Grenoble, 1973), 2 vols. For the lower south, Gaston Galtier, *Le Vignoble du Languedoc méditerranéen et du Roussillon* (Montpellier, 1961), 3 vols. For general studies see, Paul Marrès, *La Vigne et le vin en France* (Paris, 1950), Leo Loubère, *The Red and the White. The History of Wine in France and Italy* (Albany, N.Y., 1978); Henri Enjalbert, *Histoire de la vigne et du vin* (Paris, 1975).

2. See Rémy Pech, *Entreprise viticole et capitalisme en Languedoc-Roussillon* (Toulouse, 1975).

3. Jean Sagnes, *Le Mouvement ouvrier du Languedoc* (Toulouse, 1980).

4. Marie Moscovici, "Le Changement social en milieu rural et le rôle des femmes," *Revue française de sociologie*, I (1960), 314-22.

5. Patrick Forbes, *Champagne, the Wine, the Land, the People* (London, 1967).

6. Charles K. Warner, *The Winegrowers of France and the Government since 1875* (Cambridge, Mass., 1960), chaps. 1-2; J. Sagnes, "Viticulture et politique: Edouard Barth, député de l'Hérault," in *Hommage à Robert Laurent* (Montpellier, 1982).

7. Institut du Vin de Consommation Courante, *IVCC, 1954-1964, Dix ans d'activités* (n.p., n.d.), pp. 9-35.

8. Jean Sagnes, *Le Midi rouge: Mythe et réalité* (Paris, 1982).

9. For southern regionalism see, Comités d'Action Viticoles, *La Révolte du Midi* (Paris, 1976), Michel Le Bris, *Occitanie: Volem viure* (Paris, 1974), Emmanuel Maffre-Baugé, *Vendanges amères* (Paris, 1976), J.R. Fontvieille, *Paure Miejour, Pauvre Midi, la révolte des vignerons, 1907-1977* (Paris, 1977).

10. See Gordon Wright, *Rural Revolution in France* (Stanford, Calif., 1964).

11. See Paul Thompson, *The Voice of the Past: Oral History* (Oxford, 1978), p. 47. This is the best study we have encountered on the methods and scope of oral history. Also useful is James Hoopes, *Oral History: An Introduction for Students* (Chapel Hill, North Carolina, 1979); David Henige, *Oral Historiography* (London, 1982).

12. Thompson, pp. 51-52.

13. Examples are Ronald Blythe, ed., *Akenfield, Portrait of an English Village* (New York, 1969), Studs Terkel, ed., *Hard Times, an Oral History of the Great Depression* (New York, 1970), Tamara Hareven and Randolph Langenbach, eds., *Amoskeag: Life and Work in an American Factory City* (New York, 1978); *Red Buffalo*, nos. 2-3 (1972); Alice and Staughton Lynd, eds., *Rank and File, Personal Histories by Working-Class Organizers* (Boston, 1973); George Ewart Evans, *Ask the Fellows Who Cut the Hay* (London, 1956).

14. This is the approach presently used in France. Pioneering collections are Léonce Chaleil, *La Mémoire du village* (Paris, 1977); Jean-Pierre Richardot, ed., *Papa Bréchard, vigneron du Beaujolais* (Paris, 1977); Louis Chapuis, *Vigneron en Bourgogne* (Paris, 1980).

15. The number of grapegrowers has been declining for some time. Those whose primary occupation is viticulture numbered 1,658,000 in 1935, but only 1,237,000 in 1965, and the number continues to go down. Some of our interviewees were quite advanced in years, and naturally the question has arisen: how accurate were their memories? Old age sometimes

weakens the capacity to recall events accurately. We are fully aware of this, but it is not a problem limited to oral sources; numerous written documents are also the elucubrations of old people. Paul Thompson has discussed this issue in some detail. See his Chapter 4 on evidence. Equally useful are William Cutler, "Accuracy in Oral History Interviewing," *Historical Methods Newsletters*, vol. 3, no. 3 (June 1970) 1–7. There are several articles dealing with this problem in the *Oral History Review* and *Journal of the Canadian Oral History Association*. Also Bernardo Bernardi, et al., *Antropologia e storia: fonti orali* (Milan, 1978); N. Gagnon and J. Hamelin, *L'Histoire orale* (Quebec, 1978); Ronald J. Grele, ed., *Envelopes of Sound. Six Practitioners Discuss the Method, Theory and Practice of Oral History and Oral Testimony* (Chicago, 1975); "Archives orales: une autre histoire? " in *Annales, Economies, Sociétés, Civilisations*, 35 (Jan.-Feb. 1980), 124–199; and Jean-Claude Bouvier, Henry-Paul Bremondy, Philippe Joutard, et al., *Tradition orale et identité culturelle* (Paris, 1980).

Chapter One
Conditions of Life

TRADITIONALLY, the vigneron has been classified as a peasant, a word which itself evokes an image of a person laboring among the vines, cultivating the soil with a hoe or picking grapes, back bent over as though condemned to this position for eternity. We can imagine this person's return to a simple and isolated lodging, too small for a family, insalubrious, for a meal of bread and soup.

This dreary image is not lacking in a certain truth; the first recollections in this chapter bear witness to the nearly primitive conditions of life early in the century, conditions which very often still existed between the two world wars. Small owners and workers both remember them clearly. And yet, if this image corresponded to a certain reality for much of the earlier twentieth century, the picture of peasant life in the vineyards drawn by those who have lived it demonstrates that much has changed.

The living conditions of the vigneron, whether in Languedoc-Roussillon, Champagne, Beaujolais, or Burgundy, have always, in some measure, been linked to the fortunes of the vine and to the struggles of workers and cultivators to survive in a highly variable viticultural economy. Although conditions have changed considerably since the beginning of the century, the most rapid changes have taken place since World War II—changes which owe a great deal not only to the wine market but also to the developing relationship between agriculture and the state, to the rising expectations of vignerons and workers, and to their struggles through their agricultural associations and unions.

Taking into consideration more general factors, change resulted from the interaction of the four major aspects of life: politics, economic activity, social conditions, and ideology. Living conditions have never been static, they have only seemed so, because change occurred so slowly that no one noticed it. From time to time there occurred shocks—societal earthquakes, so to speak—that jarred traditional practices and encouraged, if they did not force, innovation. Such was the phylloxera, as well as recurring economic crisis of major proportions, as in 1907 and 1934–35. In response men and women recognized that they had to do something if only to save themselves. As a result conditions among vignerons have evolved mainly for the better. Vignerons participated in the modernization process, perhaps even more intensely than peasant farmers in general, because they were necessarily involved in commerce and exposed at an early date to the new technology that was largely instrumental in modernizing the conditions of daily life. In this respect governmental action, such as the building of electrical networks, brought a source of energy that alleviated the harsh conditions of labor and the obscurity of dwellings. Mutual savings banks, often politically subsidized, provided cheap credit and the incentive both to save and to borrow that made it possible for vignerons to improve their homes and their furnishings and even to bring their plumbing indoors. How are we today, when indoor plumbing, electrical lighting, and gas heating and cooking are regarded as normal, to imagine what an immense advance of comfort such changes brought to rural folk?

To be more specific, what do we mean by living conditions? Certainly we are referring to housing, diet, work, recreation, the fundamental features of material existence; the impact of modern capitalism on the lives of vignerons and their ability to participate in modern industrial consumer culture. But we are also referring to their mentality, their perceptions of their situation, their culture, their attitudes towards work—perceptions for which there can be no substitute for the words of the vignerons themselves. And the first interviews in this chapter provide these words. The lives of the vigneron and the vineyard worker are above all shaped by hard work, worry, debt, and a concern for the future and by the ambivalence of seeing young people leave the land for schooling and jobs in towns and cities. They are profoundly marked by the experience of seeing a culture which, although in some respects improved in material terms, has undergone a not always positive transformation before their very eyes.

Perhaps the most notable changes in the conditions of life of vignerons since the beginning of the century have been in their diet, housing, and basic material conveniences. Bread, which for centuries was the staple of the peasant diet and the main item of consumption, has seen its part in the diet considerably reduced. White bread, which in the nineteenth century was a luxury commodity, if it was seen at all, now makes its appearance on the vigneron's table more frequently, as does butter. While meat consumption has definitely risen over the century, it is pork, rabbit, or chicken which is commonly eaten rather than beef, which remains a relative luxury, as the individuals below tell us.

But the diet of the vigneron changed slowly and as late as the 1930s remained simple: soup, fruit and bread at breakfast; meat and vegetables at lunch; soup, fruit and bread again at dinner; meals not very different from those which might have been consumed at the beginning of the century. What has changed recently is the introduction of variety into meals; variety in diet which has been made possible because of improved transportation, post World War II increases in production, and membership in the Common Market. Vegetables and fruits, even out of season, can be quickly imported from former African colonies or other members of the European Economic Community.

Finally, if the vigneron of the south, around the turn of the century, drank primarily second wines *(piquettes)* made from a second fermentation of the grape residue left in the vats, in the interwar years real wine was consumed at home and, increasingly, beer. But, for most vignerons as for other peasants, increases in income have not necessarily been translated into great change in diet. After basic needs have been met, there is little money left over for luxuries, and food remains relatively simple.

Housing has perhaps changed relatively less than diet for the great majority of vignerons. Although, since the Second World War, houses with floors of beaten earth have all but disappeared, homes of vignerons in southern France still lack central heating despite the fact that winter temperatures can sometimes hover around freezing. Overall, construction of new housing is rural France in the twentieth century, in viticultural as well as in other areas, has lagged behind the construction of barns, toolsheds, and wine cellars. In the period between 1919 and 1929, the number of newly built barns, and wine cellars, was twice as high as the number of newly built houses for rural France as a whole; so slow was the progress in building new rural housing, that as late as 1968, only 8 percent of rural dwellers lived in homes which had been built after World War II.[1] The greatest change in housing between the wars was the introduction of electricity into the countryside beginning in 1921. By 1946, 82.5 percent of rural homes had electricity; on the other hand, only 20 percent possessed running water. Progress was uneven and improvements in sanitation came slowly. In 1962, less than half of the farms in rural France were linked to a common drinking water supply; in the majority of rural homes, water had to be carried from a well, fountain, or cistern. Only 9 percent of rural homes had indoor toilets and only 6 percent had an indoor bath or shower.[2] But these figures, intended to illustrate the rural world in which many vignerons lived, do not reflect the living conditions of all vignerons and workers. Small vineyard owners for example, are often more comfortable than workers who have no income other than their wages.[3]

Although we look more directly at technology in the vineyard and wine cellar in another chapter, it is important to note here that technology has had an obvious impact on the living conditions, daily lives, and attitudes of grape growers and workers. The post-World War II years have certainly seen important progress in the availability of the products of consumer technology: gas stoves, radios, televisions, and refrigerators. By 1972, more than seven rural homes out of ten had the three basic pieces of modern domestic equipment: a television, a refrigerator, and a washing machine. Although many peasants long resisted making purchases on credit, credit purchases have become more common and even necessary for acquiring major household appliances. The willingness to buy now and pay later has therefore made it possible for vignerons and workers to enjoy the benefits of advanced domestic technology. Conversely, technological developments have had a psychological impact on the lives of vignerons.

Vignerons and vineyard workers have never really been isolated like grain farmers or shepherds, or as our traditional picture of the French peasant might suggest: ". . . physically, socially, [the vigneron] is more of a villager than a peasant. . . . In distinction to the isolated tenant farmer, he tends to live in groups. . . . The 'long road' of the Burgundy hills, the groups of vineyards pressed together in Lower Languedoc and the plain of Roussillon, are not de-

Fig. 8 The home of Mr. Pierre Guerre, in Venteuil, Champagne, perched on a cliff. The *cuverie* is below in the cliffside.

mographic improvisations of our time. . . . professional life imposes on the vigneron repeated human contacts such as those of the business world. He is at once producer and merchant . . . an emissary of the town." [4] Yet it is clear that many of those who live on the land feel isolated from large urban centers and urban life. In this regard, if the railroad played the major role in transforming the viticultural countryside in the nineteenth century, in the twentieth century the automobile was perhaps the decisive element, as some of the recollections below suggest. Indeed, in rural France as a whole in 1972, 76 percent of the households of small peasants owned an automobile, a development which, along with the television, has done much to reduce the perceived sense of isolation of the vigneron from centers of urban culture.

Although the ability of the vigneron to participate in the consumer culture of the modern industrial world is surely a product of national economic growth, mass production, and the availability of goods on the market, it has also owed a great deal to the developing relationship between peasants and the state. Gone are the days when state intervention into the affairs of agriculture was denounced as tyranny against the freedom of peasant life. The decision to electrify the countryside in 1921 marked a major application of state policy to rural life designed to increase production and improve the living conditions of peasants. It was hoped that electrification would, over the long term, encourage them to stay on the land. Although the latter objective has not been reached, electricity has helped to increase production and it has also increased the leisure time of rural dwellers.

A second major area of state policy concerns the extension of agricultural credit facilities to vignerons and workers. Although the foundations of agricultural credit were laid in 1884, the system remained relatively undeveloped and was not widely used by small peasants until the twentieth century when the Office Nationale Autonome du Crédit Agricole was established in 1920. But it wasn't until the post-World War II period that the system was used generally by small vignerons, not merely as a savings bank, but also as a way of using short or long term loans to buy winemaking equipment, tools, or land. In fact, the Crédit Agricole has also made it possible for propertyless vineyard workers to become owners of a few hectares of vines themselves. Efforts such as this on the part of the government to promote the modernization of small farms and vineyards has gone hand in hand with rising expectations of the part of vignerons themselves and with their desire to live more comfortably, *comme en ville*.

It would be a mistake, however, to imagine that the state's interest in vignerons or improvements in living conditions have dropped like manna from heaven. Clearly, the efforts of the state to improve agricultural credit, electricity, water, and sanitation have been undertaken in order to improve production and preserve a sector of French society and culture which is essential to the life of the nation. Yet, the interests of specific groups such as the vignerons have required hard work on the part of grape growers and their viticultural associations such as the Confédération Générale des Vignerons du Midi. As Monsieur Coca relates below, the vineyard workers' unions have played an important role in improving living conditions of workers and other employees on the vineyards.

The above picture of progress in the living conditions of those who labor in the vines must be tempered by other factors. Among these, the state of the wine market is perhaps the most fundamental. The years between the end of World War I and 1926 were relatively prosperous; the average price of southern table wine rose from 98 francs per hectoliter in 1921 to 190 francs per hectoliter in 1926. But the late 1920s and 30s were years of great disequilibrium as they were in virtually all other sectors of the economy. A combination of good harvests and the development of the North African vineyards combined with the world-wide economic depression to cause a serious glut of wine on the market. Prices fell to 154 francs per hectoliter in 1929 and continued to fall, reaching 128 francs per hectoliter in 1932. By 1934, the national average price of wine had plummeted to 50 francs per hectoliter.[5] Even though the wine market stabilized and wine prices increased in the post-World War II years, other factors such as declining domestic consumption of wine and overall increases in the cost of living have caused most vignerons and vineyard workers to find themselves in a position of relative insecurity, although, as the vignerons themselves suggest, this insecurity is perceived and experienced differently from region to region. Southern table wine producers and workers are more likely to feel the impact of imports of Italian wines and each year, actively protest, sometimes violently, against the depressing effect of these imports on southern wine prices. These are pressures which do not affect the vignerons of the Beaujolais or Burgundy regions for example, for whom Italian table wines pose no competition.

Overall, in terms of the material aspects of their lives, French peasants in general may be less comfortable in relation to workers in urban areas or those in the professions. From the end of World War II up into the 1970s, agricultural households, for example, continued to spend a larger portion of their budgets on food than urban workers' households.[6] Despite the fact that leisure time of those living on the land has increased over the years, those who work the land are still bound by the rhythm of the seasons and the demands of the vine, whose cultivation still requires constant attention, despite technological modification. Indeed, the fact that the lives of vignerons and workers are still lives of hard physical work and relative insecurity, helps to account for the continued exodus of younger generations from the land, pulled to towns and cities by the hope of higher paying jobs, more education, professional advancement and the promise of an easier life.

Finally, in addition to changes in the material conditions of life, vignerons' recollections also reflect the considerable qualitative transformation of their lives. The decline of traditional celebrations and community rituals which has been noted for peasant France as a whole has been seen in the vineyard regions as well. Local, regional languages, such as Occitan or Catalan, have almost disappeared in the recent past—although efforts are now being made to revive them; in Languedoc, for example, special schools and courses have appeared, seeking to rehabilitate Occitan language and literature. Religious life, never especially strong in the southern vineyards, has declined, as has the power of religious authorities within village society. The passing of religious observance has also meant a change in village sociability, inasmuch as religious holidays and even weekly church attendance traditionally constituted important occasions for community gatherings.

We must notice the sense of debasement, a kind of loss of innocence, felt by some of our interviewees, as regards mechanization in the vineyard and the wine cellar. The use of the tractor in the vineyard and the introduction of electrical power in the wine cellar have been as revolutionary in the vigneron's professional life as the gas stove and vacuum cleaner have been in domestic life. We must emphasize here the role of machines as factors in the transformation of living conditions. The enormous role they have played in part explains why some older men are distrustful of them. Looming larger than life, they can assume the proportions of a new messiah, promising salvation from pain and worry. Vignerons know that while mechanization can bring an easing of labor, it can also bring burdensome debts and overproduction of grapes. It is important for them, given their love of the land, to accept only those devices that do not abuse it. Many are prepared to make sacrifices to acquire land—landed property to them is not a legal abstraction but a real, palpable possession—they are doubtful of the worth of their sacrifices to purchase machines. But then, most of the people we interviewed make up a transitional generation, between the old style of life with its basis of human labor and low material standards, and the young who are conditioned to the machine and higher standards. The older generation makes sacrifices to the new generation, if only to placate and retain the young on the land. Where the young are leaving the family village, the importance of the soil, of its possession, grows weak; it becomes merely another instrument, useful, but not an integral part of one's psyche.

Fig. 9 The new house of a vigneron in Champagne; a modern adaptation of a traditional style.

Of course, while social conditions were often eased by material comforts, human contacts were sometimes loosened. When women no longer gathered to do the wash at the village washing shed or to collect water at the common well, both arduous physical labors, they nonetheless lost some of the pleasure of communication and sociability that had been their traditional heritage.

Material progress has also had an ambiguous effect on social life. Television and radio, by now commonplace in the home of even the poorest worker, have done a great deal to bring vignerons into contact with the rest of France and the world. At the same time, however, such technology has made its own contribution to the decline of community sociability and the privatization of social life. Although vignerons and workers offer more complete reflections on this aspect of their changing experience in another chapter, the passing of communal sociability is yet another feature of changing conditions of life which reappear regularly in the recollections of the people of the vines.

1. Georges Duby, ed., *Histoire de la France rurale* (Paris, 1976), Vol. 4, *La Fin de la France paysanne de 1914 à nos jours*, pp. 213, 276.

2. *Ibid.*, p. 276.

3. Even this assertion must be qualified, although precise data for vignerons and vineyard workers is not available. A 1966 agricultural inquiry showed that the heads of farms of 5–35 hectares lived in homes which were less well-equipped, in terms of running water and sanitary facilities, than the homes of agricultural workers. *Ibid.*, p. 277.

    4. Ernest Labrousse, *La Crise de l'économie française à la fin de l'ancien régime et au debut de la révolution* (Paris, 1944), pp. 598–599 (trans. L.L. Frader); Duby, p. 281.
    5. Philippe Gratton, *Les Paysans contre l'agrarisme* (Paris, 1976), p. 126.
    6. In 1971, agricultural households spent around 45 percent of their budgets on food, whereas the national average was 37 percent and less than 40 percent for workers. *La Consommation alimentaire des français* (Paris, 1972). Good general studies of rural conditions are: A. Dauzat, *Le Village et le paysan de France* (Paris, 1941); Henri Mendras, *The Vanishing Peasant, Innovation and Change in French Agriculture*, trans. Jean Lerner (Cambridge, Mass., 1970).

I

Mr. Jean-Marie Valayer, a grower of Richerenches in Upper Provence, has seen a notable transformation in the life of vignerons in between the two world wars. His view of the progress of material conditions is shared by nearly all producers, from Châteauneuf-du-Pape to as far north as Champagne—a long chain of prosperous vineyards.

Mr. Valayer: It is certain that today the vigneron is better lodged. He has a modern kitchen; his wife, it is evident, works in very good conditions in her kitchen. There is a refrigerator, a washing machine, quite often there is a freezer, and apartments are pleasant, spacious, there is a livingroom in most houses. It is certain that this is completely different from twenty-five or thirty years ago. Comfort is greater, and life is so much more agreeable.

    These last twenty years have permitted this progress, this improvement of both housing and living conditions. It is because of mechanization that life has become much more pleasant, labor less painful. People go out more often, they take off in cars, they entertain one another.

    [But even while acknowledging general improvement, Mr. Valayer, like many others of his age, misses several aspects of his life when he was young.]
Mr. Valayer: My father had fifteen hectares [of land]. That was already quite a lot for the time, but we did not cultivate only vines. While now, in many properties, one cultivates practically nothing but vines because vineyards have expanded so much. I don't know whether I told you, but at the start of 1935, they made 4 or 500,000 hectoliters, now we make a million and a half, a million eight hundred thousand hectos. Thus vineyards have grown considerably, despite yields perhaps a little less high on average than they were perhaps thirty-five or forty years ago. Which means that in a holding that now has thirty hectares formerly there were fifteen hectares of vines, which was more or less our case. And there were places that were cultivated in cereals, [others] that were cultivated in forage. For when we used to have horses, we didn't need oil tankers, because we had our own oil at home with our forage, you

understand. Only we needed two or three hectares of forage that we cut, that we mowed, that we carried into our hay barns, and a horse ate that forage for a year. And we were much more independent; they could have closed the Suez Canal [in 1956] or I don't know what, that wouldn't have prevented us from working on our vines, monsieur. Now, if fuel is cut, we couldn't do it, that's the real drama, you understand. In the Côtes-du-Rhône you'll find [no more than] perhaps ten or fifteen horses and mules; but that's a catastrophe, that is. While in former times we had three or four horses and mules on the holding, there aren't any more. There is a tractor, but if one doesn't put fuel in the tractor it is no use. Oh, but that's very serious.

Mr. Loubère: Before the progress that you have spoken of, were there also times of crisis?

Mr. Valayer: Yes, there were crises. I remember '35–'36 well, our produce sold badly, very badly. Now, when produce sells badly, well now, you don't make any money, and you have to live all the same. Now, I told you, formerly, if you like, crises were felt less. Why? Because they did not have as many needs as we have now. Which meant that in a year when there was less income, all right, instead of buying a suit for a child or if the good wife felt the need to change her stove, which used to be wood-burning or coal stove, well we waited until the following year and we were patient. But now, there are so many demands, you see, it is necessary for the eldest son to be dapper, rigged out, it is necessary if the wife wants to do this or that, to change the furniture. . . . It must be done. There is television and if one doesn't have a television set, one isn't à la mode, you understand. In such a case there are imperative forces that make it impossible for us to accept a year of losses. There are debts. . . .

Mr. Loubère: Everything is bought on credit?

Mr. Valayer: Not everything but a part. When we had horses, I'll tell you the difference that there was. It's this: when we had horses, we used to buy a young horse each year, that cost us 1,200 or 1,500 francs, I mean old francs, francs of fifty years ago. Well, that young horse grew up on the property and little by little we accustomed him to work. Then we sold the oldest [horse] and sold it for more money than we spent for the young horse. This means that we did our work, we bought no fuel, and we still earned money on the horse that was now working for us. Now it's just the opposite, because you buy a tractor, when you sell it you lose a great deal of money, and this money has to come from some place, it is far wiser to increase production so that products sell better. Those are the imperatives that one faces now, and, in addition, the horses belonged to us, while right now the tractors often don't belong to us or not entirely; they belong to the Crédit Agricole.

Mr. Loubère: You make monthly payments to the Crédit Agricole?

Mr. Valayer: Yes. Workers, and not only workers, there are white collar people who buy autos on credit, you pay so much each month for your auto, you pay so much per month for your refrigerator. . . .

Very well, we've copied the Americans a little. I don't know if that is a good or bad thing; that's the way it is. What is certain is that that has nevertheless brought important benefits. I'll explain myself. When I married, I didn't have a house built right away; but when I had a few pennies, because credit did not exist at that moment, I had a house built and I had it constructed within the limits of my wallet, you see, and then afterward I had it enlarged. But now I have my grandson, my sons, when they set themselves up they said: 'Alright, we're going to build a villa, we're going to build something.' They couldn't build, but they arranged for a loan, which means that they repay the loan but they immediately enjoy the well-being that they wanted, voila! Whereas formerly, for me, that didn't exist; we waited to sweat it out, we waited until we had the money in our pockets to buy this or to buy that, to buy a refrigerator if you wanted a refrigerator or a radio. This means that credit has evidently much embellished life, I find.

Mr. Loubère: Did that make life more demanding?

Mr. Valayer: Of course, you understand that when something does not exist, you don't want it because it doesn't exist; but when it exists, when you know that somewhere there is a fellow who has a car, for example, well, you have no rest until you have one too. On the day when there was an auto in the village, I remember, it was one of the first Citroëns, fifty or fifty-five years ago, very well, at first there was one, soon there were two, then there were three. Then, the person who could not buy a little larger one bought one a little smaller, but everyone wanted a car, and before long everyone had a car. And then, as soon as there was a better model, we wanted that model; that's human, what do you expect! Credit has made that possible.

Mr. Loubère: Have there been any crises since the second World War?

Mr. Valayer: In viticulture, there have been difficult times but no crises. Even now when the Côtes-du-Rhône is a little underpriced, when prices are not exactly what one hopes for, even now there is no crisis yet. I don't know what you have been told up to now. Has anyone spoken to you of a present crisis?

Mr. Loubère: I've just come from Languedoc-Roussillon and they are continually in crisis, at least they say they are.

Mr. Valayer: I'm going to tell you, I'm a peasant, a viticulturist, we are unfortunately inclined to complain, to moan; you mustn't always take that for good money. It's certain that in Languedoc there were crises there, there were true crises, but to say that they're always in crisis, there are all the same, some moments when they lived well, they were comfortable. There is a proverb, I don't know whether it's known in America, but there is a proverb that runs: 'Help yourself, and heaven will help you'. Now, you understand, if you always wait until manna falls, often you'll miss out. Above all I think, when there are problems, you must tackle them boldly and there's always a solution to problems. You have to will it, and you must sometimes make some sacrifices, that is something understood. But in the end, I think that all the same you always hold a part of the solution. Sometimes you have to pass through difficult times; in agriculture, you must average out, but it's certain that no one accepts these averages now. No one admits that one year can be worse, less good than another. Why? Because there is indebtedness, we're used to a certain level of life, no one wants to lower it, that's understandable. But all the same, we must accept that there is no such thing as perfect regularity. In certain years the harvest is better than in others. We've always had fairly good harvests. But we must realize that in one year it will sell less well, another year perhaps it will sell better.

Mr. Loubère: The vigneron who has a better life, has the government played a role in its improvement?

Mr. Valayer: I think that it is rather our viticultural organizations that have played a role, but it's clear that the state, through certain measures that it has taken, has nevertheless facilitated certain movements, as for example, the establishment of young vignerons, or sometimes by the investments of the Crédit Agricole, its favorable loans. All the same, the government, in our cooperative wineries, has granted us subsidies. Let's say that the government has, according to the times, helped a little. Because I think that in agriculture in general, and even in industry as well, at present everybody goes knocking on the government's door.

II

Mr. Sabon, viticulturist at Châteauneuf-du-Pape, finds that mechanization, highly praised as the only means of progress, has probably brought many unwanted results. He doubts that the development of machines has contributed to the extension of liberty. The tractor, on the contrary, appears as a quasi-historical force determining the lives of farmers. Mr. Sabon shares the opinion of Mr. Valayer. Mechanization has created too many problems.

Mr. Loubère: Do you think that the quality of life is better today than in the past?

Mr. Sabon: Personally, I think [the past] was a good time because, you see, one had time for oneself, there were far fewer expenses than there are now. We did not seek to obtain very big harvests; we worked the vines well, we were masters of our work, because my father having a passion for vines, he managed to get fifteen hectares. He reasoned: 'I have three sons, with five hectares each, they will be able to live well!' But now, with five hectares of

vines, how can you manage to live? Well, let that go. Then, I had two horses
all year long, and at the beginning, we had forage. Afterwards we plowed up
those meadows to put in vines, because it was more profitable to make wine
and to buy forage; we made a profit. Good, no more problems. We bought
forage, we needed 8 or 10,000 kilos of forage a year. We first went in search
of it, we traveled around; then, little by little, there were bales of forage, we
had bales brought in, then they were carried in by truck; that was paradise,
that; in one day, you brought in your forage and the horses ate all year.
Later, we went in search of straw. And, of course, on Saturday or twice a
week or every day, it was necessary to curry the horses. That was a job! But
in the morning, I had a worker, in the morning, I used to go myself, if he
had not finished currying, brushing, the horse, I gave him a hand. We had to
put on the collar. At noon we brought back the horse, it rested two hours, two
hours were needed to feed the horse. And during these two hours, I went to
the house, I ate, and I had some time for myself. I went over to the public
square.

But now with tractors, we stop the tractors at noon. If there is a worker he
returns at two o'clock, but if it's the boss, he has to fill the gas tanks or
something. If it's the boss, he stops at noon, he dines and he leaves again.
Me, my sons never stay now for two hours, while I always used to have two
hours, and this time of the year, I had four hours. And you left and you
returned in the evening. Sometimes I returned in the evening and it was dark.
Life is no longer the same.

Now we've done away with the horses, but it is necessary to invest millions
and millions in equipment, so you've got much heavier expenses; you have to
expand to recover these expenses. Look now, with one of my brothers we
shared the expense of a sulphate machine; afterwards my brother took it for
himself. I joined two friends, we bought another machine, but when they
wanted to sulphate, I needed it. You understand, these machines [are useful] if
you have a large property of sixty to seventy hectares; you begin on one side,
you finish on the other; you direct yourself. But when there are three of you
with three [holdings] of twenty hectares, and the material is owned in common,
that can't work. Each man needs his own equipment. When he needs it, you
need it too; when he picks grapes, you are obliged to pick also. We have
enough equipment in Châteauneuf to work ten times the amount of land there
is, but we need it, there's nothing to be done, we need it.

That's evolution. My father bought his first auto in 1929. Now I have three
sons, and now, as for cars, there are five at the house. Me, I had a bicycle
and I was happy when my father bought the bike for me.

III

*Mr. and Mrs. Serrurier of Venteuil in Champagne tell us briefly how diet has
changed. Or rather, how buying habits have evolved over the past two
generations, since the 1920s.*

Mr. Loubère: Have you noticed a change in your diet over the years?

Mrs. Serrurier: Oh, you bet, because today we eat things that we didn't eat twenty years ago. Today we eat a lot more shellfish whereas before we didn't eat any, even fruit from foreign countries, like avocados. All that we didn't eat before, while today we eat it, things like that.

Mr. Loubère: Formerly, did you grow your own food?

Mr. Serrurier: Not completely, but let's say a part. It was much healthier, much more, how shall I say it, natural.

We have chickens, we still do gardening as always, and there is fruit, not of all kinds, but let's say that we have some fruit. And there is meat, we have rabbit, we have pork. But all the same we buy a lot you know, we buy.

Mr. Loubère: Do you buy more today than in the past?

Mr. Serrurier: No, it's about the same as the time you were speaking to me about. Even so we buy a lot more meat than our elders bought in their time; they lived off the land, so to speak, which we don't do. For us, it's supplementary and that's all.

Mr. Loubère: Is the consumption of more meat the only improvement in respect to the past?

Mr. Serrurier: As regards the past, yes, oh yes. In the past, in the time of our parents, they didn't buy meat like that. They bought beefsteaks once a week, and then, a *pot au feu*, you see, to make soup. Roast beef, young turkey, you see, all that meat that we have now, that we don't call special; it's for every day.

IV

Workers have also seen an improvement in their living standards, as witnessed by Mr. Raspaud, a worker-owner at Tautavel, an isolated village in the high hills between the Pyrénées-Orientales and the Aude. Yet, like Mr. Valayer, he too feels that certain changes are more loss than gain.

Mr. Raspaud: Let me tell you, at the beginning of the century, housing was not very different from now, since there was lighting. We had running water already, since the water tower was constructed about 1935. But all the same there were bad wood floors and it was difficult for a housewife, keeping things clean, and there were practically no housekeeping appliances. You had wood fires, therefore you burned old vine roots, and the traditional array of utensils with pots and pans and everything you wanted, all installed. While now, if you visit workers' lodgings in Tautavel [village of the Pyrénées-Orientales], and elsewhere in the region, they're the equivalent of a kitchen in Perpignan or elsewhere. Everybody has appliances, whether it's a refrigerator, or a washing machine and a gas stove. Every household comfort exists in the agricultural worker's house—but at what sacrifices!

In former times all that didn't exist. The wood fire, it was the center, it was the place where the family gathered, either around the table or around the fire, the hearth. It was there that discussions took place, all the family was there. Me, I felt it. It was difficult for me when I equipped my modern kitchen. I felt that the fire was missing because it was there I had received the first guidelines of my life, from my father. It was there that he advised me, it was there that he encouraged me, it was there that I first heard the savory anecdotes that formed a part of my childhood. So you see, all things were concentrated about the fire. And now there is an oil stove in place of the fire and there is something even better than that, there's even electric heat, and so it's neat, clean, everything you want, but it's nearly inhuman; it hasn't a soul like a fire.

[Our parents] lived on their own produce; in practice they did not buy much, apart from basic products, oils, and again, most of them slaughtered a hog, despite this not being a region of stock-raising, so they had a provision of pork meat for the year and grease, lard. Everybody lived off a pig, and off a garden, vegetables and kitchen garden produce. In practice, they bought as luxury products of the time a little sugar, olive oil. Not everyone cooked with oil since they had a little pig fat. There were reserves, but no refrigerators. How to preserve? Exactly, because pork you know very well is preserved by salting, like all coldcuts; so they made a part of the pig into coldcuts: paté, sausages, blood sausage, everything you could want, and then the hams that were salted of course, so what remained was fat. And in summer, I remember that despite the absence of refrigerators, workers were rather smart about drinking cool water, for example, or in preserving certain foods—they all had cellars, and consequently hard dirt floors. There were many who had water before there was a water tower; there were many houses that had wells, because in Tautavel there's a lot of subterranean water. So they had wells and a pump, and there were many who kept their food fresh in the wells.

V

Today's comfort strikes us principally in contrast to the lack of comfort of the past, and Mr. Darricade, of the Médoc, recalls briefly for Jean Sagnes the housing conditions before the war of '39. Those were years of general crisis and lack of sales for wine, even the great growths.

Mr. Sagnes: You were talking of comfort. About forty years ago, during the 1930s, how did one live in the village? Was there running water?

Mr. Darricade: Oh no, there was no running water, no bathrooms, no toilets inside the house. There was only an outhouse in the yard, made of wood, that's all. There were even some folk who had a pretty house for the period, but they had no inside toilet. Electricity [came] in '25–'27; let's say, to avoid any error, after the war of '14–'18. Yet, as regards housing, it was deplorable here in the region as much for the small landowner as for the worker. The small proprietor's house had a kitchen, a large bedroom, no bathroom and no water at the time. For the worker, it was even more sparse. Now at present all that has changed, but what needs to be said is that many houses were ready to fall into ruin, because no one could pay for repairs. Among the small owners, sometimes [there were several bedrooms or kitchens], but among workers that was rare. This was the typical house for the worker: a bedroom, a kitchen, often smaller than the bedroom, and in some cases what was called a storage area, that's all there was. And no large window in the bedroom, and an attic. That was the typical house here.

Mr. Sagnes: Did married children generally live with their parents?

Mr. Darricade: Yes, while waiting to look for housing, or they were housed by their employer, because 90 percent of the employers housed their workers.

VI

Mr. Coca, a worker from Coursan in the Aude, also remembers important changes in living conditions, but changes which he sees as less the product of government action or the passage of time than the product of concrete efforts on the part of workers themselves.

I remember very well during the harvest, employers brought in foreign labor . . . either people from the mountains or, since they [the mountain folk] come less and less, Spanish workers. I also remember that these people, who were workers like everyone else, slept on straw. Some employers, more sensitive than others, made mattresses, others provided nothing at all. When they came from work, the men and the women were obliged to wash at the same spigot in the courtyard. After a while, that too was part of the evolution of union activities, because . . . the unions took up this problem. The union saw that from the social point of view, it wasn't good; that from the standpoint of health, it wasn't good and we succeeded in obtaining a ministerial decree requiring that hygiene be respected on vineyards employing seasonal labor. We succeeded and now it's a requirement that employers have apartments, comfortable lodgings, with bedding, chairs, tables, showers. Let us say that from this point of view things have really improved . . . but I emphasize that it is thanks to the union's action that we were able to get it, because the employers would certainly not have done it otherwise. . . .

VII

In this selection Mr. Raspaud, joined by Mr. Montava, also of Tautavel, and a worker-owner, express feelings which have less to do with changing standards and more with dimming expectations. Both struggled hard to purchase a few parcels of vineyards. Now they ask whether it was worthwhile to impose so many privations on themselves to become owners. A small parcel augments income, but after the age of sixty it becomes a burden for the aging worker who cannot pay anyone to work it until he reaches sixty-five, when he can retire, and who must in consequence nearly kill himself still trying to cultivate it. He increases his chances of dying before retirement. This is a terrible dilemma. The other dilemma, just as sad, is the departure of sons and daughters from the village. Why bother accumulating land, workers now ask, if the young no longer remain to inherit it?

Mr. Loubère: Do you remember anything about conjugal life in the past? At what age did you marry twenty years ago?

Mr. Raspaud: Not very young; I was twenty-three. It was above all military service that influenced marriage. After returning from military service, generally young people got married. This was true of agricultural workers.

Like everyone, agricultural workers aspired secretly in their inner souls to become small landowners in order to become free, let's say, of the tutelage, of the constraint of the employer, to want to struggle for independence, for autonomy. So it was known that for a couple, the earlier they began, the better it was. Well me, I'm speaking on a personal level—but really, I think that this was more or less true of everyone. I know that during the period, let's say, when we courted (I don't know what that's called now, if it's flirting) we looked to the future. From the moment we [began to have plans] what we said was: 'Very well we're going to orient our life like this; we're going to try to put aside each day a gold coin to try to buy a piece of land. It will produce little ones; we'll buy another piece. One day we'll be the boss. Thus that meant we'll be working for ourselves; with a little crop sharing we can succeed.'

Now the government has erased all these aspirations. Myself, I believed that around the age of forty I would be a small producer, but for nearly ten years I've not bought any more land, because I've asked myself this question: whether it's better to be independent to work for myself, or to be both; to work my property and earn a salary. Well, I don't think that I'll reach retirement, see it arrive while I'm independent. I believe that I'll die an agricultural worker. And this is something important for me, because we had dreamed of flying with our own wings. I believe that I've narrowed my aim to adapt myself to the new situation.

Mr. Loubère: Are you also married, Mr. Montava?

Mr. Montava: Me, no, I'm a bachelor. And today I ask myself whether a
certain liberty may not cost me too dearly. I think that you already lose
certain advantages, if you're independent. Now, the employer pays all our insurance, that is my case. If I had been able to buy a little more, given that
I'm a bachelor, and I retire on my own account, I would lose the advantages
of insurance, I'd lose the advantage of the few vines that I have. I work them
at the same time I work [my employer's] property. That's to say that I can
just as well go work for my boss tomorrow, Sunday, if a job is urgent, and
Monday, for example, go to work on my account. That's the liberty that I
have. Now, if I retired to work for myself, already I'd not have the possibility
of working my land [with the employer's equipment]. I'd have a little more
liberty, but there are advantages all the same that I'd lose, large advantages.
And I go about asking myself, like my comrade, whether this liberty can be
paid for too dearly.

Mr. Raspaud: You'll meet the same problem that our comrade Fagi met, because you are fifty-seven years old. So being optimists we hope to have our
retirement at sixty. For farmers, for the moment, it's at sixty-five, but we hope
for sixty. But you're going to reach sixty and you will be condemned to have
to work [five years more]. All your life you've worked, at sixty you'll have to
work your piece of land. Before, an agricultural worker who managed to get a
family-sized vineyard [five to seven hectares], his physical condition no longer
permitted him to labor for himself. He paid a wage worker, not full-time but
from time to time he could hire a worker to assist him with heavy work, and
even then, he made some profit. So there was no problem for agricultural
workers, since they had descendants, there was a helping hand, there was the
child who was present and who took over the property. But even those without
children, they could pay [for help]. There were low salaries, there was no
heavy social security [premium]. While now, when you reach sixty, you'll see
[landless] workers who have nothing under the sun, sitting on benches in the
main square, and you, you must go on working.

Each year counts when you are a few years from retirement. If you persist
in working in the vines, which is still rough work, you risk ruining the little
health still remaining to you. There are some around now who are having
difficulty reaching sixty. If you go walk in our cemetery up there, they're fifty-
seven, fifty-eight, there are many who did not reach retirement age.

Mr. Loubère: When large estates are divided, is there an opportunity for viticultural workers to buy small parcels?

Mr. Raspaud: Yes, if they have the money, the financing. Up to now there
were possibilities of borrowing, but given the present policy of our government,
there is a tightening of credit, so the faucet drips drop by drop. There are
certain criteria now for those who are to be favored with loans. For the new
generation of farmers, they demand agricultural diplomas. The acquisition of a
property requires a minimum number of hectares, so you must already know

the outline of a project, the planning of work, know how you will be in a position to work. That's to say that there must be investments, self-financing to put into development. And that requires enormous financing. Land is very expensive and so is material. So it's very difficult for the son of an agricultural employee to set himself up on his own.

Mr. Loubère: Are your sons leaving the land?

Mr. Raspaud: Practically there are few left. Those who have gone for the moment, some of them talk of returning to their roots, but for the moment, at Tautavel, that has hardly begun.

Here, [among] the young persons who departed, there are a few who went to the capital. But there are many who didn't go far and they come back quite often. For the week-end they come to the house, but they come to renew their provisions of wine, of produce, to have a family meal, but they live well. Sometimes they went off with a village girl, both of them expatriated themselves. Or sometimes, they met a woman after, in Lyon, or in Toulouse or in Bordeaux, or in Perpignan even and they come in their cars, as I said, to the native village. They cling to it. When there's a festival, for the village festival of August 25, they are nearly all there.

But their parents mustn't count on them for help; they are well separated. They live their life, and the parents, they live from hand to mouth.

Mr. Loubère: Are workers' sons leaving the land?

Mr. Raspaud: There are only a few who remain on the land. There is a slight break on the rural exodus, because you can't reduce the personnel any more. There are employers who also work. There were ninety-two workers in '55, but in 1900 there were many more; there must have been 150 workers in Tautavel. And now there are only thirty-one workers; you can't cut back any more.

VIII

The factor that most influences the quality of life of all vignerons, as of all peasants, is land. Access to land, the source of well-being as of personal liberty, is a powerful stimulant, both for small landowners and for workers. Like Mr. Raspaud, the Guillemards of Pommard in Burgundy recall the difficulty of acquiring it, the obstinacy which generations put into its purchase, and of the decline of former bourgeois proprietors, which facilitated access to it. Having become medium owners in a prestigious commune, they are more optimistic in outlook: their roots are deep in these fine vineyards.

Mr. Guillemard: My father, my grandfather, and I have always belonged to a family of viticulturists. My wife, her father was a viticulturist since his youth.

But they were not [originally] viticulturists; they were people who came to Pommard toward 1900. At the beginning, they were workers, vignerons hired on large estates and over time they bought little bit by little bit and they ended up freeing themselves, by becoming proprietors. That was extremely difficult.

There are 90 percent who are viticulturists now, fellows who were once wage workers. And now that has become very difficult for one reason: because prices have made property, nearly inaccessible.

It is very, very dear. Families who are not settled there, for a young man, to create a property, it's difficult. So one needs to work hard, to have initiative. While in past times, the one who inherited a little of something from his family, well, my goodness he attempted to expand very slowly. Land was not so dear in the past. You had to renovate it. You did everything by hand; all you needed was a pick and a spade. Now, it's machines like bulldozers, power shovels, all mechanical work. Now all that has nothing to do with what you did in the past, when it was all manual work. Until 1910 there was not a horse, everything was done by hand.

There was a certain bourgeoisie, you understand, which had nearly all the property and controlled the workers. It was a hard time, that time. The bourgeoisie, of necessity, had all the property, it had nearly everyone all around depending on them. Then, there were no social laws, no nothing. Definitely all those big families, that held the territory of Pommard, well they've all disappeared, there are no more or only a few.

Mrs. Guillemard: You understand: they did nothing with their hands at all. It turned out they could no longer live, for it cost them too much, hand labor did. It turned out that property no longer paid, so they gave up.

Mr. Guillemard: But for a good reason; they no longer harvested any crops.

Mrs. Guillemard: So, at that time, it was all the employees who bought [the land]. It was fairly well shared out. There are still one or two or three families who are like that, important, otherwise, really, it is all shared out among the vignerons.

IX

Mr. Emilien Soulié, former director of a large estate in the department of the Hérault, and residing there in the village of Montblanc, sees the same evolution in the Midi as Mr. Guillemard observed in Burgundy. We must keep in mind, however, the trying conditions, the privations of several generations, imposed by the purchase of property. Cooperative wineries, the oldest of which are found in the lower Midi, have aided this evolution by making wine with the grapes of petty vignerons, thereby dispensing them from the need to buy at the same time both land and wine-making equipment. The term gavaches *is*

*an opprobrious one for poor peasants from the Cévennes Mountains, and
sometimes from the Pyrénées.*

Mr. Sagnes: Is the passage from the rank of agricultural worker to that of
petty owner an exceptional phenomenon at Montblanc?

Mr. Soulié: I believe that one can generalize. When, at the start of the century, the *gavaches* came down, it was a regular process for all those who
settled as agricultural workers. As we say in our language, if you are a worker
you don't remain an agricultural worker. The possibility of acceding to property
is a possibility, even for big owners of twenty or thirty hectares. Their grand-
fathers came, they were laborers. At the end of the last century, how could
you buy a thousand vines? An agricultural laborer's wage never allowed workers a decent life, that is, to satisfy the most immediate necessary needs after a
day's labor.

You began like that, one thousand vines, that's one thousand vines. Perhaps
you even went into debt, or you didn't pay for them [at once] but were able
to acquire one thousand vines more. Such things became easier with the installation of cooperative wineries, because the problem was not only to have land
to work, it was to have a minimum of wine-making equipment.

And the Spaniards, all the Spaniards came in three or four periods of emigration, and the last emigration began in '56. They are numerous in the village, they are now forty to forty-five years old, fifty. All are owners and they
rent additional land. And that's a fact that doesn't surprise us. We've known
that with all those who've come here as agricultural workers.

Mr. Sagnes: In between there was the position of tenant farmer?

Mr. Soulié: Ah, but they were both.

Mr. Sagnes: But in the beginning, there was no money. How was it that an
agricultural laborer could buy land while he couldn't pay for it?

Mr. Soulié: Because of this: the Crédit Agricole for an entire period [was
helpful]. Now, with restriction on credit, with certain conditions for the installation of young people, you must already own three or four hectares to benefit
from the advantages of an agreement called the installation of young people.
So the owners sold. My parents did like that, and the persons who sold, they
made them pay an interest that was probably usurious. Buyers labored; they
deprived themselves. Spaniards did like that; they deprived themselves, and
they began every year to pay a little over, two or three years. Then those
who paid off their land, their concern was to have more. This is love of the
land. Moreover I believe that this is a particularity of the laborer, of the
agricultural laborer. It's that he really belongs to the working class, but he has
the soul of a peasant, of a land dweller, because he has the possibility of
becoming an owner of land. While the factory worker, the worker in a large

enterprise, masonry or other, he knows that he will never be an owner of a factory. Several may get up a small business, but after all, that's the exception. While the phenomenon of the agricultural worker is generalized. When you go back over all the families of Montblanc, of one generation, or two or three generations, their antecedents are all Aveyronnais or Tarnais (natives of the Cévennes Mountains north of Languedoc), and that's it.

X

A condition of life among peasants in the past was isolation, both as a material fact and as a state of mind. Means of transport of course determined the degree of isolation. Generally, wine-producing regions, because wine had to be sold in an external market, were rarely as cut off from the outside as more self-sufficient rural communes. Yet, lacking easy transport, even they were far from urban centers where it was widely believed that peasants feared losing sight of the village church steeple. This was the case of the Guillemard family in the village of Pommard, who sensed their isolation until the first automobiles appeared.

Mr. Loubère: Did there exist, just after World War I, a feeling for the native village? Did people feel at home in the village?

Mr. Guillemard: Oh, there's always that business about the local bell tower. Each vigneron had a sense of belonging to a village.

Mrs. Guillemard: He stuck to his village.

Mr. Guillemard: No one left the village often. What do you expect, at that time, where was anyone going to go? To a family gathering or to a patron saint's feast day. One profited from that to entertain all the family. There weren't many means of travel. You had to go on foot.

Mrs. Guillemard: You traveled with a horse or a wagon or a bicycle.

Mr. Guillemard: Only if you wanted to go ten kilometers. My grandmother, she died without going to Dijon (head town of the Côte d'Or). She never went to Dijon; she died without going to Dijon. There were no autos to go on the roads.

Mrs. Guillemard: Then, what brought people out of their houses was when the automobile came along, all the same it was the automobile.

Mr. Guillemard: Also the railroad.

Mr. Loubere: Did people marry chiefly in the village?

Mr. Guillemard: Very much so, very much so. There are families like that. There are at Volnay, even at Beaune, people who have the same name, who are neither brothers nor sisters, who are local people.

XI

Isolation not only encouraged marriage within the same village, it also preserved local usages, among which were local dialects as well as regional languages such as Catalan, Provençal and langue d'Oc. Mr. and Mrs. Casadamont, viticultural workers at Fourques in Roussillon, remember this aspect of their youth. In contrast their son stands at the end of an ancient linguistic tradition. Here, the introduction of television has reinforced the influence of the automobile to end the sheltered life that had preserved an old culture with its own language. Even the village as a collectivity has been weakened.

Mr. Casadamont: Formerly all the families spoke Catalan. Now many families speak French to their kids. Before, no, there was not a family that spoke French to a kid.

Mrs. Casadamont: And now they're learning Catalan again in school.

Mr. Loubère (addressing the son): Do you speak Catalan?

The son: No, not really. There are several persons in the village who are really interested in Catalan.

Mr. Casadamont: Among themselves they speak only French. Before our time, we were young, they spoke only Catalan; it was rare that anyone talked in French even in school. In school, too, we spoke in Catalan. If the teacher heard us speaking Catalan, he punished us. While now, everybody talks in French.

Mr. Loubère: When did you stop speaking Catalan? Was it before the war?

Mr. Casadamont: Since we've had the kids. Right away after the war, '46–'47.

Mrs. Casadamont: And the children, they don't have the same pronunciation as we do. We, when we speak Catalan both of us, with my husband, they understand everything that we say, but they aren't capable of translating it.

The son: We can't speak it correctly. But there are many Catalan groups that try, eh?

Mr. Loubère: When you used to dance, did you perform Catalan dances, the Sardane and all that?

Mr. Casadamont: Here, generally no. For example, for November 11, in the morning before noon, they played the Sardanes, but even so no one danced them.

Mrs. Casadamont: The Sardane is danced rather at Thuir, Céret (small mountain towns in the Pyrénées), you see.

Mr. Loubère: Rather in the mountain villages?

Mrs. Casadamont: Up there the tradition is well preserved.

Mr. Casadamont: Here, there were only the Spaniards who danced, they
danced the Sardane very well, the Spaniards.

Mrs. Casadamont: Ah, but it was a pretty dance. It was prettier because young
people stayed in the village, and when there was a festival in another village,
we went there. That was almost cameraderie you see, we were more united,
more grouped. While now everybody goes their own way, everybody goes off.
There is the *télé*.

Mr. Casadamont: Everybody has a car, everybody goes off. While before, for
the festival, everybody remained in the village.

Mrs. Casadamont: Our values have evolved from the point of view of comfort,
from the modern point of view. But from the human point of view, from the
point of view of conscience, from the point of view of friendship, we've made
a step back of thirty–thirty-five years toward the past. As I told you just a
while ago, of a summer's evening, in that season, we went out after supper,
we discussed things. What did we talk about? We talked about the old times,
we talked about the grape harvest, we talked about Christmas, we talked about
the festivals to be prepared. While all that now doesn't exist. We no longer
discuss things with our neighbors; we are drawn back on ourselves; we no
longer express our feelings, our ideas.

XII

*Outside of Roussillon where Catalan is still spoken even if it is losing ground,
other old languages have given way more rapidly: langue d'Oc, as Mr. E.
Soulié affirms, and Provençal, as noted by Mr. Valayer.*

Mr. Sagnes: Fifty years ago the langue d'Oc was spoken widely, and in particular for work.

Mr. Soulié: For work, yes, in the *colles* [work gangs]. As for me, I remember
that at [the domaine] St. Jean de la Cavalerie we were fifteen who were
working with sand. There were some old fellows and we gave them nicknames.
There was one called 'Jaurès' (socialist deputy) because he spoke without stopping, and there was one of the first, I'm talking about '35–'36, who had
condemned the socialist party, we called him 'Cachin' (a leading communist)
and he told stories about times before the war of '14. He spoke patois of

course because he was Occitanian (Occitania was much of France south of the Loire River). Yesterday, in a newspaper, I saw an article [in langue d'Oc], I was incapable of reading it.

In our villages, apart from a few where one made a great effort [to revive the langue d'Oc] there is a following, but there's been no takeoff, only suspicion. After all, when I went to school, I was pinched because I had spoken one word in patois. Now, trying to start up the tongue again, you can't start up again just the tongue, you must revive the whole ensemble, all the culture; if not, it won't work. The tongue is dead, why try to make us speak Occitan? Well, and it's true, I think, that it comes from above, from the intellectuals. But at the bottom, there's no following.

*

Mrs. Loubère: Did everyone speak Provençal when you were young?

Mr. Valayer: Ah, madame, I'm going to tell you, me, I never addressed a single word in French to my father or to my mother. It would have seemed to me to insult them to speak to them in French.

My father had been to school, but unhappily until nine or ten years of age. Me, I was there until twelve, but he not so long. But they could do their accounting, they knew how to speak French, they knew how to read newspapers, they could write. But we didn't speak [French] among ourselves. Me, I still have friends with whom I speak Provençal; I could not bring myself to talk to them in French; these are friends of my youth, you see.

Mrs. Loubère: And the language is dying out among the young?

Mr. Valayer: It is dying out.

Mr. Loubère: Your sons, do they speak Provençal?

Mr. Valayer: Alas, no. Me, I talk to them often in Provençal. They understand; they even speak it, but very little; they're not fluent. Oh, what a pity! It's truly a pity. Precisely, yesterday, I attended a soirée in which there were nothing but Provençal songs; I had a great time. There were fifes, tambourines. You've seen the *galoupet* with the tambourine?

[At this point Mr. Valayer sang *La Coupo Santo* of Frederic Mistral. Mistral was a poet and the leader of the movement to revive Provençal as a culture. He composed the poem in 1867 to celebrate the union of Provençaux and Catalonians. We include here our translation of a few verses. The *Félibres* were defenders of the Provençal language and culture.]

Provençaux, here is the Cup
That comes to us from the Catalans:
Each in turn let's drink together
The pure wine of our plant.

(Refrain:)
Sainted cup
And flowing over,
Pour to the brim,
Pour freely
The enthusiasms
And energy of the strong.

Of an ancient people proud and free
We are perhaps the last,
And if the Félibres fall
So will fall our nation.

Of a race that itself renews
Perhaps we are the first buds;
Of our fatherland perhaps we are
The pillars and the chiefs.

XIII

Like the old languages, religion and the church have declined. Everywhere vignerons have recognized the weakening, but they draw a distinction between practice and relief. This fine distinction is recalled chiefly in regions where priests still enjoyed a large influence in the earlier century, as in Châteauneuf-du-Pape, where Mr. Sabon lives, and in the Médoc where Mr. Darricade recalls the bond between religion and politics. Conditions differed in the lower South where the anti-clerical left won some of its outstanding victories and which churchmen look upon as a missionary land to be rechristianized. The chances of that are slim. The memories of Mr. Coca, of Coursan, reveal to us the part played by religion in class relations.

Mr. Loubère: Has religion played an important role in Châteauneuf?

Mr. Sabon: Yes, if you wish.

Mr. Loubère: Are people still church-going?

Mr. Sabon: Less and less. There were many more practicing people when I was young than at present. People are still Catholic, but many don't practice anymore.

There is a priest, there is a church. In past times there were processions for St. Marc's day, there were rosaries, because there were sanctuaries dispersed in Châteauneuf. We have a chapel two kilometers from here, the chapel of St. Peter of Luxembourg where last Saturday there was a procession, in the evening after supper.

Religion has not disappeared, but has become attenuated. The young are no longer practicing; the young don't give a damn. First of all young men now don't get married, they take a woman, and keep her, no?

Mr. Loubère: Is that true even in the villages?

Mr. Sabon: Yes, even here in the village there are several.

Mr. Loubère: That's a little extraordinary in rural France.

Mr. Sabon: That's because there's no longer the religious instruction that there was in past times. There is only the communal [lay] school; well you know that that is the communal school. Now, there is catechism, the young make their communion; there are maybe some who don't make it, I don't know. And that's all, after, it's finished. It's no longer as in the past. First there is evening mass now at 6 p.m. Me, I don't go to the mass at 6 p.m. I don't hide it, I was a church-goer, my mother was very church-going, my grandparents were pious people. I've a brother who still goes. Me, I used to go a little and I gave it up. Note that for the big holydays I go to mass; but I'm not one of those who say, 'Me, I'm a believer.'

Mr. Loubère: Do your sons go to church?

Mr. Sabon: I have one. He is Catholic, but I can't say that he's practicing like that. And I'll tell you, life has changed so much that on Sunday morning there is always work to do; one doesn't have time to go to mass.

*

Mr. Sagnes: It's said that viticultural areas have a strong republican tradition. Is that the case in Médoc?

Mr. Darricade: In Médoc, I don't believe so. In the Midi, yes, and in Entre-Deux-Mers also more than here. In Médoc, it's rather clerical, really, there are clerical roots. Let's say that people are no longer practicing as in former times, but there remains something of it. [In the 1930s it was more conservative]. There was Corpus Christi day, street processions and all.

Mr. Sagnes: Was there also the influence of the large chateau owners during the interwar years as regards politics?

Mr. Darricade: There was a certain influence.

Mr. Sagnes: And the wholesalers of Bordeaux?

Mr. Darricade: No, no more, in our region, no.

Mr. Sagnes: Was it above all the village notables?

Mr. Darricade: We, in our village [St. Christoly-en-Médoc] it was the Monsieur, Monsieur of this, Monsieur of that. Well, you have in each village, or here for example, you have five or six proprietors who, with four to five laborers, had nothing to do; they lived with nothing to do. How did they spend their time? I used to know two or three who spent the day behind their workers, not to urge them to work, but to talk about things, wearing a greatcoat, these great-coats you know, in winter of course when they [laborers] were pruning. But five or six workers, that enabled them to do nothing. [Today, fifty years later, the role of the notable is] less important. That's to say, after the war of '14, the larger proprietors were eliminated because they wanted to continue their way of living, to live ordering three or four workers, not to give a damn. They gobbled up everything, they ruined themselves, that's true. Well, it was laborious workers who bought one parcel, two parcels. There were now many, many little owners.

*

Ms. Frader: In your opinion did people go to church much? Did the priest have a role in the village?

Mr. Coca: Yes. Let's say that Christian thought was rather important. There were more Catholics than now. At present, there are some, but I really have the impression that fewer people go to church than in past times; that's a personal impression. Because, there also, was perhaps where employers had a hold. The employer insisted that his workers [go to mass] and some, fearing to be frowned upon or fired, often went to church. Perhaps they did not have a profound belief, but they went anyway, you see. Well as regards such matters, that practically no longer exists; I don't think that there is at present that kind of pressure by bosses on workers. Now I must point out that Coursan, from this point of view, has been the flag-bearer of secularists and of those who don't like anything religious. There was a grouping of free-thinkers that was very powerful in Coursan, maybe the most powerful in the department of the Aude. I don't think I'm exaggerating; at least among the most powerful.

Ms. Frader: And who were these free-thinkers?

Mr. Coca: There were many workers, perhaps some owners at the time, but in general, they were many workers who were free-thinkers. Now I think that this group has disappeared. There are still some free-thinkers, but I don't think that their organization exists in other localities.

Ms. Frader: That is very important, because it is not much disassociated from the traditions of [class] struggle.

Mr. Coca: Precisely it was that tradition of struggle which formed the anticlerical spirit. And here, since there was a rather important nucleus of anarcho-
syndicalists, and you know that they were anticlericals, that added all the same
a certain strength. And even in syndicalist struggles, I mean, without pointing
a finger, but when a worker went to mass or to church, he was a marked
man. They didn't throw stones at him, but really he was stared at. Now, that
doesn't exist anymore, that sort of thing.

Ms. Frader: Well, when people married, early in the century, were these civil
marriages?

Mr. Coca: There were some civil marriages, but the great majority went to the
church in order not to vex the parents or to vex the young woman whom
they loved, so they got married in church, but without any deep conviction. In
my view the fact of marrying in church does not imply systematically adopting
the religion. I don't think so.

Chapter Two
Labor in the Vines

THERE IS a certain poetic aura to the expression "laboring in the vines;" there is also a moral injunction stemming from the age-old belief that hard labor over long hours leaves no time or energy for getting into mischief. Victorian capitalists believed that work was the most effective means to discipline factory hands and accordingly showed little sympathy toward reform movements aimed at improving labor conditions. Nonetheless, governments gradually accepted a tutorial role and enacted laws that reduced hours and improved safety in factories and to a lesser extent in workshops. Their gradualism, however, was even more pronounced in regard to agricultural labor. Toward these men and women who cultivated the land their sympathy was limited, their attention short. Few politicians were familiar with the conditions of rural life, and most of them in France had a romantic view of the countryside. They saw in the man with the hoe the very basis of a stable society, the preserver of sacred tradition, the laborer in the vineyard of the Lord.[1] In the representative chambers in Paris, rural spokesmen were conservative and generally indifferent to the plight of farm workers. On the other hand, they were solicitous of the landed peasantry, the artisans of the soil.

Unlike general farming, viticulture has always been an artisanal pursuit, a good reason, many advised, for leaving it alone. Under this persuasion, politicians refused to extend protective legislation to vignerons, and that even included the high tariffs that were supposed to safeguard the cereal and beet growers. As several of our interviews bring out, even labor on large estates—often called wine factories— has retained much of its artisanal character; there are still too many tasks that are delicate and require expert hands to carry them out successfully. Work under these conditions is quite different from that of a true factory with its assembly line, routine, and boredom. It is understandable that factory workers become bored, become alienated, as Marx long ago observed, from work routine, from the product of work, from fellow workers, finally from society and themselves. Gross alcoholism is the result.[2]

In contrast, the absence of excess alcohol consumption is a hallmark of grape-growing regions. Vignerons, whether laborers or small owners, do not feel alienated by their work. On the contrary, growers even in the lower south, where large

estates are everywhere, struggle and riot in order to remain on the land and to
work it. The laborers as well as the cultivating owners among our interviewees,
look upon work as an expression of their skills, as an extension of their personalities.
It is their work and the land that define the human psyche, enhance its full
creativity, bring out the sense of pride that distinguished the true craftsman. We
note this even in the testimony of the wage-workers with little or no land. In
their eyes a man's standing depends on his skill as a cultivator.

Wage workers, of course, did not always experience pleasure in laboring in
another man's vineyard. Their number has declined steadily since World War I.
Apart from the disappearance of so many of them on the battle-field, their wages
have been too low and their living conditions too precarious. As noted in several
interviews, rural labor has always fallen short of the ideal picture that agrarians
have painted of it. Work in the open air may be healthy but winter pruning can
bring on pneumonia. It may be nice to never work in the rain, especially when
farm laborers had nothing but old sacks to cover themselves, but when there was
no work there was no pay either, and it was with bitterness rather than pride
that a worker trudged homeward with empty pockets. As we noted in chapter
one, vignerons feel that living standards have risen and that their struggles have
brought more legal protection from arbitrary employers. They have moved far
beyond the pre-World War II condition when it could be dangerous to be a union
militant. Yet the profession still has its victims, when a sudden hail storm destroys
a year's grape crop as well as the vines. Then there is neither work nor wage.
At such times indoor factory work appears preferable for it offers that which is
lacking in farm work: security. In the vineyards merely excess humidity provokes
rot that can reduce a year's harvest by one-third, even one-half, and then there
is less work, or the owner cannot afford to raise wages because his income has
fallen.

When work is available on a fairly continual basis, it involves several elements
that the worker experiences. There is the time element, and there is a wage
which is determined by time, a given number of francs per hour. Raising wages,
like raising grapes, has been one of the chief pursuits of workers, along with
limiting their work-days. Another thrust has gone into lessening the physical effort
of vineyard tasks. In this respect little could be accomplished until the introduction
of labor-saving machines, as well as new cultural practices. The reverse side of
the coin of progress, however, is that machines reduced the need for workers. A
tractor which needs only one driver can replace from three to five men and
reduce the number of work days; it can drag several plow shares between vine
rows and complete all the spraying in a fraction of the time needed. A practice
called "nontillage" can even lessen the need for plowing by preventing the growth
of weeds which are discouraged by long plastic sheets laid down along vine rows.
Spraying the ground in between them with herbicide complements the plastic
sheets. Save for pruning and grafting, most other tasks have been simplified enough
so that cheap foreign labor can be hired to perform them. As Mr. Valayer points
out, as the need for skilled workers declines the need for skilled management
rises. Certain kinds of work therefore become more complex. The great physical

effort of former times is being partly replaced by great mental effort, and this is as true in wine making as in grape growing. All this, it is evident, had modified the working class.

There is need here for a few words of caution. Save for a few areas of high vine concentration, as we note in the short introductions preceding each interview, there is no rural working class comparable to that found in areas of industrial concentration. There is a sizable percentage of workers who possess enough land to supplement their wages significantly and who are therefore owner-workers or vice versa, depending on how much land they own and the extent to which land ownership has influenced their outlook.

When reading these interviews it is important to bear in mind that viticulture has been evolving at a rapid pace since the late nineteenth century. In particular several factors should be kept in mind:

The introduction of mechanical devices, at first horse-drawn then motorized chiefly after 1945;

The steady emigration of agricultural workers to urban centers;

The gradual break-up of some large estates, for lack of workers, and the increase in the number of small owners, at least until recent times as this trend is becoming reversed;

The introduction of a sizable foreign labor force that had its beginnings during World War I;

The important differences that exist between the mass-production vineyards of Mediterranean France and those elsewhere that emphasize quality over

Fig. 10   A rototiller is used for cultivating the soil in small vineyards.

Fig. 11   Horizontal endless screw press.

quantity of production. Low alcohol wine, for which the lower south is noted, has always been made elsewhere too, but the excess yield of southern wines has created a condition of almost continuing crisis in the form of low prices and lack of sales.

Equally notable is the great attention to time, the detailed descriptions of the temporal divisions of the workday. Unlike most modern factory workers, conditioned by the unidimension of man-made time, and less concerned with solar time, the grape-growers, like all farmers, adhere to two time dimensions. The sun determines when to begin and end the workday, while the human-operated village clock indicates when they shall rest and dine. And, of course, woman's work is never done, some of it has simply become mechanized.

This chapter, devoted to the problem of labor in the vineyards, attempts to reveal three aspects of the problem. First we hear from viticultural workers, that is, men who earn either all or a major part of their income from wages paid by an employer. Many of these men come from the vast Mediterranean vineyard where large estates are worked by gangs made up of both permanent and day laborers. The work force in these cases approaches or equals that of a small industrial plant, for indeed they are big capitalistic enterprises. One senses among the workers an outlook that is proletarian and class conscious. A second aspect is that of an employer of workers who vividly reveals to us his outlook on labor relations, which, as it turns out, is the essence of paternalism.

Fig. 12   A carrier unloading grapes for transport to a near-by winery. At left a future vigneronne eating grapes.

Finally, we learn about the work performed by small owners, who are, so to speak, "dirt farmers," men who cultivate their own vines growing in their own soil. Labor on the land is a way of life to them and vine culture is a noble art. They are not exploiters of the soil, do not like large, complicated operations and are symbiotically part of their holdings. Their labor is one of love, an extension of the inner being, the reason for living.

1. For the agrarians see Pierre Barral, *Les Agrariens français de Méline à Pisani* (Paris, 1968).

2. Edward Shorter, ed., *Work and Community in the West* (New York, 1973), chap. 1.

I

Mr. Quilis came from Spain. His recollections inform us about the conditions of foreign workers and how it was possible for an industrious immigrant like himself to become integrated, to marry locally, and to win the esteem of his employer—while never losing sight of his origins, class consciousness, and pride. He also provides some excellent insights into labor relations on a large

*enterprise as well as the matter of language and communication. He was
employed on the estate of Céleyran, near the wine town of Coursan, a domaine
that for a long time belonged to the Tapié family, of which Toulouse-Lautrec
was a member and who often visited there when he was young.*

Mr. Pech: You arrived in France in 1915, during the war. Was there a
shortage of workers?

Mr. Quilis: There was no one; everybody had gone to war. As for me, at that
moment, I was eighteen years old and we had been asked to come here. I
went to work at the estate Céleyran in the month of June 1915; I remained
there forty-five years. I was foreman of a work gang, *mousseigne* [in Occitan],
head of a gang of Spaniards, of Frenchmen, of everybody. At one time I was
the director who gave the workers their pay. In my team, we were fifty. That
was the gang of the estate of Céleyran; they were wageworkers. There were
only foreigners: Spaniards, Italians, Moroccans. I led some Moroccans, I led
some Tunisians.

Mr. Pech: Did they do different tasks from the French?

Mr. Quilis: Yes, the French, they were there to prune vines. The Spaniards,
we put them to doing the heavier work, for example, cleaning out ditches,
piling earth over roots, making holes, they did the planting. But the others, the
French, they were there to make grafts. These were specialized jobs.

Mr. Pech: Were there differences in the workday?

Mr. Quilis: No, it was the same. The wages were the same. They were all
unionized. Ah, not all! As for me, I was always a member of the C.G.T.
(General Confederation of Labor). But there were others who were afraid to
join. But me, I did my work; I wasn't afraid of the boss because I did my
work. As for the others, I didn't meddle in their business. If they didn't want
to be active in the union I didn't try to force them because each does as he
wants.

Mr. Pech: Why were they afraid of joining the union?

Mr. Quilis: Because they were foreigners and they risked being expelled from
the territory of France. For the least fault they committed, for example, if
they fought among themselves, all that; they were put in jail for two months,
but if they were in prison for over two months, they were expelled from
France.

    There were some foreigners in the union. In 1934, some Spaniards were
brought in to pick grapes; they were common laborers, hired by the day.
When they came here, they were taken in charge by a contractor from Narbonne. This contractor from Narbonne was a Spaniard, but all the owners had
confidence in him, they gave him all their work. That year they arranged with

him for grape-picking at a fixed sum *(à forfait)*, and he agreed. [But] he brought in foreigners who believed they would work by the day. Only, when they were here, he had them work at a fixed sum.

Well, at the end of four or five days, there were women, there were children, there were parents, and they said, "This can't go on." There was a strike; they went on strike. They didn't want to work. As for me, I was on their side. The contractor, he wanted to put me in charge of those people, to get them to work. *Mousseigne*, I'm that all year long. The owner, he suppressed their ration of wine since they wouldn't work. He had given them three liters of wine each day. And me with my brother—he's dead now—we had wine in reserve and the strikers came to us to get wine. So there, we gave them all the wine we had.

And then I asked them: "Listen, are you unionized in Spain?" Some of them told me, "Yes, we're unionized." They showed me their C.G.T. cards. Then I told them, "You're to go to Narbonne," not in my name, because I can't do that; "You're to go to Narbonne to see the labor inspector. You're to demand your rights." They went to Narbonne, and when they passed on to the Labor Central *(Bourse du Travail)*, the Central told them, "Listen to us, remain at Céleyran. If you want to work, work, only you don't need to do more than work by the day." The contractor, he was blamed on that day there. Only there were families, there were men, children, women, and all that, they acquiesced, that is, they hurried to find some work at Coursan. Because at that time, there was a shortage of laborers everywhere, so for grape picking they found jobs. They didn't ask for compensation, nothing like that. In '34, it was at that time.

Mr. Pech: And in '36, were there any strikes?

Mr. Quilis: No, that is, at Céleyran we could have struck, at that time there were strikes elsewhere, but all of us, we worked, that was on the estate. We worked all the time, only we were seventeen to harvest at Céleyran. An estate like Céleyran, that year it produced 30,000 hectoliters. There were 250 hectares [of vines].

Mr. Pech: So you worked only for Soulas as employer?

Mr. Quilis: No. I hired on in '15 with Tapié; I carried on during the years of '16 and '17, that was the first picking. It froze in '17, there was a storm, it carried off the harvest. He thought he would harvest 8 or 10,000 [hectoliters], I think that he just barely got 4,000 from a harvest like that.

Mr. Pech: Did you have good relations with Soulas?

Mr. Quilis: Oh yes, for me, yes. Each time that he came to the vineyard, I was at the head of the workers, he called me over to talk about work; we spoke Spanish both of us. He spoke Spanish, Mr. Soulas. He remained forty-five years in South America. As for me I went to South America, I stayed three years in Argentina. Mr. Soulas was a good employer for me.

Mr. Pech: He was tolerant? He accepted your being in a union?

Mr. Quilis: Oh yes, he wasn't concerned about that, about politics, he wasn't concerned about it. I even knew workers here, so I found some personnel. So I said; "You know, they're anarchists." He said to me, "So long as they do their work, I don't give a damn that they're the pope."

He even gave me a vineyard, Mr. Soulas. I sold it later. It was a field; I planted [vines] in it and all. He had told me, "Well now, you'll go to the notary, and you'll say, in my name, that I give you the field." I went to the notary and I told him: "*Voilà*, Mr. Soulas is giving me a piece of land (there were 1,000 or 1,200 vines), you must make out a bill of sale. So I want to know how that's arranged." At the end of several days he came to Céleyran, the notary, he gave me the deed. After the death of Mr. Soulas, the director came to me and he said, "You've got papers to prove that the vineyard belongs to you?" "I've got the deed at home; if you want I'll show it to you." "No, no need, I believe you." If I didn't have those papers, after he died everything belonged to Céleyran, they would have taken my land back.

*

Mr. Pech: Did you work every day of the year, even Sundays?

Mr. Quilis: Sundays, no. On Sundays we worked sometimes because it was necessary, we worked by agreement. We were seven or eight, and on Saturday I said to my pals, "Do you want to work tomorrow?" "Yes, yes we'll work." We worked only a half-day; at noon we cleaned up. At the end of the week I counted up what we'd earned, and Sunday was counted as if we had worked the entire day.

Mr. Pech: Were the Coursannais scornful of Spaniards?

Mr. Quilis: NO!

Mr. Pech: Did you speak in patois in the vines?

Mr. Quilis: Always, even the director, we spoke to him in patois. [Even the Spaniards spoke patois] but there were some who didn't understand. I translated. [The owner] spoke French and Spanish; he spoke German too. Among ourselves we spoke langue d'Oc, and the director, to give orders, he spoke also in patois.

Ms. Frader: Were most directors and foremen French or Spanish?

Mr. Quilis: It was all the same, only they were obliged to hire Frenchmen because Frenchmen did the complicated tasks, and we others, we did the hardest work; that was normal. And for plowing, there were *domestiques* (live-in workers) but they were always French, rarely Spanish.

Before 1914, there were a few Spaniards at Coursan; they're all dead. They were deserters from Spain, from the war of 1898.

Ms. Frader: In the past when the domain was very large, did workers think of themselves as proletarians?

Mr. Quilis: I'm going to tell you. There was a cellar master, the one who made the wine, a blacksmith, a *ramonet* (foreman), stableboys—they were fixed to the estate—a director, a subdirector; they all were the fixed cadre, they all lived on the estate. They were all on the side of the owner; not one was in the union.

But the rest of us, the laborers, we were in the union. Anyone living in Coursan was in the Coursan union. Anyone from Salles was in the Salles union.

Ms. Frader: But even those who were not unionized, did they follow the union members?

Mr. Quilis: Ah, yes. Listen, for May First [labor holiday], when I was foreman, for May First I got up early, I departed for Narbonne on my bicycle. . . .

Mr. Pech: For the labor headquarters?

Mr. Quilis: No, to walk about, I visited the sights. But at Céleyran, they all had to work; until after the war things were improved a little. There were workers who went to the stables to lead the horses out, to go plowing on the first of May. I arrived, I said to them, "Where are you going?" "*Eh bien*, we're going to plow." "But don't you see your comrades, they're celebrating, and you, you're going plowing!" And after, there were 80 percent who preferred to go work.

II

Mr. Emilien Soulié was for many years a wine laborer on several large estates. His native village of Montblanc (Hérault) lies in the region of large estates which mass-produce ordinary wine. He was accustomed to working in large gangs, each directed by a foreman. He gives us an additional glimpse of the place of foreign workers in the lower South and the problem of their integration into village life.

Mr. Soulié: As for me, when I began work in 1933, because my mother put me out, I got myself hired at [the domaine of] St. Jean, in a *colle* (work gang). I had to buy a bike, I rode to St. Jean, I did seventeen kilometers, and if it rained, I returned in the rain. *Bon*, only in '36 did I begin to have some kind of assured wage, with a permanent job.

But there was really a split between agricultural workers and viticulturists, there was a break. Agricultural workers lived among themselves; they represented a social force. At Montblanc there used to be 150 workers; now they're only thirty-two, I think. Now you don't know where the agricultural worker is, save for some Moroccans who aren't numerous.

There were some Spaniards who arrived in 1914. Well, evidently, to marry a Spaniard, that was a crime of *lèse majesté* for the French. There was xenophobia. I don't think it was racism. But that, for example, I experienced it: no Spaniards in the town hall, neither in the cooperative winery.

I lived through that, but at present that has disappeared, because those who arrived at the beginning of the century, they've been integrated, and they became the most xenophobic toward the Spaniards. I saw on the walls of Florensac after the last immigration, in fifty-six, in sixty: "Spaniards have come to devour the Frenchmen's bread. They don't fight our war, they don't do any military service." That's surely kept up.

Mr. Sagnes: Today, there are Moroccans on the estates.

Mr. Soulie: They're very discreet; you don't see them. They don't get married. Here, we had three or four young Tunisians who were on the soccer team. As for me, I've never seen an outrageous, calculated expression of racism.

III

Mr. Cabrier became a domestique *or full-time live-in worker in 1904, when he was fifteen years old. All his working life he labored on large estates. He gives us glimpses of living conditions as well as the complex relations between workers and employers in the area between Narbonne and Béziers, where there was the largest concentration of agricultural laborers in France, a true rural proletariat.*

Mr. Pech: What kind of work did you do?

Mr. Cabrier: Everything was under the orders of the director. There was a *mousseigne* (foreman) and his wife for the workgangs (women as well as men). At times the day was long, there were days lasting ten hours. We began at four in the morning [in summer]; at seven o'clock we stopped for a half-hour; then we continued until eleven o'clock. At eleven o'clock we quit until two o'clock. Then we worked until five o'clock in the evening. The *ramonette* (woman employed to feed workers) fed only the *domestiques*, not the day laborers.

There was all kinds of food. For me it was extraordinary: meat at every meal—but no coffee. I spent a year at Aubian [estate near Cuxac]; we were twenty *domestiques*. In the morning we had thick soup, well prepared. Listen, there's another thing, if we began work at 6 AM [in fall or early spring], then, at 10 AM, there was soup, a stew with a bit of meat, a dessert. At one o'clock a snack, at six o'clock soup, stew, dessert and all the wine you wanted, a wine that seemed like velvet.

As for labor conditions, when it rained, we went "to mother's," that is, we weren't paid, that wasn't human, that. There was no work to do. Today that has changed. During the grape harvest, if it rains, if there is mud, the owners want their grapes picked anyway. It's only just, in my opinion, that owners employ workers to labor even in times of rain.

I worked for De Martin (on the domain Ricardelette) for 32 years.

Mr. Pech: Was he kind, the owner?

Mr. Cabrier: Yes, the old man. My wife was very sick for nearly three years. You couldn't fool him. He was severe, but *enfin*, he had a cow of his own and he sent milk to my wife. He said, "As for me, I can do without it, but your wife loves milk, *voilà*." When she began to work, the owner gave her half-day work in the garden with the gardener—light work.

Mr. Pech: Were there many workers?

Mr. Cabrier: There were fourteen men and fifteen women, plus thirty contract laborers in Balagna's crew. He was Spanish. These laborers sabotaged the work. The contractor earned more; he took five francs from each of his men. Balagna made the rounds of Céleyran, and the Pech, 300 men in all [1920–1940]. There were some who did their work well.

I didn't belong to the union, but I wasn't against it. In 1905 old man De Martin (granduncle of the present De Martin) wanted to lower wages; he wanted the *domestiques* to work Sundays. But Sunday—it belonged to the workers, of course. A conflict came about. Stammering Athanase and his brother decide to stop picking when the *comportes* (wooden tubs) are full. The director asks why they're stopping. "You're not hitching up today?" "We're not hitching up because Sunday belongs to us. If you don't pay us for Sunday, we're not hitching up." Finally the conflict was brought before the owner. Bearded, hatted, in his carrige, he looked like a great lord. The owner says to me: "Work or I'll give you what!" Me, I say, "This work, I didn't look for it." The *seigneur* asks me, "What is it you want?" "We want Sunday work paid. If you won't pay, we won't work." The owner says, in langue d'Oc, "Don't work!" And there it stood. Finally he came back, saying, "I've changed my mind." So he gave in. There would be twenty-five workdays per month.

IV

Mr. Raspaud, Secretary of the Workers' Trade Union at Tautavel, has a vivid remembrance of working conditions and of the control exercised by landowners before and shortly after World War II. By dint of hard labor and economies he acquired a few parcels of vines, which classes him as worker-owner.

Ownership, however, had not changed his sense of class. Tautavel is a small village, tucked away in the high hills known as the Fenouillèdes, northwest of Perpignan. There are no large estates and no big gangs of laborers. Today nearly all the workers are of Catalonian Spanish origins; they attended the interview. Mr. Montava is also a worker-owner and an associate in the union.

During our exchange, which lasted over three hours, Mr. Raspaud described the conditions of work of his father and the changes that have occurred since the interwar years. One of the notable changes has been the numerical rating or coefficient of workers according to their tasks and skills. These ratings are used in collective bargaining carried on by regional agricultural trade unions and employer associations.

The interview underscores the importance of work schedules rather than of work itself. All these unionists are full-time wage workers, but nearly all of them also own small vineyards, and it is essential that they allocate some of their daylight hours to cultivating their own plots.

Mr. Raspaud: Almost no agricultural worker owned a house, save if by marriage—if he married a landowner's daughter. It was nearly everybody, surely who was housed as part of the labor contract. This was a yoke for workers; employers—there weren't the same relations as now—they were more genuine, but they were tougher. There was a class struggle in its full meaning: on one side was the boss, on the other was the worker. Nowadays it's more subtle, it's more dangerous. There's more paternalism, let's say, things have evolved. They're less aggressive and they're fully as dangerous.

But at the time there wasn't any permanent employment. That's to say that in our youth we knew winters more rainy than now and more frigid, so there were conditions such that the worker couldn't go outdoors. O.K., to get the most out of an investment, the employers—certain large outfits—provided work, such as chopping wood, sawing wood, work in the cellar. But employers who had only one worker, who had no such particular jobs to give, O.K., they didn't give any work. There were workers who labored only two days out of a week, or three days. And you had to make both ends meet. Fortunately there were spuds in the garden that filled your plate. But our children, they didn't eat much in the way of luxury products as they do now, like chocolate. We ate the black-pudding or a sausage, and like grown people, we ate the principal dish, the *ouillade* (Catalonian soup made of cabbage, fat and potatoes). And now, this lodging was precisely an important pressure. As soon as a worker manifested, for example, his wish to improve himself—despite that he had only let's say elementary schooling, which didn't mean that he didn't aspire to social progress—so if ever he showed [resentment] for example, when his boss left him with a week of only two days work, he made him aware of his feelings, when he returned to work, [by saying]: "You know, all the same, as for me, I've got a family to feed; you were a little stingy."

The [boss] would say: "Alright, eh, if you're not content, eh. . . ."

So it was a yoke, when I say a yoke, I intend the full meaning of the word. If ever you made another demand, whatever it was, at once he let you know: "Don't forget that you're housed on my place."

As a result of this constraint which pressed on agricultural workers, each one, at the cost of enormous sacrifices, let's admit it, managed to buy an old hut from an employer, who was well housed, and who had a shanty ready to cave in, well, he took it. But afterward, the employers noticed that this was helpful for the workers, this liberated them, those workers who bought them with time payments, at an enormous sacrifice. The worker felt himself under his own authority and more independent. Other employers accused those who sold houses. As for me, I know through my father at the time, that the president of the employers [association], it was his boss . . . , well, he made known to other employers, he said:

"Fools! You mustn't ever sell a house to a worker, it's emancipation for him, it's independence; we won't hold him anymore."

You see the state of mind. That's significant, eh? As for the workers, they persisted along this line, but you'll see some who are still lodged by the boss, there aren't many. Nearly everyone tried to have his own house because that meant independence.

Mr. Loubère: Was your father an agricultural worker?

Mr. Raspaud: He was an agricultural worker, he was a stableman. That's to say, he had permanency of employment from the fact that he was a stableman, from the fact that he was connected with animals, that he drove a horse or horses. So the stableman had the mission of caring for the animals. It was he who got up two hours at least before work began, or three hours, so that the animal had time to absorb its food, to be cared for and curried. He was in charge of the work team on the estate. So he was permanently employed because even on Sunday, it was necessary to feed the beast; it ate every day. So, as for him, he was under some constraint, but, on the other hand he had the advantage that he could already calculate his budget; he knew that there were twelve months in the year, that he earned so much each week. He was paid each week. Even when it rained he had to get up and feed the horse. As a result he went about keeping up the material: he greased the wagons, he greased the harness. He gave on such a day a more careful dressing to the horse; he manicured the hoofs. If some material needed a few repairs, he did it himself, or he brought it to the artisan, the blacksmith, at that time. So that's what a stableman was.

Then there was the worker *tout venant* [general worker], let's say, who is the equivalent of our present 125 coefficient [rating], that's to say, the worker who trailed behind the horse and who did the tasks not accomplished by the plow: he cut trees, he bared vine roots and he sprayed [vines]. He sprayed because we sprayed by hand at that time. That has evolved also because there are some who do it with a turbine [mechanical sprayer] but as yet at Tautavel, there are at least 50 percent who still do it by hand. Women there, they came, they lent a hand for this job of spraying, if you wish. And then, sulphuring was still carried out with the back-pack sprayer, as they still exist.

And how did we become agricultural workers? Most of us, we didn't have any choice; it went from father to son. Moreover, in other trades, it was a little of the same thing. Fifty years ago, you well knew that if the father was a notary, infallibly, if the son had some grey matter, he became a notary. If the father was an agricultural laborer, you didn't have much choice, because you couldn't continue your studies farther than the elementary studies certificate. That wasn't because you lacked grey matter to continue, it was because it was necessary to pay for those studies and, good Lord, an agricultural worker's salary didn't permit that extra. There were some who accepted the sacrifice up to that point, and we've got some children of agricultural laborers who've become teachers, who've become professors even. But you can count them on the fingers of your hand. They were really exceptionally intelligent.

But from 1950 on we've known a rural exodus *en masse*. All my comrades that you see there, except one, there's not any who are really from Tautavel; they're all immigrants, they are. As for me I'm from Tautavel, I have Tautavel roots. They're Spaniards, because all their names have a consonance, these are Spanish names. They're immigrants, either because their fathers had already immigrated, or because they themselves had immigrated in '36, '39, '40.

After the civil war they came into concentration camps (set up to house Spanish republicans fleeing the armies of General Franco) and later brought their families over. And now, even among them, there are many who left the land; they've gone into construction, or they're wage workers in the plain.

But here, we reorganized our union in '55, because there's always been a union, that's traditional in Tautavel. Only it was dissolved during the war. It continued awhile clandestinely. Then, when there were Germans, all that, there was too much danger, it fell through. It wasn't me who was secretary at that time. There were ninety-two workers in 1955. Now [1977] at Tautavel, there are thirty-one not in the union. You see an example of what's come about. Now the playing of foreigners against Frenchmen has been frustrated because among them we've got authentic Frenchmen now because they've become naturalized. So, taking account of the naturalizations, out of the thirty-one workers there are in the village who're not all organized, I'm being precise, there are two foreigners and twenty-nine Frenchmen.

Of these thirty-one, there are thirteen tractor drivers. In truth, they are workers who drive machines, with a rating of 140; they're really tractor drivers, whose rating is 140. Or there are those with a rating of 137 who drive vehicles but who don't drive tractors because those who practice nontillage weed with herbicides. Well as for those fellows they drive vehicles, either a tractor with wheels or a truck, but as a form of transport. And then we have sprayers on wheels that they drive; well they've got a classification somewhat higher than an ordinary laborer, with a rating of 125. Then we've got, which

I didn't point out, ten to twelve ratings of 137. That's how our working population shapes up.

Mr. Loubère: What was it like, a typical work-day for your father? Did he begin early?

Mr. Raspaud: My father? That depended on the season. Stablemen were very scrupulous about hours. The employer was more strict for animals than for men. At present, stablemen, you know, if any still remain, well, whether the horse eats a half-hour later or an hour later, he doesn't say anything; nor does the employer. But in the past there was a schedule like the tides, it was very precise. On the hour you saw all the stablemen, you saw all their windows light up at the same time. All pumped water at the same time. All distributed oats at the same time, hay at the same time. It was synchronized, it was like the tides. In the evening it was the same. Spreading litter, if it was for eight o'clock, for example, it wasn't for eight-fifteen or eight-thirty. He left—even if he had some guests who retained him to talk or anything else—he left his soup on the table; he went down, because it could happen that the boss arrived and he could have said: "Listen, you've come down ten minutes too late. If you begin that you can draw your last pay."

So a stableman's day, practically, began at four in the morning, it ended at eight at night. And the actual day of labor in the vines: well, in winter, it began at seven o'clock solar time. There were more breaks than now; the day was more divided. But in order to make a full seven-hour day of work, well you had to spend at that time fully ten or twelve hours on the job. In winter no, in winter less time because it wasn't daylight yet. We were synchronized with nature. In the morning you couldn't begin promptly, not before seven o'clock because the sun hadn't risen. So they waited, they left, the workers, exactly on the hour and they waited in the vines. They lit fires and made, in Catalan what we call *gra de l'ail*, that is, they cut a slice of bread while waiting for the sun to rise, and they carried a piece of garlic while waiting and they rubbed it [on the bread], and they nibbled that, it was a snack.

Then they worked an hour more or less and at eight o'clock—I'm referring to solar time—they stopped to breakfast for an hour. Then at ten o'clock they halted ten minutes. In winter it was ten minutes, a pause to go drink a shot. They worked until eleven-thirty. At one o'clock they returned to work; at two o'clock on the dot, a break for ten minutes. At two-thirty they stopped a half-hour, to have a snack, and then at about four-thirty, they returned home.

But now, there's another method. In winter we work three and a half or four hours in the morning and three hours in the afternoon, without breaks.

Workers still respect a schedule more or less, because employers themselves are less rigid from the fact that at times they help one another out with family cultivators, and then they've come to understand—they're, after all, rather intelligent, these employers—they've understood that we're not robots. So they leave us to our convenience. But all the same there's an established schedule. We understand that there are no more breaks. We remain fewer hours on the job, but they're full hours. In effect, we've turned the schedule around.

From May first on two systems exist: there are those who do three-fourths of the work schedule in the morning and one-fourth in the afternoon. Others, of which I'm one, we do seven straight hours of work in the morning, but we begin at four o'clock solar time. We stop at seven-thirty for a snack and then work through until eleven-thirty. You see, now each one does as he wishes.

Mr. Loubère: Do you live far from the vineyards?

Mr. Raspaud: The farthest is seven kilometers from Tautavel. Today that's not far because we have motorized vehicles and it's only a matter of ten minutes to go from home to work. We're all motorized. Even the horse, if there is one, we carry it in the truck; he doesn't go on foot.

Mr. Montava: It's simple, in winter everyone used to lunch on the job at noon. Today, no one stays outdoors. We come home at noon, even with the horse, in the truck, of course.

Mr. Raspaud: As for horses, there are hardly any, four or five. Nontillage and the tractor do all that's needed.

Mr. Loubère: What were your feelings about work, and how did you learn it?

Mr. Montava: We learned by doing, that's it. My father, on Thursdays because there were no classes on Thursday and I was very young, my father led me to the vines and taught us, with the love of his trade. For me that was to plow; I was thirteen years old.

I was proud to drive a horse because not everybody could drive a horse. That was it, that was work. We all learned on the job. I had my father, I had his employer, who both gave me lessons. When I was young my employer always told me: "You want to learn how to work, to do it well, because to do it badly you don't have to learn from anybody."

Mr. Raspaud: Plowmen, to support what he says about professional work, plowmen insisted on meticulous work. They found it a diversion; on Sundays they gathered together, to go for walks, they went to observe the plowing of one another, and if they could find fault, they were severe. The furrow had to be really straight. They even, and this I have from old men, according to old men because I never saw it, they had the cleverness to attach a branch behind the plow to sweep the furrow—you could have seen a rat running in the furrows. And it was shameful for anyone to plow furrows like a cord in a sack (swerving), that fellow became the laughing stock of the village. He was nearly rejected by other workers.

Pruning you were taught to do, your father taught it to you like that, with a true love for the work. Well, we always walked to work; we made our way through vineyards—one vineyard was five minutes away, another ten minutes, we knew the distances and the time needed to reach them. At times we set out, two or three together. Going into one area, we observed, "Look how that fellow trimmed." With vines, we know who had trimmed those vines, because we knew who worked for whom, and we looked at the vines, and we were critical, "Oh, that fellow there! "

And later in the café, all we talked of was work. "You saw that, that fellow, he did only that many vines." This was self-criticism of each of us. So each of us knew it and we put all our efforts in our work, we did our best. Then the fathers were very scrupulous and if there was a son who betrayed the profession, his father had nothing to be proud of.

Mr. Montava: A job that was not completed, I saw, for example, employers make their workers return to the job next day to finish a vineyard because two furrows had not been completed—I mean two furrows, a ten-minute job. And it took a half hour to get there.

V

Mr. Hervé Galinier, native of the wine town of Capestang (Hérault) was by profession an agricultural worker from 1921 to 1969, save for the years 1939–1944 when he was a war prisoner in Germany. For all of his professional life he was active in the trade union. Here he brings out the diversity of labor conditions and wages of agricultural workers in lower Languedoc between the wars and tells us about some strikes that profoundly marked the life of his town. Like Mr. Coca (in chapter one) he is convinced that trade unions have been the necessary instruments of social progress.

Mr. Galinier: Between the wars there were differences in working hours be-tween each locality and even, sometimes, between properties. There were also big differences between wages from one property to another. Today we're gov-erned by a departmental collective convention which unifies our conditions of labor and our level of wages, whereas in former times, there were some work gangs that pretty well protected themselves and they had advantages that oth-ers didn't have. In the period when our union had to struggle, we tried, with the means we had, to equalize wages at the highest level of pay. After the strikes [of 1903–04] and the grand demonstrations of 1907, all the proprietors had promised to give wine to their workers. But these promises weren't kept. If they were kept, it's when the proprietors gave only the left-over at the bottom of their barrels, which wasn't saleable. That explains why, when all the agreements were signed later, the workers introduced the phrase: "the wine shall be authentic and saleable," in order not to get the residue of the cellars.

The first departmental collective agreements were signed after 1945, but before the war, relations between wage workers and employers in all the towns were often regulated by accords coming after strikes and bargaining between employers and workers. And they were mostly respected by all the owners. Sometimes certain employers gave even better conditions.

As for social legislation, it didn't exist. Here's one example. Through their action, through their trade unions, workers in commerce and industry got insurance for industrial accidents [1900–14] while in agriculture, we had to wait twenty-one years to benefit from a law on accidents during work. That means that if an agricultural worker lost an eye, broke a leg or got killed by accident, he couldn't claim any indemnity to pay the doctor. His family had eventually to pay the expenses of his funeral.

Not only was there no insurance against industrial accidents, but there was no assistance in case of unemployment. In the past it wasn't rare to lose from two months to two and a half months of work because of bad weather, even in full summer. This made it necessary afterward to get jobs for our kids from nine years old on to go pick grapes and recover a little of our wage that was lost in the course of the year.

I came to know the *combatif* labor movement in 1924. The union decided to demand a raise in wages (I don't remember how much). Given that all the proprietors—this was habitual—loaned a horse and the labor force to harvest a little vineyard, it was hard to get the agricultural workers to take part [because they owned these little vineyards]. What's more, the foreigners who came to "earn four cents," as we say, didn't understand the necessity to go on strike. It lasted only one day; it was my first strike.

In contrast, the strike of 1926 was very well prepared. The officers of the trade union met together, then the general assembly. Two weeks later another meeting was held, three days later even another. They had begun with twenty agricultural laborers, but at the fourth or fifth meeting there were nearly three hundred workers present.

At the time our union was the CGTU (Confédération Générale du Travail Unitaire, a revolutionary union of communist leaning). And our demand was for 20 francs. At the end of twelve days of picketing, or fifteen,, we obtained 20 francs a day, plus a rest of ten minutes per hour that was called the *buvette* (refreshment bar). That was a rather well-organized strike, there were pickets at each exit of the town. All the little owners respected the watchwords of the union not to go to work, and each evening there was a gathering before the town hall and a parade with drums and bugles in the village. All that was accompanied by the songs, the "International" and the "Carmagnole." If there was a recalcitrant owner we went in front of his domicile to let him knew that we were there. At two o'clock in the morning there were always thirty, forty, fifty comrades awake to man the pickets at the village's exits.

I remember that it was at the Auberges, that is on the road that goes to Carcassonne. A certain Ginies arrived with his horse; his workers didn't want to drive him because he was a militant against the union. He showed up with a revolver in his hand before our striking comrades who were manning the post. That revolver landed in the ditch in less than two [seconds].

The result was that this strike ended by an accord based on 20 francs per day, that is, 2.50 francs an hour, while we used to earn only 2.20 francs before. After that strike you had to wait until 1933 to have another important union movement. It was a setback. That was a very hard strike, very long; twenty comrades were imprisoned and five were sentenced to five years of prison. But given that an accord was reached (the authorities went to work, all the municipal officials) there were requests for pardons, and at the end of forty-two days everybody was free to go home. I lived forty days as an outlaw, changing identity three times and hiding out with comrades.

VI

Mr. Valayer, native of Richérenches in the Côtes-du-Rhône, is a landowner and a manager of the bottling cooperative "Celliers des Dauphins." During most of his life he was a medium-sized producer and now describes the labor that was required of a family vineyard worked by the father, aided by his sons and a few wage workers. Numerous family sized vineyards have always existed throughout France. What tends to be absent, outside of the lower south and parts of the Bordeaux region, is the very large estate with gangs of day laborers. The work routine and conditions described by Mr. Valayer are those of men who love and also own their land. The same conditions prevail for Mr. and Mrs. Arnaud, whose village, Ste. Cécile-les-Vignes, is only a few kilometers from that of Mr. Valayer.

Mr. Valayer: The father's role in a viticultural family was in a way the same as today, but with different means. That is, it was always the father obviously who decided on the work to do, who directed the little family enterprise, formerly, as today. For formerly when I used to cultivate, conditions of life and work were all different from what they are at the present time. I remember that when you had to leave for the vines, you got up at three or four o'clock in the morning. You had to give forage to the horses and then have them drink and then curry them. That is, it required nearly two hours of work before departing with the plow and being in the vines. You see the large amount of work that gave you. And then, when you were in the vines, you made one furrow after another; for example, between two rows of vines, if you had ten furrows to make, *eh bien*, you had to go and come five times with the plow. To plow between two rows of vines with a tractor at the present time, in one stroke it goes faster, to do the entire alley. What's more, if you want to begin work at seven in the morning, alright, after you've had breakfast, you sit yourself on the tractor, you start it up, and you're ready to go. Just see the difference. And more than that, as for work, you pay more attention when working with a tractor, but it's much less painful than working with a plow. You had to press on the footstep of the plow. Have you seen men plowing? *Enfin*, it's a job that's painful. At present on a tractor it's painful too, but it's not at all comparable; the physical fatigue is much less.

Mr. Loubère: Has there been a change in attitudes toward work? Does it seem more mechanized, more impersonal?

Mr. Valayer: No, it's the same in viticulture, above all in our region, it's still part of the profession, it remains artisanal. Even I'd say it's not large scale agriculture just because the vigneron has a tractor. It remains necessary all the same for him, himself, to take part in the work. There are only very few vignerons who can permit themselves to hire laborers and then twiddle their thumbs. You see what I mean, the vigneron participates in the work on vines.

Mr. Loubère: Can you recall how you learned to cultivate vines?

Mr. Valayer: My dear sir, I'd say, oh yes, that is learned, but it comes from heredity. Look, when you've got a father who grew vines [you begin] as soon as you—I won't say as soon as you've learn to walk—but as soon as you've done your studies. First of all, schooling, formerly, was much shorter than now. As for me, I left school at twelve. My sons quit school at eighteen, and my grandsons, at twenty-five, are still in school. So it's not the same, that. As for me, when I was twelve years old, I was still a kid, and already I has a taste for life. And once you've gotten a taste for a job, that's a job that you'll do well, that's a job that's not painful to you. Because what's most painful in a job, it's to be obliged to do a job that's not suited to you. But when you do work that you like, it's not hard. Even when it was painful with horses, with a sulphur tank on your back, when you had a taste for it, you saw the vines growing, you saw the grapes developing, well then you have the satisfaction that fully compensates you for the trouble you took.

I learned on the job, I didn't go to agricultural school. Take note, there are now viticultural schools and I think that it's necessary because actually, all the same, a vigneron remains a vigneron, but he has to do his accounting. Life's not the same as it was before. Formerly we lived nearly off the holding. As for me, I didn't have to buy fuel, to buy tires. You see, there was less bookkeeping than now. Now you have nearly to be an accountant because you've got to know how much you'll pay for fertilizer, how much you'll pay for chemicals. And today there is so much progress in fertilizers, or in sprays, that you have to keep informed about all this evolution. So the vigneron is obliged, at least most of them, to know more about agriculture in general and about viticulture in particular, and to do a little accounting also, because there are also taxes that used not to be so important and which now have become important. And then, there are those who have personnel, you have to calculate wages, play with the withholdings that have to be made, etc. At present, that's complicated from the point of view of accounts, whereas that used to be simple. You had a worker, you gave him so much per day and then it was finished, there were no social payments, nothing. At present, there's all that grafted onto and complicating a little the vigneron's life.

Mr. Loubère: Are there fewer workers hired today than formerly?

Mr. Valayer: A few less workers, yes. Mechanization has clearly diminished the number of workers. But all the same, you need a rather large work force in comparison to agriculture which demands very few laborers. While in viticulture there are all the same two sorts of work, there's grape picking—picking has not been mechanized, or very little—and pruning the vine. For that you need an enormous work force. Depending on the size of the vineyard, during the harvest, you must have fifteen, twenty, thirty pickers, and to prune vines, you need three to four workers during two or three winter months. So you see, for that you need a very large work force. But for heavy farm work, for spraying, there you don't need many workers because that's mechanized. We have a great need of a seasonal workforce.

Mr. Loubère: Are native French workers disappearing?

Mr. Valayer: There are still a few but very few. This is not special to viticulture; it is equally true in fruit culture. Well, there is an enormous Spanish and Italian labor force. First they were Italians who came, then Italians stayed home as progress came about. And after, it was Spaniards; they come less now. And we have a labor force from the Maghreb: Moroccans or Algerians. I can say that I've got four sons who cultivate vines. My son-in-law has a Spanish worker; one of my sons has a French worker, and the two others have Moroccan workers. I think that's pretty much how they're divided.

*

Mr. Arnaud: We presently bring in Spaniards to pick our grapes. We can't find the labor force we need in France. We used to find them, but for the past fifteen years, since 1962, we bring in Spaniards. Well, we built lodging, very simple lodging. You know, where we kept horses, and storage, we built a kitchen, we built a refectory, we built a dormitory and since 1962 brought in a Spanish crew. For twelve years I had the same crew; it was always the same person in Spain who sent me my grape pickers. Then one year they didn't come. This year will be the fifth consecutive year for the team that now returns.

Mrs. Arnaud: They come from Granada; the former ones used to come from Alicante.

Mr. Arnaud: They come work a month for us.

Mrs. Arnaud: When there was a change, the others didn't come, the employment agency at Orange had us make anonymous contracts: we don't put down any names, they put in the names. So when the workers arrived we didn't know them. And they made us pay much more for these contracts, because someone was paid to find the workers.

We used to have less surface (land area) you understand [when I was young]. People helped one another [in those days]. As children, we began school later and people harvested later because we were less concerned with quality, we didn't get many degrees of alcohol. My father had a little cellar of his own. Very well, we went to pick for two days at one neighbor, two days at another. We were paid and took off for another. There were many people who did like that at that time. I must say that you could take on many more people than now-a-days. Now, there's insurance and all that. Before, good lord, the neighbor's children, they came to help out, but we paid them. Overtime pay didn't exist. At that time, people worked from sun up to sun down, as we say, and you were paid by the day. When we were married, there were people paying 20 or 22 francs per day.

VII

Mr. Darricade lives in St. Christoly-en-Médoc, and his recollections take us to another great area of wine production. Like Mr. Raspaud, he reminds us of the former importance of animal power, oxen in Médoc, in the cultivation of vines. He also gives us a glimpse of female labor.

Mr. Darricade: Until the year 1930–1935, more or less, you cultivated vines with horses or oxen. For the worker and the small owner, it was necessary to get up early in the morning to attend to the beasts. Oxen ate slower than horses, for example, so you had to get up even earlier. In summer that meant three o'clock in the morning. Oxen ate for two hours, then you had to water them, and then they ate again after drinking. Well, that means that in order to start out at six o'clock, you had to get up at daybreak. What's more, here in our region, there were communal pastures, and in the evening, after work, the laborers and small owners, after feeding and watering their cattle, led them to spend the night in those pastures at a distance of fifteen hundred meters. So that in the morning you had to get up early to go find them, and at times it was not easy, because they ran in those common fields, where there could be one hundred head of cattle. You had to get up early to be on time, in case you couldn't catch them easily, because while there were docile beasts, when they saw their master, they came to the fence, but there were other kinds.

After all this in the morning, and then the time needed to get to the vines, the question of hours of work didn't come up. You worked until twelve o'- clock; when the steeple bell rang in the village, you stopped work. Then in summer you started again around three o'clock perhaps, because you had a little siesta. Then you worked until nightfall. The workers worked less, but small owners went on. In all about ten hours.

Mr. Sagnes: Were there several categories of workers?

Mr. Darricade: There were those who took care of the animals, since there were in a property a little larger than a small property, there were those who plowed and those who did the rest. There was a plowman, and we estimated that a good worker, in a property of a certain size, could do about three hectares and a half. Three hectares was the norm. For example, we said, if there are ten or twelve hectares, you need three workers to work the property. Even more, in winter, you needed the women to help do winter work, that is, put in the stakes. Here we call that *nastes*, that is, the branch that you leave, you bend it over the stake; well the women bent them all winter, and gathered branches also, they made little faggots. We didn't burn canes outside as we do at present. The canes were collected, you tied them with osier, and afterward you carried them back. You made one pile for the owner, one pile for the worker for the year. They served in the fireplace. Besides that work women helped to do what we call here *tirer les cavaillons*. Well, that's done when you remove soil from around the vine roots *(déchausser)* by means of a special hoe, which is rather hard, above all when the vine is dirty and there are weeds. Women did that also.

Afterward came the period of sulfuring and spraying. Well that, evidently, you saw women do that rarely. It was men who did that with sprayers on their backs, and we estimated that when a worker in a half-day has used up a barrel—that's 225 liters—a barrel of mangnese sulphate [or copper sulphate] he had worked hard. In the afternoon he began again, he used up another barrel, or two barrels a day. Now, it's clear, here you had a sulphate sprayer with a special system, with a lever handle, that was very very fatiguing. Well sometimes there was a woman who helped all the same; she helped to fill the machine, because otherwise the worker was obliged to take off the machine, to fill it and to put it again on his back; that was fatiguing. Because when there was a woman, there was a chair on the side, without a back, he sat under the faucet of the barrel and the woman filled him up. Because at the same time she had to roll the barrel so as to stir the mixture, that was called a *branleur* here. She had to mix in advance when she saw the worker coming, afterward she filled him up. That was less fatiguing.

There were also some tasks that women helped with during summer. That was the hay harvest. For oxen and horses, and you know for cows, you need a lot of hay. There were fields along the banks of the Gironde here. So we went to cut hay and women tedded the hay by hand; at that time you tedded by hand as yet. And then they helped to bring in the hay, that was women's work. The same when vines grew in the month of April and May; they attached the branches [to stakes or wires], they helped to cut vines, they cut the tops of vines. They were busy nearly all year.

Mr. Sagnes: Was there work for children?

Mr. Darricade: You know, that was rather rare, apart from grape picking. Children picked when very young, at twelve or thirteen years of age. That must be general, twelve or thirteen to harvest. Me, at twelve, I harvested. And school started after the harvest; that aided poor families, you see, one or two children, everybody was fed, that aided worker's families.

Mr. Sagnes: Were there work crews to pick grapes?

Mr. Darricade: In our region of Médoc, there are already lots of local folk, but we found pickers in Les Landes, not only in the department of Landes, but in the Girondin Landes also. There was someone who organized it, a gang chief who recruited members. We went to pick them up in carts, at Hourtin which is thirty kilometers away. We installed benches on each side of the carts. They were in general people from Les Landes. It's not like now; we've got a labor recruitment service. That was absolutely different. From the point of view of the labor force, it was good; we had men who were known as heads of gangs. While now, they send you someone, you don't know him, you don't know where he comes from, you understand?

Wages of women, in about 1900, were 20 *sous* per day, one franc. Men earned double, about 60 francs a month; 65 to 70 francs with [wine and some other things].

VIII

Mr. Jean-Paul Gardère has been the director of Château Latour since 1963. Here he gives us his views on labor relations, which are quite different from those expressed previously; he gives us the employer's side. As director of one of the large first-growth wineries of Médoc, he is in direct contact with a sizeable labor force of both men and women. A man of considerable experience and administrative expertise, formerly a wage worker himself, he reveals the wisdom and magnanimity that one would expect from so great an institution as Château Latour.

Mr. Sagnes: I've heard that on some estates certain workers have some vines for their own use.

Mr. Gardère: That's not the case here.

Mr. Sagnes: What advantages do workers have? Is there lodging, is there wine?

Mr. Gardère: First there's the wage. Here I pay workers by the month. I had proposed to them monthly pay when I began here. They said no, and I understand them because as I often told them: "Everything you've done, I've done also, so I know your reactions." I reacted as they did.

Many workers [elsewhere] are not paid by the month; they do piece work: so much pay for this task, so much for that task. Women here are still paid by the task, because I haven't guaranteed the jobs of women: yet I arrange it so they're fully employed. And I proposed to them monthly pay when saying that in the notion of piece work there's a notion of cheating. As for me I did piece work, I know what it is to do piece work. In our viticulture, in construction companies that make cement, mortar, pitch, paint, etc., you understnd that where it's possible to cheat, men will cheat, even if you use piece work.

When I proposed monthly pay they said no. I think that I would have had the same reaction if I'd been in their shoes. [They thought:] "He's proposing that, there's a reason, it's in the boss's interest. So we must distrust him and say the opposite if we want to save our interests." There was this very solid attachment to old ways. People used to be paid some years ago, by the *sadon*. The *sadon* was a measure still used in 1900. There were twelve *sadons* to the hectare. That dates from before the Revolution. Ask any old men around how many vines are needed, most are going to say, "I worked so many sadons."

Well I said [to the workers], "Listen my children, if you wish we're going to study [this matter] together, we're going to study work time, work norms that ought to be applied to specific tasks, and you're going to propose some work norms for us. What do you consider the time that's necessary, for example, to prune one hundred vines, so that they're *pruned*, I don't say *cut* the wood, *prune?*" Because pruning shears, they're primordial to the vigneron; when he knows how to prune well he preserves the old vine stock.

We needed two years to introduce monthly pay. They came back, we studied. We used the averages of the last five years: stormy weather during pruning, how much one could prune; I mean pruning from daybreak to sundown.

Monsieur, one vine with two canes produces a half bottle of wine. If this bottle of wine is worth, let's say, 60 francs, then one vine produces 30 francs of wine every year. There's the problem, you understand. A mechanical harvester loses 5 percent of grapes. We lost picking by hand 1.5 to 2 percent, and I try to find a means to lose half of that. One and a half percent lost grapes out of the best, the most ripe, we've lost fifteen barrels of wine (225 liters each) and fifteen barrels of wine at 60 francs a bottle, well you calculate it.

The problem lies in the best harvesting, the best yield per vine, the safeguarding of old vines. We're always seeking quality in harmony with our search for quantity, but quantity disappears before quality.

So the workers came back and said, "We can prune 600 vines." I could have said 650, and they would have done 650. All the norms they proposed I accepted. Why? Because this is Latour. So I arranged monthly pay with them, we put in two years studying together. There's no signed agreement, it's a moral contract. And since these are serious, proud people, everyone respects it without problems.

The women are not yet paid monthly, first because while I arrange to give them full-time work, I don't want to guarantee their jobs, even though by the number of hours it's practically guaranteed, because they are the wives of our vignerons, they are the women of the property. They want to be paid monthly, but I'm not yet ready for that because women are much more given to cheating than men.

Mr. Sagnes: Ah *bon*, you're distrustful!

Mr. Gardère: Yes, even though I especially watch over the women, given that above all we've mechanized men's work, what we call heavy tasks. We haven't mechanized women's work, the lighter tasks. Formerly we carried sprayers on our backs, cut paths with picks, planted with shovels.

I bought some goggles for the workers, jockey's goggles, because you know jockeys when trotting rip up many pebbles and Lissac had made some unbreakable goggles. All the same one must wear them. Of course I know that you need windshield wipers because when you work with a pick you sweat in the goggles. [So the workers would not wear the goggles]. If the labor inspector passes, I'm at fault, I'm cornered, so I'll say, "Inspector, sir, take the pick and the goggles, you're going to see." Now with the stroke of a pick and bursts of pebbles, there's one who had an eye put out, another who nearly lost it. Now that danger is over, thanks to an earth drill.

At a given time I put women, for certain tasks, on the men's pay scale. When I said to the worker's delegates, "For that, that, and that, women will earn like men," they all said "How's that? " There were three delegates and three supplicants, I united them all: "Go on, you make me laugh, you've just reacted like your cave-dwelling ancestors; you've just had a male's reaction and what's more, it's a matter of your wives, and more than that, you're delegates. Then they burst out laughing; that all happened amicably, you understand. They all thought at the beginning that their wives would tell them one day, "You know I earn as much as you for that." I said, "Any way, women are superior to you in some ways. If you're told to label bottles you'll do fewer; if you have to sew buttons you'll do fewer; if you go about bending vines you'll do fewer. Because they have an attention to detail in their fingers that we don't have and never will have. What's more, they'll always be superior to us, they make children, we'll never make any." So all that ended in that way.

Well I must, you see, watch over what I call labor capital here. Perhaps because I'm from the soil, because I'm like them, I feel it even more. Here the office of welfare is my office. If there is a sickness in the family we've only to telephone the clinic, they'll come. And that'll work as long as we maintain this familial climate. Sometimes people say that I'm a paternalist. Yes I'll act paternally because when there are seventy persons and not five thousand or seventy thousand persons we all know each other, and some people have been here for twenty years, thirty years, fifty years. I try to remain human and when there are problems, we settle them.

As for grape picking, we harvest with people on the estate, on the one hand, and on the other, people from outside, from around Paulliac, whom I pick up in a bus. I set up a child care service because for the little household that works in an enterprise there's a month' vacation: fifteen days for leisure and fifteen days to go picking, because there's a good wage. They're well fed, food's abundant; there's enough for all the family. In the child care center there are sometimes thirty, forty, fifty kids; I've three women who watch the kids, I feed the kids. I started that some years ago.

We bring in harvesters from all over. Here we spend 1.45 francs per liter to harvest grapes and to make wine. There's a banquet every day. They're fed morning, noon and night. I've a service of provision; I've eleven women who do the cooking and who serve the tables. At this moment [August 1979] we have 180 people to feed. This is the critical moment. I've set up a service. People sit down, they have as much bread as they wish, as much wine, coffee, chaser *(pousse-cafe)* for each repast. On the last day of harvest there's a feast. They're paid, but they have the day off, I arrange a dance. That's part of a way of living that this privileged soil permits. Now I'll tell you that with wine like that at Narbonne at two francs a liter, I'd buy mechanical harvesters because I couldn't spend 1.45 francs to harvest. But I think that Latour does it and finally, I've got very good pickers.

Voilà, the people are well off, they've no wish to leave, they have good wages. Today a chief tractor driver, in the vineyard, earns 4,000F a month, housing included; they're housed on the estate, they have wine included. We offer a salary of 3,300F and add about 500F for housing if they live off the estate on their own. If they live on the estate we keep that and for the wine we presently take 17F per month; they get two liters of wine a day. Why do we give wine? Because its a part of the benefits long written into contracts and we won't go back on it. Why was so much wine given in former times? In former times there was very little money in this region. During periods of crisis when the worker asked for a raise, the custom when they couldn't pay him, was to have him drink, and they gave him a lot of wine because it was so cheap. Well that remained among the benefits.

We give them end-of-year bonuses that vary from three to five weeks pay. At first we gave them monthly bonuses, but we perceived that we encouraged the hare-brained and discouraged the good worker. Well, now we give grades; I know well that this can be criticized and in a factory of 5,000 workers you couldn't do it, but here there's seventy persons in all. With good conscience we do it, we give grades for human values, professional value, exactitude, initiative in work. I don't say that it's perfect what we're doing, but what we've seen above all is that the hare-brained have been discouraged and the good encouraged, especially when the wives become involved because the fellow who obtains the maximum bonus of the year and who then fell off, we'll tell you that we count above all on his wife to pester him for six months.

Women's work is too dispersed to be paid on a monthly basis. They work on everything, they work on the vine, they work on bottling. Of course we work perhaps in a not very efficient way; we don't have a group for bottling. I keep that for my women. We bottle by hand. We have two phases. First we draw wine into the bottles. Then comes the dressing: labels, capsules, wrapping

in tissue paper; I keep that for winter. Because when they're finished cutting
the bands that attach vine branches, when they've gathered pruned branches,
they come to indoor shelter, they are warmed, they can earn their day well.
That's their recompense. If I hire a group of women, they're going to do poor
work in the vines. I know that from the management point of view this is not
highly profitable, or the greatest concern for management. Well, we do it, my
women are content with that. What is needed in this work, in this highly
specific work, of highest quality, it's above all to care for the human capital.
In these domains, as I tell you, there is land as capital, prestige as capital and
labor as capital. If you look after the third, the first two will go along well
with men of quality, good workers. A good worker is never overpaid, the pin-
head is always overpaid. Between a vigneron who prunes reasonably, wisely,
while watching over them, he has a value not comparable with the pin-head
who massacres a vine. The capital is there, it's the vine, and to preserve that
capital you must care for your human capital who trims that vine. All the rest
is literature.

Mr. Sagnes: What do the costs of labor represent in a domain like this?

Mr. Gardère: Between 60–65 percent. Labor costs have gone up considerbly.

Chapter Three
Leisure and Festivity

THE FESTIVE ASPECT of life, the play element, has always assumed a large role in every society. Until the First World War festivals and other forms of amusement that most directly and frequently influenced vignerons were local, a product of their own making or of the neighboring villages, and combined traditional practices with more recent creations: story telling, card playing, and the maypole, with the newest music and dances. The pattern and pace of village life, its limited contacts with the outer world, determined the form and substance of recreation. The isolation that was part of rural life gave to the various styles of play their rootedness in the locale and their naturalness, their authenticity.

Viticultural France of the 1920s was not greatly different from the France of the "Gay Nineties." In wine villages and small towns the pleasures of life had not changed much and were still enjoyed as part of village life.

We are referring to the open or public activity that went on after work. Within the village setting, vignerons relaxed and sought pleasure both on a day to day basis and during certain seasonal holidays.

After their daily labor, growers often attended a *veillée* or *chambrée*. The *veillée* was a gathering of the members of a small village or several families, each bringing some form of artificial light and beverage and food for sharing. Here, the village elders told stories from ancestral lore—often about calamitous vintages or ghosts that shook grapes off the vines or a local achievement still part of the collective memory. For the vignerons of Champagne there were the disasters of war, 1870 and 1914, and heroic harvesting in the midst of falling bombs. These experiences, lived and remembered, integrated or bound the group together. Entire families took part in the *veillée*, and young people carried on their courting and decided who was to marry whom. Beverages were usually cooked wines or wines fortified with alcohol.

Equally important was the café or barroom. Even a small village had at least one café and small towns boasted several. The village café was usually a grubby, ill-lighted, smelly place frequented mainly by local peasant males after work. Married men went there to escape their cramped living quarters and their families.

Bachelors went to seek companionship. These were not singles bars. Women rarely set foot in them until recent times.

The café, regardless of its decor, was a place for locals to meet. These men did not drink much during the winter and the beverage would more likely be coffee rather than alcohol. They talked and joked and played cards or dominos and, if inclined, read a newspaper provided by the café owner. One cup of coffee lasted the hour or two that its drinker remained among his pals. Grape growers were not big spenders; very few of them made much money and they went early to bed. During long summer evenings and on Sundays, their favorite game was *boules* or outdoor bowling in the backyard of the café. The drink on these occasions would be more decidedly alcoholic: a vermouth or brandy in the north, pernod in the south.

Sunday lunch and various celebrations (marriages, birthdays, anniversaries) were family and often village events. Here, wine, homemade to be sure, came into its own. It is here one sees the important role of wine as part of the ceremonial activities of rural life—a role that goes back to ancient Greece and Rome. What the French (and the Italians and Spanish) inherited from these very distant ancestors was the notion of wine as part of the ritualized aspects of society. Marriages, births, anniversaries were rituals—formerly religious rituals or ceremonies. Wine was a necessary ingredient in religion and both Greeks and Romans worshipped wine gods (Dionysus and Bacchus).

We do not want to give the impression that grape and wine growers were given to excessive drinking. We discovered no recollections of Dionysian drinking contests or Bacchanalian orgies. To the question, "Were winemen heavy drinkers in their reveling? " we can answer no. To be sure the French accept wine as a desirable part of life. Wine is older than France. It was brought to ancient Gaul— from which France grew—by the Greeks and the Romans. Like them, the French have always believed that wine is a gift of God, unlike many Anglo-Saxons who have been convinced that it is a trick of the devil.

As a gift of the Christian God, wine has played a dual role in French life. First, it is a divine food. In former times the father of the family, before cutting a loaf of bread, made the sign of the cross over it as an act of gratitude. Wine was part of this meal and this sense of gratitude. Among a people who for centuries were more poor than rich, whose diet was often limited, wine was a divine gift of calories.

But wine was more than a food, it was also a part of the ceremonial side of life. This aspect of its influence undoubtedly arose from the Catholic tradition of France, for wine was an essential element of the Catholic Mass, which was for centuries the unifying ceremony of both rich and poor. From the holy altar, wine moved to the dinner table as dining became a ceremony. Since World War I, most French growers have abandoned the sacred altar of the church, but they certainly have not yet abandoned that other altar, the dinner table—nor the wine bottles standing upon it like holy candles.

They drink wine with a certain reverence, but chiefly with meals. In consequence, drinking has been limited. Wine growing regions were not and are not now beset by alcoholism, because much of the wine consumed is home grown and is low in alcohol. It is as much a part of work as of play. Vignerons consume as much as two liters when working on their vines. They rarely drink that much when dining or during an evening's entertainment. Wine is a natural accompaniment to banquets and growers generally organize several social banquets. On these occasions, each member brings a bottle and passes it around. This is home grown, untaxed wine. Most growers do not possess a great deal of wine for their own consumption and the best of it they jealously reserve for seasonal festivities.

In February, many villages in the south celebrated carnival. This has always been a time of true reveling, and festivities went on for a week before Ash Wednesday and the beginning of Lent. Sometimes the reveling went on for a month because February was not a time of work. There were parades with decorated floats made on harvest wagons drawn by mules or oxen. There was dancing in the dirt streets and the cobblestone square. Young people dressed in odd costumes, all wearing masks. In villages with an imaginative population, there were theatrical farces. These were occasions for the village wit to bring laughter by sly allusions to the illicit acts of his neighbors: the watering of wine, overcropping, sugaring of musts, cheating in trade, and love-making among the vines. There was often a troupe of young men dressed in voluminous nightgowns who performed traditional and comic dances that were centuries old.

The grape harvest was also a time of frolicking. Before the advent of mechanical harvesters, picking grapes was a hard, backbreaking task. Yet, every evening the youth of the village gathered for dancing and merriment. Music was provided either by a mechanical piano or by local musicians and their instruments: accordion,

Fig. 13 Festival and procession in a Champenois village.

fiddle, trumpet or flute, and drum. Dances were the waltz, mazurka, polka, and a lively quadrille. In the 1920s came the tango; in the 1930s came jazz and jitterbugging.

Up to World War II (1939 for France), amusements were determined by the technological level of society. In many wine villages, transport was extremely limited. Therefore, people had to amuse themselves. They could not rely on outside entertainment. Even a village or town ten miles away was very far away when the only means of transport in the evening was walking or a bicycle. Very few grape growers owned automobiles until the 1950s. The Saturday night village dance, therefore, was about the only form of weekly communal fun as distinct from seasonal festivities. Until the 1930s, local musicians provided the music, which consisted of peasant songs that everyone could sing; and there were singalongs as well as dancing. By the 1930s the juke box made its entry. The village could rent one and everybody contributed coins to feed its hungry mouth. It was placed on the village square, not because it was cheaper than live musicians, but because its recordings offered "city music." Peasant songs were now in disrepute, old-fashioned, fit only for "yokels."

We have not found a fully acceptable reason why this change in taste occurred. Perhaps it was a result of the economic crisis of the 1930's. Young men and women who had fled their villages in the 1920's to work in the city were suddenly without jobs. So they returned home and brought their big city ways with them. Naturally, the local folk wanted to imitate them. Peasants learned the Charleston, the jitterbug, and the blackbottom. This tendency was reinforced by the spread of radios in households as rural electrification made headway. The advancing technology of communication rapidly broke through the isolation of village life.

This change took place more rapidly and easily in wine areas because they were generally located on lines of easy transport and communication. Communication was and still is all important in the entertainment business. Before World War II, however, that business was centered mainly in larger cities. In the countryside, it was more of a craft than a mass production enterprise. It did not center itself in one place, but had to be peripatetic; had to travel to its audience—as did the wandering peddler who carried his wares on horseback until the 1930s, when he began to arrive in a huffing and puffing truck. Entertainment arrived in the same way: the traveling circus as well as the traveling cinema and vaudeville show. Save for the movies and kerosene lamps, such troops of actors and acrobats had been carrying comedy and drama to rural villagers since time immemorial. The notable feature here is the communal or public character of entertainment. Peasants had fun as part of the village community. They had fun together—this was togetherness as a normal part of life. Housing conditions probably encouraged people to go outdoors and entertainment was largely an event of the warmer months in wine areas. In colder months, there was the *veillée*.

Since World War II all of this has changed. The automobile and television have ruined the traveling theatre and destroyed the integrity of village life. The little community has lost its reason for being and, therefore, its economic independence and cultural creativity. The local craftsmen and merchants have been put out of business by mass produced goods and supermarkets in the cities. Automobiles have allowed peasants to drive into cities to buy manufactured articles as well as groceries at prices much lower than in villages. The village has become a place where people work and sleep; it is no longer a place where inhabitants play. When vine dressers come home from work, what do they do? They dine and go to bed. There are, of course, a couple of hours in between dining and sleeping. These are devoted to television. Villagers no longer visit neighbors for gossip or exchange of jokes—they stay home and watch the *télé*. Communal life hardly exists; the new technology of entertainment has fragmented the community. Television keeps people closed up in the home; automobiles carry them away from the village.

The technology of transport has also separated generations. Once, young people organized village festivities. Today, they get into automobiles to escape the village. At reckless speeds they rush into the city's cafés and discotheques, leaving their parents at home to watch television. More than ever before, technology has separated the young from the old. In the past, the youth of the village were keepers of the flame of fun. Today, in an age of canned entertainment, they have abandoned that role. Disco dancing is a symbol of the now generation. There is little physical contact; there is barely communication with others. Each dancer does his/her own thing. Hindu philosophers were supposed to attain nirvana looking at their motionless navels. Today's youth attain an exalted state of excitement while beholding a navel that is rocking and rolling in rhythm with sounds so ear-piercing and frenetic that they could turn good wine into vinegar.

I

In this chapter, the intimate connections between viticulture, festival, and religion become evident. Even in the Mediterranean south where anticlerical forces greatly weakened the role of church and priest, most festivities have their origins in a belief in God and his saints. But since the late nineteenth century, lay holidays, such as July fourteenth and May first have acquired a larger and larger place in the life of villages and towns.

Mr. Emile Bélet, a vigneron and music teacher, and his wife, also a teacher, live in Capestang, in the Hérault department. They know particularly well the amusements of former times: they were not only observers and participants, but also creators, being both musicians and poets.

Mr. Bélet: There were in our village two bands *(harmonie)* and two choral groups. They were the red band and red choral group, the white band and white choral group. They were the right and the left, the royalists as one called them at the time, and the republicans of course. They had a fight one day, striking out with their instruments; but that's a detail. At that time the war of '14 broke out, and during the war all those entertainments, let's say artistic affairs, of the village were abolished of course. So then, for entertainment in the village there was not much; those who liked to read had books of course. And me, I began at that time to play music because the municipal band, which was the red band, republican, because the socialist party ran the town hall at that time, well they trained students. As for me, I took private lessons with the assistant leader of the band, violin lessons, you see. That's to say that when war was declared, there remained in the village only the republican band, the others having disappeared entirely, and even the republican choral group was disbanded. The right wing band went to play in the church and the choral group also went to sing in the church. And the others went to participate in the republican demonstrations of July Fourteenth, and May First.

Well, after the war there were demonstrations "in memory of," as one says, and then certainly there were large turnouts, and that continued afterward, for Armistice Day. There were local holidays, these festivities attracted crowds, since there was nothing else. And as amusements for the young there was naturally the silent cinema, and then there was a dance every Sunday with an orchestra, in which I played from the age of eighteen.

During the week, at the village café, there were young people who danced in the evening to a player piano. So, those were about the only amusements there were in the village.

The dance we began in 1924. We were the ones who had begun to form a jazz band, as it was called at the time, jazz. Then training was no longer the same; the other kind of training was with the violin, clarinet, baritone, and stringed contra-bass.

That was the orchestra of a time when they played polkas, mazurkas, waltzes, and quadrilles. We were the first to make jazz. We dethroned the other kind of orchestras, because young people no longer wanted polkas and all that. So we began to launch "melodic jazz," as it was called. As instruments there were the violin, the piano, saxophone, and cornet at first, because the trumpet came after, and drums of course. Then as dances, we did the one step, foxtrot, java, tango, and waltz. The waltz held out and the java, in sum it's rather like the mazurka used to be, not with the same air, let's say. That was melodic jazz as they called it.

Mrs. Bélet: And then we played a series of dances, then there was an intermission when they went to the bar. After the waltz they did another dance, because the waltz, not everyone danced it. I, who like to dance, the waltz makes my head turn, I don't do it. And so, there was a dance that they called the invitation dance. Then, you understand, everyone had to participate, to be invited. So with the invitation dance, it was in general the young man who was courting you who invited you in order to spend the dance time with you, of course. It was a march, a very easy dance so that everyone could do it.

Mr. Bélet: On holidays, they never began before nine-thirty, ten o'clock [p.m.] like they do now anyway. But they lasted until five o'clock in the morning, even six o'clock sometimes. [But there were numerous intermissions].

Mrs. Bélet: And at festivals, they ended with the snail. The snail, it's a dance in which they make several arrangements with chairs, with a ladder, they did *farandoles*, then they [a couple] climbed onto the ladder and kissed, it was an opportunity to kiss each other. Then they would duck down over there, then another couple would skip to the rhythm, then at the end, they would duck down again or kiss.

Mr. Bélet: And then it came to an end, they made the snail, then it unwinds, they unwind it by passing underneath. The person who becomes the prisoner, who's in the middle, the prisoner in the middle rejoins the line by sliding under the others and the snail unwinds.

The municipal band is still going strong. I was put in the schools to teach singing and music. I remained thirty-two years. I began in 1927 and I resigned in '59, and that's still going on.

Mrs. Bélet: The municipal government of Capestang, although backward in many things, it's always paid someone, very badly paid but all the same, it's always paid someone to train students in music. That dates from 1905, I think. There are night courses.

Mr. Bélet: We had, when I was a young man, after the war, in the 1920s in Capestang, three artistic societies. They were very clearly divided: *Le Cercle*, *L'Aurore Littéraire et artistique* (petty bourgeois, since the rich had *Le Cercle*) and *Los Amusäires* (the amusers, they were agricultural workers). Formerly the people of *Le Cercle*, they were called rich and some of them were not really rich. That is going to interest you because formerly a proprietor who produced 300 or 400 hectos, even less, had a worker or two and he went to see them in the vineyard with a suit coat, a tie, and cane. He did nothing. He lived, I know how he lived because the workers, he didn't pay them much, and clearly he had enough in profits to be able to live without doing anything. While now he can't live if he doesn't "knead the dough."

Mrs. Bélet: And precisely, the other day, when I was taking a walk with some ladies, we spoke about it and recalled all those fellows in *Le Cercle*. Well, they've all disappeared, they were all ruined.

Mr. Bélet: They used to fill the town café there. There were about twenty families. They put on theatrical works, there were men singers and women singers, you understand. And then there, they had a symphonic orchestra since there were a piano, violins, clarinets, woodwinds; they had every kind of instrument available at Capestang. They put on three shows: one in autumn, one in winter, and one before spring.

They put on the *Flibustier (The Buccaneer)*. They hired me, you can say, because I played in the theater, I sang, I played comedy at that time and I played the violin. So you understand I was useful in all departments, to such a point that they wanted to pay me, in fact, to send me to Paris so I could go to the Conservatory. And my mother did not want it because I lost my father in 1917 and I was alone with my grandparents and my mother.

Well now the second group; it was the *Aurore Littéraire et Artistique;* they had a library where they gave out books. They put on *soirées* like the others, at a rate of three or four per year. There, they played works by Courteline and Labiche, you see, unpretentious plays. They also had singers, of course.

And the *Amusaïres*, the other, it was nearly the same, only, as I told you, they were workers. I went there too. There were also some petty landowners.

The aim of each was the same, it was in sum to amuse the population, you understand. Now there were some people who went to the *Aurore* and who went to the *Cercle*, but who did not go to the *Amusaïres*. Evidently those of the *Cercle* did not go at all to the *Amusaïres*, but as for the *Amusaïres*, there were some people of the *Aurore* who went there, you see, because all the same they were radicals and socialists. [Radicals were Jacobin republicans].

Mr. Sagnes: So, their activity was theatrical above all.

Mr. Bélet: Yes, above all theatrical.

Mrs. Bélet: But *Los Amusaïres*, they also did, I know, a parody of *"Cloches de Corneville."*

Mr. Bélet: They played those military plays, trooper's comics, you know the type.

Mr. Sagnes: Did they use only French?

Mr. Bélet: Ah, they used langue d'Oc also.

Mr. Sagnes: Did you use langue d'Oc?

Mr. Bélet: No, in major plays, no. There were those who read monologues in langue d'Oc, and they put on short sketches.

Mr. Sagnes: Was it you who put on all that, who composed all that?

Mr. Bélet: Composed, no.

Mr. Sagnes: Was there a regional repertory?

Mr. Bélet: Well, they took Emile Barthe (author using langue d'Oc). One year at the *Amusaïres* they played, if I remember, *"La Fille de la Mer."* They played Emile Barthe once, you see.

Ah, they were determined to put on shows in all three societies, because everyone put his all into it, and there were people of talent at all levels. And as entertainment there was only that, and silent films on Saturday. That's all there was here.

For the *Cercle*, of course, since it was the rich, as I said, you had to go dressed up, in a tuxedo, women in evening gowns. While at the *Aurore*, there it was a little more free, let's say. Everyone went as they wanted. And at the *Amusäires* also, they didn't go, by Jove, in work clothes, but after all, they didn't wear tuxedos or evening gowns. There now, that's the difference in dress in the three societies. Now, the *Aurore* disappeared about 1932–33 or '34. Les *Amusäires* disappeared at nearly the same time. There was only the *Cercle* that held out until the war, let's say, until the declaration of war in '39.

Now as regards jazz, that was going on in '25. And then at that time they had many village festivities, that is the celebration of summer here at Capestang. It's in the month of August, 3–4–5 August. And the carnival, certainly the carnival was properly celebrated. And we used to have a *félibre* (an advocate of Provençal language and culture) from Toulouse; his name was Boullard. He wrote songs in Occitan for the carnival. They always wrote carnival songs in Occitan.

For the carnival before the war of '14 they made a float, they made a locomotive. In 1925 at the birth of jazz, of the jazz-band, as they called it at that time, Boullard being dead, it was I who began to write songs in Occitan for the carnival. I wrote a song on the jazz-band. I'll translate it for you in French:

> With the jazz-band all in chorus
> We've come to expect you,
> All this music of the Summer
> We're happy to receive you.
> That's a change from the old dances,
> The old polkas, waltzes and mazurkas.

And after there was:

> Long live the jazz-band for girls and boys
> Long live the jazz-band that all the young love,
> Long live the jazz-band that sets all Capestang going.

At the end of carnival, the last day, Ash Wednesday, Carnival was put on trial, always using Occitan. So Carnival was brought to judgement. They accused it of all the bad things that happened in the region during the year. It was accused of introducing an evil spirit into people's minds.

Mrs. Bélet: If there had been hail, for example, or if there were frosts, or if fire had broken out someplace, it was accused.

Mr. Bélet: And it was blamed for wine, for the lack of sales, or because of the events of 1907.

Mrs. Bélet: And if there were infidelities, cuckolded men, it was responsible.

Mr. Sagnes: How was the trial carried on?

Mr. Bélet: On the square. There were people dressed as lawyers. There was the lawyer for the defense and the one for the prosecution, and witnesses.

Mrs. Bélet: There were picturesque people in disguise. One came to confess that she made her husband do this or that, or that he always made his wife burn the soup, tricks like that.

Mr. Bélet: When in the course of the year, something happened to a native, a misadventure, they dragged it out.

Mr. Sagnes: But weren't they careful enough not to make allusion that would have angered a part of the village?

Mrs. Bélet: It wasn't mean, all the same; they didn't go too far. They didn't go beyond acceptable limits.

Mr. Bélet: These limits you know them too, by Jove! There were political limits because there at the trial of Carnival, the *Cercle*, *Aurore* and *Amusäires*, all were involved in the matter, young people above all.

Mr. Sagnes: But no one mentioned names; no one made allusions? For example at Capestang in 1933, there was a very widespread strike. Did the carnival of 1934 allude to it?

Mr. Bélet: No, because it was serious, it nearly became a tragedy. You know, there were gendarmes, and there was the adjutant of the national police who was in charge of what they called "sabres drawn." There were workers in front of the mayor's office who carried on the strike and who, in the end, began demonstrating.

Mrs. Bélet: The strike marked too many people; they don't like to talk about it; it was too serious.

Mr. Sagnes: So there was an "auto-censorship."

Mrs. Bélet: It was too serious, no one wants to talk about it. People suffered too much; there was real poverty; there was hate.

Mr. Bélet: All that ended after the war, in '45–'46. In the following years they didn't do much, carnival wasn't celebrated too much. Then after, at a certain time, during ten years, the Rugby people took over the carnival, that meant that they became responsible for organizing the carnival. Well, at that time, they acted to restore old traditions, to revive the judgement of Carnival and all that. Now none of this is done.

Mr. Sagnes: A moment ago you spoke of more personal problems, for example of *cocuage* (cuckolding). How was that passed off and tried?

Mrs. Bélet: All right, there they referred to so-an-so. . . . In the end, people whom one could attack if their affairs were a little too. . . .

Mr. Bélet: They named no names all the same; they made little allusions. So every evening during the holidays, which lasted from Saturday until Ash Wednesday, we put on sketches. At midnight they stopped the dance and we put on a sketch that I directed and that I created as well. We did Nounours, a sketch at that time on Allarix the Gaul, because it was for Asterix the Gaul, and because we had a president named Albary, I did that sketch of Asterix the Gaul. It was a hunting scene in the lagoon. Ah, well, all that for laughs!

And then I did one, a little as a joke, it was more in the popular singer style, that was called "The Ballet of the Buckets," because we had put on the ballet of the little rats of the Opera. So, you see these little rats, they were rugby players, the half-pillars [of society] and all that, dressed as little rats with ballet skirts. That's funny. Then the other was to poke fun, "The Ballet of the Buckets," at the inertia of the municipal government for cleanliness in the village, because we still have outhouses, and we still had them for a long time after, until barely seven years ago. You see they had the "everything in the gutter" at Capestang. It was the ballet of the toilet buckets, sung to the air of the "Washerwoman of Portugal." It ran: "And scrub, and scrub, and scrub little broom, and scrub, and scrub, and scrub, it's a true palace. . . ." There was more to it than that, that was a part of the refrain. It began with the air of "L'Arlésienne": "Early in the morning, we're going to put buckets at street corners and public squares. . . ." I don't recall any more, but they were going to put out the toilet bucket as good women did every morning, before the pick-up wagon passed. The village government took umbrage.

Well, these traditions were broken after, in '68 I think. The rugby team no longer did the carnival, it all caved in. Now the rural club has taken it up, they do it moreover with the rugby team, they got together again. They do the local festivals.

Mr. Sagnes: Were there theatre groups of this type in other villages?

Mr. Bélet: No, but they didn't have them everywhere. There was one at Puisserguier; it was good. At Nisson, one that still exists, is *"Los Rousegaïres."*

Mme Bélet: But at Puisserguier, they put on three-act plays that appeared in *"La Petite Illustration."* You see it was on a rather high level. They played "Thaïs"; they put on good plays.

Mr. Bélet: But for our part, I'm going back to '44, we put on "L'Arlésienne" at Capestang. That, you see, was for the benefit of war prisoners, and I didn't bring in politics, you might say. I took people from the *Cercle*, the *Aurore*, the best of the three societies, but I had participated in the three, you see. Then I was very comfortable, I knew them all, and I took talented people and we put on "L'Arlésienne" with chorus and orchestra, all complete.

During the occupation. We began in November '43 after the grape harvest and worked for more than three months and played it in '44. We had rehearsals in the House of the People, and there was a curfew and stoppage of electricity. We had to obtain permits because sometimes rehearsals went on till ten o'clock, when curfew began. So as not to be trapped by German patrols, they procured two *Ausweise* for us, for the actors, so someone conducted all those going west and I conducted those going east. We were never arrested. Do you know how we rehearsed when there was no light? We used miners' lamps.

We did two shows at Capestang, and we went to play it for the prisoners from Béziers at the Municipal Theater of Béziers, on Ascension Thursday.

Mrs. Bélet: All the orchestra seats were taken by German officers; we played before German officers, and they rose to applaud us at the end. To be sure we played throughout the region, because all the same, we had put it on in a masterly fashion. All the roles were well acted, we played with much sincerity, with conviction.

Mr. Sagnes: Didn't the Resistance take umbrage at this kind of . . . ?

Mr. Bélet: It was for the prisoners of war, for the benefit of the prisoners.

Mrs. Bélet: We played until, I don't remember the date exactly, but the end of May, and on June 9 the manager was deported, so we could not continue.

But you spoke of resisters, there is something serious there; it's the business of Fontjun. [When some resisters almost openly departed to join the Maquis, local informers warned the Germans, who ambushed them at a place called Fontjun. German troops took Capestang and deported 183 men]. Emile [Bélet] was denounced by some people from here, and denounced in a calumnious way. He was denounced for having put on "L'Arlésienne" to enroll youths in the Resistance because we put on the *farandole* (a peasant dance) of "L'Arlésienne." In the *farandole* there were all the young people of Capestang who came, the girls and the boys of Capestang. Since it was known that he belonged to the Resistance, the collaborators deduced that he used "L'Arlésienne" to set up a resistance network.

Mr. Sagnes: Well now if we can go back in time.

Mrs. Bélet: Well, to the *Cercle* in 1924. The *Cercle* one year prepared a review on Capestang to play during a soirée and this review was high class because in the Cercle there were some very cultivated people who knew how to handle a pen and who had the gift of writing verse, even though three or four got together to do it.

Mr. Sagnes: Were they all viticultural landowners?

Mrs. Bélet: They were all viticultural landowners, but they were cultured all the same.

Mr. Sagnes: Did they complete secondary school?

Mrs. Bélet: Oh yes, yes. And there were personalities all the same. The theme of the review was Capestang. And that review was somewhat humorous. It dealt with members of the *Cercle* above all, with the life they led, of lovers, then with favored places in the village, with amusing things. For example,

about Mr. Tabouriech who was an aristocratic person, who had a polished
tongue, who was a gentleman, they said:

So Tabouriech
With anger taken suddenly
Bawled out the passers-by
Like a *répétite*.

The *répétite*, she was the fishwife. Afterward there was the man who was not
very valiant, who never did anything. Then of course there was also the lady,
Mrs. Doumerque, who had a bus there and who piled passengers in carelessly:

But Mrs. Doumergue
Smilingly offered me
A seat quite as soft
As an oriental cushion.

That's because in the diligence, as you know, no one was very comfortable.
And then they referred also to the fountain that we have here. It provides
Capestang with its drinking water because at that time [1920s] there was no
other water in the village save that of the canal. The only drinking water
came from the "Fountain of the Terror." So in verse, they referred to the
fountain.

To the *pech* come when dies the day,
At night I sleep almost without veils.
The sole cloak of my attire
Where the dew places its velvet
Is the golden cloak of the stars.

That's the fountain speaking. And there also is a nymph who speaks, the
nymph of the fountain. And then also they glorify wine:

Listen to the wine bubble in the pot-bellied vat
And marry its gurgling to the rhythm of bared breasts.
Where Phebus poured the fine gold of his burnishings.
Come and thou will kiss reddened mouths
Ripe like fruit saturated by the sun's rays
Come cry out on the vermilion slopes
Where the dancing olive tree hides in the hollow of branches
The songs of the cicadas.
Come and thy pale hands will gather at will
The fruits of our gardens,
Our supple-bodied women and
Thou will drink our wines
So that, the evening come, while dancing our round
Thou canst get drunk to the health of the world.

There were also personal allusions:

What, you still don't have in hand
The recent work from the pen of Mr. Doumenc!
And it's entitled "The Maladies of Vines."
Which arose from the railroad, neighbor to his vines

> Whose smoke, it seems, arrested their vigor.
> He combats it. How?
> By a gigantic fan
> Installed along the track
> That takes the smoke
> And toward the lagoon sends it.
> It's very ingenious.
> But yet the *grangette* is at the lagoon.
> Ah, do you believe that stops him?
> He ably captures this smoke down there
> And spreads it in April to prevent frost.

There were clever things like that, you see. There also they recall the old diligence of Doumenc.

Mr. Bélet: There were diligences until after the war of '41. There were still diligences after the war. The first buses came, I don't know exactly, toward the 1930s.

Mrs. Bélet: Well then, they recall the time of the diligence, to the air of *"Temps des Cerises."*

> My wheels are rusty, so tarnished my gilt;
> And I'm out of service for so long now
> I've finished my job.
> Those were the good times; the dusty road
> Bathed in sun was all mine
> And I was happy bounding gaily
> Like a trotting carriage
> My trembling windows told of my emotion.

Mr. Sagnes: In these three societies did they use French as well as the langue d'Oc? Because all this smacks a bit of the humanities, secondary studies. Did little owners and workers speak Occitan?

Mr. Bélet: Well, they spoke a lot of Occitanian patois.

Mr. Sagnes: And the big owners, what did they speak?

Mr. Bélet: They spoke French. If they let fall some words in patois from time to time, that was rare. You understand, it seemed vulgar to speak in patois.

Mr. Sagnes: Were there festivities connected with the grape harvest, for example, or with wine?

Mrs. Bélet: There was the dance of the grape harvest.

Mr. Sagnes: Can one consider that the importance of all this artistic life has a connection with the leisure that the vine provided? Because you had to rehearse, you needed dozens of hours of rehearsal?

Mr. Bélet: We had no radio, we had no *télé*, we had nothing, so that helped us pass the time.

Mrs. Bélet: And then it was in the evening, it wasn't during the day.

Mr. Bélet: Here, we had all our evenings free, the agricultural worker and everyone.

Mr. Sagnes: And in summer more than the evenings?

Mr. Bélet: In summer we had some of the afternoon, because they made it *de longue* (nonstop) as they said. Here they began at seven o'clock in the morning and finished at two o'clock in the afternoon.

Mrs. Bélet: Listen, as for me, I always heard it said at home and around me, that viticultural work was the most despised and the hardest; that's what it was, they said. It was even urged that we give up vines. And I'm going to tell you something. Alright, in the upper school when I was asked what my parents did, I was a little ashamed to say that they were vignerons. I found that if a girl said that her father was a mailman, that was better. You see the mentality that they formed for us.

Mr. Bélet: You know, I always heard my father say: "It's the most ungrateful and despised work." Well, I was a bit slow in maturing to become aware that this was true. But when you have a little property, it's a profession in which you have to count pennies; and then there are the uncertainties of weather, it's a profession without security, that's true. But as work, frankly, you're outdoors; it's interesting work I find, healthy work, interesting, and then it leaves you some pleasure.

But the petty owners, but those of the *Amusaïres*, the wage workers, they labored *de longue* as I said to you, and they were not well paid and they still aren't, not yet, and they carried on *bourrados* as it's called, that is supplementary work. They went to do contract work, they went to prune or dig holes for others, to earn a little money. And they arrived home for supper in the evening and that didn't stop them from going after supper to rehearsal.

Mrs. Bélet: The vine demands constant care, but all the same the little owner, if he wants, he goes to the sea in July and August, he goes back and forth. And then after the harvest he hunts in November.

II

Mrs. Rachou, who lives in Quarante in the Hérault, recalls all the holidays of the year, and her recollections, given her eighty years of age, are exceptionally lucid and lively. It is remarkable how, before radio, cinema, and television, villagers knew how to entertain themselves. Perhaps those in the environs of Béziers, which includes Capestang as well as Quarante, were more imaginative and influenced by that rather sizable, lively, and wealthy center of the wine trade.

Mrs. Rachou has set out to review all the local holidays or festivals, most of which were also national or regional. What we discover is that politics permeated every aspect of life in the lower Midi. Festivals, dances, pig markets and so on were all influenced by considerations of party. This was the Midi: there was a left, there was a right; in between there was nothing that was willing to serve as a middle ground. From New Years to Christmas all was politics. Such was life in the grape-growing south of France.

Mrs. Rachou: For the New Year, we did as we do now. We played lotto, and there were *réveillons* [late night eating and drinking], dances.

Mr. Pech: Did they give presents to children?

Mrs. Rachou: Yes, they gave you two *sous* or a paper cone of candy. Then young men went to wish a happy New Year to the girls or to friends, and they had a little nip. Sometimes they were tipsy.

Then, after, there was the fair of 29 January. That was the pig fair; there were 200–300 pigs weighing eighty to a hundred kilos. Only pigs were sold, by true pig dealers who arrived from Marseille. For 100 francs you had a pig, even 90 francs. That was a good sum; you had to economize all year, 20 sous, then another 20 sous in the money box, to be able to buy a pig.

In addition to pigs there were merry-go-rounds, there was candy, there were dolls, all that you wanted.

There was the dance of the rich and the dance of the poor, as always. There were even singers who came. One café owner hired comics. At a certain café, he hired women dancers who raised their leg, as they say. The orchestras were local and played for the Sunday dances. There were five musicians.

They learned music in the village. There was Bec who taught music and who taught the young to sing. There was an *orphéon* [choral society] at Quarante, and you had all the men of Quarante who went to sing in the chorus. Only they didn't know how to read or write [music]. They learned by memory and they went out to win. Some time ago they went to Lyon and they won; this time they lost. At Lyon someone gave them printed songs to sing, and since they didn't know how to read, they lost.

Every Sunday there was a dance at the Café de France; it was the dance of the poor. Then there was the dance of the rich at the Café Sidobre. There, you had sons of proprietors, and girls who were poor, who went with the rich, who believed that the rich would marry them. There were also the Café de la Patrie, the Café Mondier, Café Cros that's now called the Café des Sports, the Café des Platanes. Formerly there was another on the square; it was old Quisset who ran it.

[Usually the large room was divided]. There was the café side, and the other side for dancing. While in the Café Sidobre there was a separate ballroom, that

was the fancy café. In summer there was the casino, in front there was a
garden. While people were in the garden, others danced in the ballroom. They
removed panels that they had for winter because it was closed in winter. There
were vases with oleander and all that. That was our Moulin Rouge as my
father said.

And then there was a platform outside, musicians put themselves there and
people danced. And where there were no musicians, there was a piano. This
piano, you put in a two-*sous* coin and the piano played the songs you ordered.

Mr. Pech: Well then, in the café, one played cards and read the papers?

Mrs. Rachou: Ah yes. There were those who did not take the paper. I'm going
to tell you something. There was Courniou, he had 300,000 francs capital at
the time, he was rich before the war of '14. Well, he went to the Café
Sidobre there, he drank coffee and read the paper. He didn't take it at home,
that was too expensive. He read *l'Eclair* [right-wing] and so he said to Mr.
Sidobre: "If it's all right with you, Mr. Sidobre, I'll give you one *sous* and I
won't drink any coffee." The paper cost two *sous*. "I'll give you one *sous*,
and I'll read the paper, I won't order any coffee." Mr. Sidobre said to him:
"You'll read the paper and you'll order the coffee, you'll pay for the coffee.
Because I get more profit if you pay for the coffee rather than the paper."
Because the coffee cost three *sous*, he had two *sous* profit.

The Café Sidobre was reactionary, it was the café of the rich. The café of
the poor where people wrote articles to put in the *Dépêche* [*de Toulouse*, a
Jacobin sheet], was the Café de France where you found Rives, Mirabeau, my
father and all the clique, you understand, that was the café of the poor. The
Café des Platanes, that was the café where you found the half-proprietors. And
the Café des Sports, my goodness, it was the café where everybody went. It
was the café where the diligence stopped. Although its owner was a socialist,
but he criticized nobody. Later the first buses stopped there. There you found
the merchants of the square, because it was on the square, and it was well
located. Merchants went there to drink coffee, and the fishmonger, who located
in front of it, went to drink coffee there. You know, no one spoke about
politics there.

Now for the Carnival, of February-March. It lasted a month. At the time
there was Laforge and he was a reactionary, a reactionary who was rotten,
who gave away so much money that he ruined himself, and he sold his estate.
He gave money to his party. He organized a band that ruined him. He also
supported the mutual aid society, a charity in which there were yellow workers
[obedient to their employer].

The red workers set up the Solidarité. Them, they arranged a carnival and
it was marvelous; I seem to see it now. At that time it was a holiday, and
you had a float of the ironers, people who ironed. It was covered with flowers,
with well caparisoned horses. There was, in the float, a table and chairs, there
was a stove. Linen was suspended, well-ironed of course. There was the float of
the seamstresses, with sewing machines and all. There was the float of the

poppies; the poppies were kids dressed up as flowers. They spent I don't know how many months making all that. There was a float of babies. I was young then, I must have been ten. That was about 1909, '10.

There was a float for Alsace and Lorraine; then came horses with girls riding behind one another. That was a wonderful carnival. The horses were all decked out, hoofs shined and all. The band was leading.

For the carnival the young men got up horns with ribbons and hung them at the end of sticks. They carried a chair, and a towel over one arm. And they paraded around the village. When they found a man they trapped him, had him sit in the chair, and made him kiss one of these famous horns. When the fellow kissed the horn, they put the towel on him and he was given a little drink and he went off. But men were not so foolish. My father, he would not have gone out because he would have thrown slaps about if they had tried to make him kiss a horn. So whom did they find? The drunkards of the place who wanted a little nip.

After the war all that ended.

There was a ball and there was the dance of the bar-keeper and another of the broom, which occurred during the ball. They arrived, dressed in white pants, white shirts, white slippers, flour on their faces and a red girdle and bellows. They arrived, five or six or eight; they arrived, they blew at one another, they turned about and blew on the others. Afterward there was the dance of the broom; the first came singing with a broom in his hand, then he tapped, the last got a blow of the broom, and in some way he turned, and they sought a way to exit. That was the dance of the broom. That took place only at carnival time.

Easter was a holiday. The little ones went to church with palms, with bags of candy suspended. You've done that. We danced as on other Sundays; there was nothing special. There was a good meal and we got together.

On Monday, young people went to make *paquettes*, that is, they went to the woods with a frying pan and eggs. They went to make *paquettes*. And in the evening they danced.

For the St. Jean, people made a St. Jean's fire. But for that there was nothing remarkable. The little ones made fires; but there was nothing special.

On May First, there was nothing, not until after the war of '14, then people didn't go to work.

For July 14, there was the retreat of the colors, the parade around town, and so on. There were games on the square. My brother-in-law was a municipal counsellor and in charge of them. For games, there was the frying pan with 5 francs in it, the pan was very blackened, and you had to draw out the 5 francs with your teeth. And the little ones were all painted. Other games were the sack race, the suspended bucket of water; one fellow tried to push it in a wheelbarrow, and with a stick another tried to push the bucket over.

In July people went to the sea, to Valras. They had wagons and it was unregulated camping. They put large hoops over the wagons and canvas over them and they slept in the wagons. And outside the wagons they raised tents of canvas. In the day they stayed under the tents; at night they slept in the wagons. But all that was before the war. After the war there wasn't any of that. There was a festival at Valras, and we went. Not very many people went there.

There was nothing special at Quarante for August 15. People went to mass. I didn't see anything.

There were no special ceremonies for the *vendanges* (grape picking). Every evening there was dancing. Presently at Quarante a barrel is brought to the church, and the priest blesses it. The socialist mayor began that.

On All Saints Day they prayed, and carried flowers to the cemetery.

For Christmas they played lotto, but there wasn't any festival, and there were dances, as we had all the time. People went to midnight mass; there were *réveillons* and there was the holy manger, of course.

At the Café Sidobre, it was a fine feast; but at the Café de France, for the *réveillon* there was tripe. Mother Fortunée made tripe, it's said that it was good; there was a good *réveillon*.

Ah, what I miss was the annual banquet of the Solidarité, the Mutual Aid. There was a supper! You paid yourself and you brought your own wine, because at this time you did not earn any wine. Someone brought red wine, another brought white. The society paid for the ball. And there was a tour of the village with *flambeaux* (torches) and children went. My grandfather took me, my grandmother took my sister Paulette and we carried *flambeaux*, and with two lanterns on each side. If there was any singing it was the Marseillaise.

III

Mrs. Rachou recalled briefly the annual excursion to the seaside. In this selection Mrs. Justine Soulié, of St. Thibéry (Hérault), 15 kilometers from Agde on the coast, provides more details about the short trips that were such adventures before the coming of swift travel in cars. Going to the beach or to a nearby shrine required considerable preparation.

Mrs. Soulié: In summer, all the young people went to the seaside. We went with the means of transport then available. Well, at that time, there were only donkeys. It was customary to let the donkey rest when halting for lunch, which we took on the grass.

At the seaside we put up provisional tents for the day, with poles to hold up the cover. This cover was made of jute sacks, sacks that had contained dung. Well we made large *bouras* of them, like a bed sheet, that we put over a frame of poles, to spend the day in the shade (there were no parasols at the time).

We brought along a little charcoal stove to heat the evening meal. We prepared the meal on Saturday, and later we had to reheat it on the stove. That was fun.

We went sea bathing. There were bathing suits that were striped; men had sleeves and women, they had pants and a kind of blouse. We were dressed when we went in the sea with a bonnet on our head to avoid wetting our hair. To the extent that people are naked today, we were dressed.

On August 2, we went to pass the night in the Notre Dame chapel at the Grau d'Adge. So we left the day before and there were those who went in carts, *carrioles*—those who had *carrioles* were the well-to-do—the others went in the large carts that they used in the vineyards. Ah, to go to Notre Dame and to pass the night in vigil was pleasant. Those who went to Notre Dame were the well-to-do; not everyone went there. The day after they went to the seaside.

The Monday after Easter, we went to L'Affrie. The chapel was still there, so we made a procession around the Virgin while singing canticles on Easter Monday.

IV

Mr. Valayer, from Richerenches in the Vaucluse (Côtes-du-Rhône), brings out that grape picking, although a time of exhausting labor, was also a time of laughter and song, the latter above all in the regional dialect. As in Chapter One he gives us another song in his extensive repertory.

Mr. Valayer: They're very important, the *vendanges*, because they too have evolved. In former times, we picked among neighbors; you see there were fewer vines than now and a larger population, so we found pickers in the village. In the village there were four or five in one holding, four or five in another. And then the children didn't continue in school until sixteen or eighteen years old; and the kids of fourteen or fifteen gathered grapes. And that always led to a celebration. The *vendange*, since people looked for a little less profit than now, was a little festival. That means that even if you gathered fewer grapes, you joked, you sang, it was a little like folklore.

Well, now we have gangs either of Spaniards, or Moroccans, or of Algerians. That means it's less of a festival, it's more like work. Formerly the harvest was work of course, but it was like a little festival at the same time. Well, now there are gangs who do the picking, yet it's always a task that's gay, when the weather is fine, and you're in the vines. Most often, at the end of the harvest, we have a feast as though we were having a wedding, with all the vignerons, even if they are Moroccan (they don't drink any wine but *enfin* we give them something else and in general we prepare a meal for them the last day of the *vendanges*, that's a little like a feast).

But after all, the *vendange* was really always something that was very gay. Formerly, also, there were fewer cooperatives. Now, all the vignerons carry their grapes to the cooperative and they go there to get their wine for drinking. I remember that we had a vat and that we made our wine. Then in the evening, when we had finished picking, it was night. We crushed the raisins, we put them in the vat and made wine. And when we drew the wine, that also was a festival. We drew wine, we roasted chestnuts; with new wine they are very good.

Mrs. Loubère: Did you compose your own music for the dances?

Mr. Valayer: No, we sang the songs that were passed down by word of mouth like that, you see, and often in Provençal. They are no longer sung, you understand. Moroccans can't sing these same songs, neither the Spaniards. I'll sing one for you, only it's in Provençal, and I'll give you the translation if you want:

When Jehovah decided
To acquaint Noah
With the virtue of the juice of the vine,
Of course he intended to warn him
That wine can be too easily drunk,
And then man's reason escapes.
(Refrain)
When we are hot, let's drink it cool,
    it's worth its price.
When we are cold, let's drink it hot,
    it renders us joyous.
When we are laboring, no more than a dram
    of two fingers
When we are festive, a good share
    but not too much.

V

The Serrurier family, natives of Venteuil in Champagne, show that rural festivities did not differ much between north and south. The difference, if there is one, would arise between generations and their respective geographies of amusement, as the family's son Didier tells us. He is twenty-two years old.

Mr. Serrurier: When I was young, let's say that my pleasure was going to the movies and then, well, to village festivals. Well, let's say that there was fun for everyone, and there was a dance in the evening. Me, I like to dance, I've always loved to dance. When we went to the festival what attracted me most was the dance, as well as the merry-go-round in the day.

Mr. Loubère: Were there songs and dances of this region?

Mr. Serrurier: That existed already, but less than now. Folklore groups you mean? No, at that time [1930s], it was not as widespread as now.

Mr. Loubère [to Didier]: The young of today, how do you have fun?

Mr. Didier Serrurier: We go to the discotheques, that's practically all we do. But that depends on your age. At first, when I worked with my parents, I went to festivals, to dances. All that is dying out; there aren't many young people who go to festivals.

Mr. Loubère: You, young people, prefer to go to the city to have fun?

Mr. Didier Serrurier: Yes, go to the discotheques.

Mr. Loubère: At school, do you sing old songs?

Mr. Didier Serrurier: No, no one taught us any old songs. I've done a little with folklore dances at the *Maison des Jeunes* (Youth Center), that's all I've done.

The Maison has been in existence for ten years. These are old songs that they found in the archives, that they recorded, records that are commercially sold. And they set dances of the period to them. After a certain age you drop out because you can't listen to them anymore; you can't go on dancing or doing what they want you to do. We prefer to go off individually.

Mr. Loubère: You did things differently from your father. I don't imagine, Mr. Serrurier, that you went to town very often to have fun; you had to find your pleasures here in the village.

Mr. Serrurier: Let's say it was rather the comraderie among local pals; it was rather our outings that were the most important. It was when you went to the neighboring village, on bicycle, to a festival or like that. Otherwise, all these new amusements that the kid just described to you didn't exist in our time.

Mr. Loubère: Is there a café in the village? And do people meet there?

Mr. Serrurier: Yes, and that depends. Me, I go there for cigarettes, for an *apéro* (aperitif) from time to time. But there are some who have the habit; when they've finished their day's work they go have a glass at the café; then they talk among comrades, among pals. But I don't frequent it much.

Mr. Loubère [to Didier]: And you neither?

Mr. Didier Serrurier: Yes, we meet among buddies; once we're all assembled, we take off. It's a meeting place on Saturday and Sunday, but in the week we go there less often.

Mr. Loubère [to Mr. Serrurier]: Do people drink a lot around here; what about your generation for example?

Mr. Serrurier: I don't think so; it's declined. That's to say that the older generation drank much more than we do. Let's say that we've occasions to drink, to find ourselves together during friendly outings, or then during parades, because I belong to many clubs, you see. So we have many reunions among pals, in clubs. There's the Maison des Jeunes, there's football, there's the firemen, the band. Well let's say that all these societies have an annual banquet. We go to all the clubs so as not to be unfair, you see. At the Maison des Jeunes, there's a cabbage dinner, the football club, there's a . . . you see, outings like that. There is a banquet and a ball; it's an evening of pleasure, so we participate in all those *soirées* there.

Each club furnishes the wine, each buys it from someone, from a landowner. And it's like that that they make a little profit for the treasury of the club.

Mr. Loubère: You pay for the meal and the drinks; like that they improve the treasury. Do you go also, Madame?

Mrs. Serrurier: Oh yes, there, the *soirées*, yes. They are our only chance to go out. They do all that in winter, the clubs, from the month of November to the month of January. That's the dead season. Oh, there's all the same a little activity for us. The Maison des Jeunes, it puts on a play each year.

Mr. Serrurier: Well, my wife, she plays in the theater. The Maison des Jeunes has many activities, tell them.

Mr. Didier Serrurier: Yes, as activity there is the theater, folklore dances, we do photography to preserve what remains of old houses in the area, to have archives, we do archival photography. We've tried model making, but that's too difficult surely. There's marksmanship. There are many activities for young people, all the same. But it's like that all over. You can't belong until you're fourteen. At the Maison des Jeunes, you remain about three or four years. As for me, I'm staying because I'm a part of the council. But otherwise, as a member who isn't active, you stay for three or four years, until the age when you begin to go out, as I go out now. Because, well, at fourteen, you don't have the right to go out. Your parents don't let you go far, so you go to the Maison des Jeunes. Once you have the right to go out, you don't go there anymore; you go elsewhere.

Mr. Loubère: Do you do a lot of hunting?

Mr. Serrurier: We have lots of game here. That's a pleasure that costs a lot, but what do you want, I only have that as a pleasure. I have stock in a large hunting ground, and moreover, I'm president of hunting in the area. I'm in charge of hunting for the village.

VI

Mr. and Mrs. Guillemard, vignerons of Pommard in the Côte d'Or, inform us that sociabilité *was not confined to the Mediterranean Midi. Societies of musicians,*

*of firemen, of former students, as well as the practice of veillées (evening
gatherings) were widespread in all viticultural regions where grape growers
lived in villages, which means nearly all of them. Revelry arose from the
imagination, from contacts among humans. Mechanization existed before the
war of '39, in the form of phonographs and merry-go-rounds, but most of the
time peasants created their own fun and games.*

Mr. Guillemard: Every winter there were festivals given by the firemen's society, there were concerts, music, there were dances.

Mrs. Guillemard: There were clubs that went in for drama; they had several
sessions in winter. And then, people had more *veillées* at each other's houses.

Mr. Guillemard: A society of former students . . . .

Mrs. Guillemard: We went visiting in the evening, after the evening meal, we
went to one person's home, then another to spend the evenings together. But
now we don't do that anymore.

Mr. Guillemard: There was a music society, that made music.

Mrs. Guillemard: They gave some concerts also. Oh life is no longer the same
now. Naturally life has evolved in a good way for us, because now people are
no longer unhappy; but you shouldn't say it all the same. People get along
more or less. The young, they go to school now more than in the past.

Mr. Guillemard: They didn't know the time of the thin kine. Today there are
cars, what do you expect? There's a month of vacation. There's no work
Saturday afternoon, that didn't exist; we worked Sunday all day.

Mr. Loubère: Were there regional dances here?

Mr. Guillemard: Do you mean folkloric dances; ah no, we didn't have that
here.

Mrs. Guillemard: They played here what was played everywhere: the waltz and
polka.
    We don't have *veillées* anymore. With television what do you want? You
know there is no more [communal] life, that television has cut it all short.

Mr. Loubère: Formerly, what did you do during *veillées?*

Mr. Guillemard: Women sewed.

Mrs. Guillemard: Men played cards. Then we grilled chestnuts, we ate them
together, and we had either tea or mulled wine.

Mr. Guillemard: Sometimes there were waffles.

Mrs. Guillemard: Yes, we had many evenings together. There were no other
distractions, what do you expect? We didn't have the cinema.

Mr. Guillemard: Oh, no, no cinema. It's true I was already grown the first time I saw movies. The first time I saw a film it was just before the war of '14. There was an ambulatory machine on the square.

VII

Drink and pleasure have been joined together since time immemorial. But wine is often denounced for being the cause of public drunkenness. Producers deny this vigorously. Mr. Guillemard and Mr. Sabon of Châteauneuf, both vignerons "from father to son" for generations, share the same point of view on the role of alcohol in festivities. Their opinion is widespread in viticultural regions where there is less inebriation than in the industrial cities of the north.

Mr. Loubère: Is it true that vignerons consume a lot of wine?

Mr. Guillemard: Oh, no, no. Wine? No, no, it's not vignerons who drink, oh not at all. No, we, we clink glasses. No, vignerons don't drink much wine. There are some who forget themselves, as everywhere, but it's not the vignerons; they're not the kind who drink. Besides they know how to drink. They have many banquets, the banquet of St. Vincent, and the like. They like to drink well, to eat well, to laugh well, and it can happen that there are some who are a little merry all the same. But that's not being drunk.

Mrs. Guillemard: During banquets like that we begin with the least good wine, we continue, and last we offer the best wine.

Mr. Guillemard: We drink the great wines, the aged wines. No one gets drunk. Because also if I let myself go, I have the occasion every day, and I put in so much time in the cellar, well I would have been in the hole a long time ago.

*

Mr. Loubère: Did people come together often to amuse themselves?

Mr. Sabon: Yes, that is, it wasn't the same then as now. During winter there were family evenings. One met among friends and went to drink a lime infusion, coffee unnerves you, so you drank lime. There were two or three of my father's friends and they went out. There were my uncle, the grandfather of Brunel, the parents of Henry Joudan, then René Paul Blanc, who is dead; so is his wife. They got together. In the evening they went here, or there to each other's house.

In winter, during carnival, there were what are called *mauresques*. You know, some youngsters masqueraded themselves and they went about in the evening. Me, I remember that at my uncle's, they arrived. Then you had to guess who it was. then they unmasked, you brought them a cup of coffee, then they scampered off. There you are, life was like that.

We had a bicycle, in 1924 or '25 or '26—I can't remember—I was given a bicycle. Then we biked around; evenings we went up the rise of St. Joseph. That's when the weather was fine. On Sunday, we went off, went up to Avignon. Sometimes we toured around the *grands ducs*, and returned.

During the grape harvest, there was merry-making every evening. I wonder how we did it. We worked all day; it was harder than now, but yet easier because we had some people from the village; we harvested with village people. Then the father of Paul Avril, he began bringing down gangs from Ardèche. Then, it was wild in the evening, those women from Ardèche, they were a little hot. *Enfin*, we laughed, we had fun because there was a dance every night. You put in 10 *centimes* and danced.

Well, the evening, when the sun set, you left the vines, on a cart, you arrived at the cellar, you unloaded your grapes, you put them in the crusher. After, you led the mule and the horse back home, and when in the stable you fed and watered them. Happily my father had a *maître valet* [permanent worker] who cared for the animals, and that meant for me, when I returned my mule in the evening to the stable, it was all over. Me, I went to the house. I washed up since there weren't any showers at that time; there was a pail of water, a wood pail with a pot of hot water, that's how we did it. I changed clothes, had supper and as soon as it was over, quick as a flash I went to the dance and boy! Every evening of the harvest.

The dances were waltzes, mazurkas, schottisches, tangos. There was no folk music. There was a *viole*, a machine; I don't know if it was electrical. You inserted 10 *centimes*. Then we discovered a trick. We drilled a hole in the coin, and when the music stopped, we pulled it out and put it in again. That's so the music would not cost too much. That was a trick but it's true, it's natural that.

As drink, we bought a bottle of lemonade and a bottle of beer, that we mixed. That's called a *panaché*. We didn't drink any wine, we would have been drunk. But we always had wine when we made a large meal. We always brought old wine, even very old wine, which gets you. When you drank a large glass of it, you wanted to drink a glass of water. I've gone to banquets when we were twenty-five or thirty, where each brought his bottle; we didn't taste as you do now. Now, you begin the meal with a white wine if there's an appetizer, and after, a young red and an old red. While before, we brought wine for the roast, there was no large meal as now, only the roast and cheese, and we drank Châteauneuf.

Chapter Four
Women and the Family

THE ROLE OF WOMEN and the place of the family in rural society have been changing for some time. Especially since World War II, the introduction of machinery in vineyard work and access to technological improvements in production have altered the nature of work, sociability, and leisure and have even affected the character of intergenerational relations. Women's activities in the first two of these areas have historically been closely tied to their place in the family, as they continue to be today.

Since time immemorial, women have occupied a central place in agricultural societies and in the family economy in the rural world. The vineyards have been no exception. In France, where prior to the late nineteenth century the family was the primary unit of production on the land, the contribution of women was crucial to family survival. From 1856 to the early 1950s, in fact, between 39 percent and 49 percent of all women in the labor force worked in agriculture; over the same period, women accounted for between 30 percent and 44 percent of all agricultural workers (44 percent in 1921), a large proportion of them in viticulture.[1] Even if, by the end of World War I, the viticultural family had almost ceased to be a productive unit, it nonetheless remained an important economic unit, where wage-earning and family consumption replaced family production as the primary economic functions. Even here, there were (and still are) exceptions; small vintners in those areas of France which produce the more aristocratic wines and which have escaped industrialization have continued to rely on family labor and especially the labor of women in the family.

In the nineteenth and early twentieth centuries, women's place in the vineyards varied according to whether they lived in areas of vineyard monoculture, such as the southern mass-production vineyards, or on the smaller, family-run operations of the Beaujolais or Burgundy regions. From the 1870s to the early 1950s the Mediterranean vineyards, with their heavy demand for wage labor saw relatively large numbers of women working on the large estates. Many of these women worked as day laborers *(journalières)*; they lived in the agglomerated villages which dot the south, and went out to the vineyards each day, taking their lunch and sometimes their children with them. During harvest, women's labor was

Fig. 14 Tying vine shoots to metal wires is often assigned to women. Courtesy of
Photothèque ITV-M. Mackiewicz.

particularly in demand, as was child labor. In fact, the contribution of children
during this time of year was important enough so that schools did not open until
the beginning of October, when the harvest was over. Most *journalières* came
from families which owned no land of their own and the wage was their main
source of income. Landownership, however, did not automatically distinguish the
activities of women. The wife of the small landowner performed the same tasks
as the working class woman who labored on the large estates. It is likely, however,
that the sexual division of labor described by both men and women in the interviews
below, was less acute among small growers, for whom necessity demanded a
broader sharing of tasks between men and women.[2] In contrast to the areas of
vineyard monoculture, in regions of diverse production such as Provence, women's
contribution to the family economy was more varied and work included care of
the fruit trees, raising of silk worms (until the 1920s) and the raising of vegetables,
rabbits, and chickens, as well as vineyard work. However, even in areas of
monoculture, women's work was often more diverse than men's work, due to the
sexual division of labor and also to slow seasons in which "female tasks" were
in low demand.

Fig. 15 Grape harvest, women pick and men carry. Courtesy of Photothèque ITV-M. Mackiewicz.

To be sure, one cannot really speak of women's experience in the vineyards without qualification. Women of the working class and wives of small proprieters led very different lives from the bourgeois wives of large vineyard owners. In contrast to the manual and often hard labor of the former, the latter's work was more often managerial. As the interviewees suggest, these women sometimes kept the account books of the estate. Their lives brought them into less direct contact with the land and contributed to the high status in the vineyard hierarchy already conferred upon them by landownership. Class perceptions among individuals differed, too. The comparative ease of the lives of women in the viticultural economy described by Mr. Valayer, a proprieter, contrasts markedly with the dominant impression of two working class women, Mrs. Cendrous and Mrs. Rouaix, whose recollections of the past were memories of hardship.

Women's participation in viticulture also varied according to the female life cycle. Women who performed wage work did so most frequently when they were single or during the early months of marriage before children were conceived. With marriage and the birth of the first child, the tendency for women to work

Fig. 16   Removing bad grapes in Champagne. Courtesy of Photothèque ITV-M. Mackiewicz.

outside of the home dropped off markedly.[3] But when child care was available from an older child, a neighbor or parent, women could more easily continue to work in the vines when children were small; many a young mother took her infant into the vines in a basket, when no child care was available. Once children were old enough to work and once primary school was finished, they might actually follow their mothers in the vines, learning the elementary skills of vine dressing. Indeed, most training for vineyard work took place within the family, skills being passed from father to son and from mother to daughter.

Work for women in the vineyards of France, as important as it was to the local and family economies, was usually not seen by women as a liberating phenomenon, but as an economic necessity. It was understood and expected that within marriage, a wife would make an economic contribution (whether or not that contribution involved earning a wage). The same expectation was made of children. Still, even though women's wage work was necessary for the family, both husbands and wives insisted on the importance of a domestic role for women, a feature of family life which seems not to have changed much at all.

Perhaps because of its importance as an economic unit, the vineyard family did not encourage young marriages. Nonetheless, ages at first marriages in vineyard regions may have been somewhat lower than the national average. In the village of Coursan, Aude, for example, the village of Mr. Coca, Mrs. Cendrous and Mrs. Rouaix, women married at about twenty-one years of age and men at about twenty-five or twenty-six years of age just before World War I, whereas the national averages for that time were twenty-four and twenty-eight for women and men respectively.[4] Within the working class as within the bourgeoisie, it was necessary for the young couple to be capable of supporting itself. In fact, economic considerations were not always entirely absent from the choice of mate. As the interviewees suggest, the requirement that newlyweds establish their own households did not mean that family connections dissolved. Families continued to provide psychological and sometimes material support in the early stages of marriage. Furthermore, parents and offspring frequently continued to reside close to one another. Close living arrangements were facilitated by the fact that before World War II, most marriages took place among people from the same locality, especially because youths, lacking transportation, could not easily meet people from other areas.

Of course, family life in the vineyards cannot be reduced to a question of work, although economic pressures have always weighed heavily upon viticultural populations. The vineyard community has always been an important locus of sociability, especially in the south of France, where the dense living conditions of agglomerated villages made it easy for families and neighbors to get together. In summer, social life was carried on out of doors, in the street, or in the public square. Popular dances were a common form of communal activity for young people in the early part of the century and after World War I. In winter, families gathered in the kitchen, where, in the days before radio and television, stories were told, or a newspaper or serial novel was read aloud. If men were able to escape to their "male space" in the wine cellar or the café for a game of cards and some conversation, for women, work and sociability were more closely intertwined.[5] Groups which gathered to knit, prepare vegetables for the evening meal, in front of the door, in the street, marked special moments in days which were filled with more solitary labor. Finally, the harvest itself was a mixture of work and leisure for both sexes, celebrated by long meals, well "irrigated" with local wine and finished off with an evening of dancing. For the great majority of workers, however, life was not marked by large blocks of leisure time and many working class men and women returned immediately to the vines to work the day after such momentous life events as marriage.

Behind the walls of villages which seem timeless in their outward appearance, there have in fact been many changes for women and the family. Since the early 1920's, the number of women in the agricultural labor force has declined. From 44 percent in 1921, the percentage of women working in agriculture declined to 40 percent in 1936, rose slightly to 41 percent in 1946 and then declined again to 27 percent in 1954 and to 19 percent in 1962.[6] Women in the vineyard areas of France no longer turn to the vines for work. The gains made by agricultural labor unions after World War I, in raising the wages of male vineyard workers have meant that among working class families, married women's wage work has been less of an economic necessity than it may have been earlier (although this, too, fluctuates, along with the vineyard economy and the national economy in general). Mechanization has also taken women out of the vines. The first tractors appeared in the vines after World War II and are now used for everything from cultivation to spreading chemicals and insecticides. In some areas of the south, harvesting machines have even begun to make their appearance in the vines in recent years. Finally, the increasing use of male immigrant wage labor in the vines and the growing opportunities for white collar employment for women in general have contributed to their withdrawal from vineyard work.

Within the home, changes have occurred, too, for women. The improvement of transportation and the availability of goods through the European Economic Community have made it possible to purchase ever more cheaply agricultural products and other goods which formerly may have been produced in the home. This development has gradually brought about the disappearance of the chicken coop and rabbit hutch and has perhaps lightened the load of rural women who previously included care of these areas in their panoply of domestic tasks. The introduction of technological improvements such as the washing machine has meant that vineyard women are no longer obligated to spend hours washing with ashes in their kitchen or at the local *lavoir;* electrical appliances have simplified cleaning and cooking, as they have for urban women. But these improvements may also have their negative side. The vineyard woman in the post World War II period may have found herself somewhat more isolated than her mother or grandmother. The groups of village women who gathered in front of the door to knit, gossip, or sew, have now begun to disappear. The same mechanization which has lightened their work load and which has been instrumental in their gradual withdrawal from the vineyards also placed women in a domestic role which is more restricted than was the case prior to the second World War. In similar ways, new forms of leisure have isolated the family from the community, as the recollections of several older vignerons suggests.

Family life in the vineyards is changing in other ways as well. Fewer and fewer children undergo the family apprenticeship to vineyard work, preferring to leave the vines and go on to higher education and higher paying jobs in business and industry or the professions. This has meant that not only is the family ceasing to pass on important skills and cultural traditions, but that the generations are becoming increasingly separated geographically as well. Old networks of family support have not disappeared, but they are certainly more difficult to maintain. Indeed, there is an ambiguity in the response of older folk: an acceptance of youth culture, with its disregard for past mores, its mobility and rocking noisiness, its virulent belief in its own values or its pride in having none; but it is a reluctant acceptance. Much of the testimony in these interviews is sad in tone: the intermittent crises of wine interests seem to have launched a permanent crisis of the viticultural family. Parental authority is flouted; the family has lost its bonds; the young are leaving the land, selling off their inherited vines without the slightest regret.

The role of the father in the family has changed as well. In agricultural families of small owners and workers, the father has traditionally had a dual role to play. He was first a father, responsible for the well-being and education of his children, the boys in particular, and in this role he could combine both paternal affection and authority. But he was also an employer of his children, usually part-time and seasonal before they left school, then full-time. This latter role is now fading, as children increasingly move away from the land.

The life course of children of grape growers followed a pattern not much different from that of all agricultural populations in France. Important to note is the long transition from the apprenticeship phase to that of vineyard helper, a long transition rather than a sudden shift, because from about nine or ten years of age to school leaving age, formerly about thirteen, children combined study and work, performing each seasonally. They attended school in the late fall, winter, and early spring, and worked both part and full time during the warmer months. Those children who had the opportunity to continue their studies beyond elementary grades were often those who left the family enterprise to enter other careers. But even they helped out in the vines seasonally, and when departing, the transition they experienced was more definitely a break from the agricultural world.

Such breaks have increased since the 1950s; the children of vineyard laborers seem to have departed in droves for other trades, but so have the children of small owners, especially the younger sons and daughters, unless they were able

Fig. 17   The harvest or *vendange* in the Côte-d'Or. The baskets or *bénatons* can hold up to 50 kilograms of grapes and are carried on the shoulders of men. Courtesy of Photothèque ITV-M. Mackiewicz.

to marry into propertied families when they would pursue a life not very different
from that of their parents.

1. See T. Deldyke, H. Gelders and J.-M. Limbor, *La population active et sa structure*
(Bruxelles, 1968), pp. 170–174.

2. For a more complete discussion of the division of labor in vineyard work, see Frader,
"The Working Class in the Wine Industry of Lower Languedoc, Coursan 1850–1914,"
unpublished Ph.D. Dissertation, University of Rochester, 1978; and Frader, "La Femme
et la Famille dans les Luttes Viticoles de l'Aude," *Sociologie du Sud-Est* 21 (Juillet–Octobre,
1979): 33–54. See also, Christine Amiel, Giordanna Charuty et Claudine Fabre-Vassas,
Jours de vigne (Villelongue d'Aude, 1981), p. 135.

3. Louise A. Tilly and Joan W. Scott, *Women, Work and Family* (New York, 1978),
pp. 124, 135, and 222.

4. Frader, "The Working Class in the Wine Industry. . . ," p. 371, and Wesley Camp,
Marriage and the Family in France Since the Revolution (New York, 1961).

5. On the sexual division of space in peasant society, see Lucienne Roubin, *Chambrettes
des Provençaux: une maison des hommes en Méditérranée Septrionale* (Paris, 1970),
especially pp. 157–197. In vineyard communities, male space was the *cave*, the wine cellar
(from which women were excluded in the nineteenth and twentieth centuries) and the barn
or tool shed, as well as the café. Women's space was the home, especially the kitchen,
and the *basse-cour* (chicken coop) and the village *lavoir*. See also Daniel Fabre et Jean
Lacroix, *La vie quotidenne des paysans de Languedoc* (Paris, 1973), pp. 249–250.

6. Deldyke, *et al.*, p. 174.

I

*Louis Raspaud, a worker, lives in Tautavel, Pyrénées-Orientales, where he is
head of the vineyard worker's labor union. He reflects on his mother's experiences
as a vineyard worker and on the changes in women's work. Although his
mother's wage work was necessary to the family's security, Mr. Raspaud still
considered her domestic role most important.*

Yes, my mother participated just as women do now. That is, from November
to the end of March, she gathered pruned vine branches, then in May she
worked eight days to powder the vines with sulphur (a treatment against mildew), then she helped with the harvest [in September]. She worked fifteen days
at harvest and that was all. Nowadays women have other choices. Nearly the
entire grape harvest goes into our cooperative winery and now we've begun to
distribute our wine in bottles. There are teams of wives of agricultural workers,
and even proprietors, who work from a week to three weeks, three women to
a team to bottle wine. But in the old days, my mother, and the other wives of

agricultural workers, did laundry by hand for the vineyard owners, to "put a bit of butter in the spinach." My mother took in washing all the time, when she didn't go out in the vines. And she took care of the house. My mother was tied to the home permanently. She never left it. We only went to Perpignan for very specific things: family business or illness. I remember that when I was a child, I had a hernia, so of necessity, I went to Perpignan to replace my bandage. Otherwise, overall, if I went to Perpignan four times, that was all. Whereas now, sometimes, we go four times a week. That's the difference. In general, it was a typical family; [my mother's] primary job was to take care of the children. There were no other jobs in the village.

II

Mrs. Anastasie Vergnes (née Cheytion), eighty-four years old at the time of the interview (August 20, 1974), was a vineyard worker. Her brother, François Cheyton, was also a vineyard worker and leader of the labor union in Coursan, prior to the First World War. Her work experience differed slightly from that of the other women interviewed, many of whom rarely left the locality in which they lived.

Mrs. Vergnes: After I left school [at age fourteen], I went to Paris with my sister to work as a cook. When I returned to Coursan, I continued to cook and also worked part time in the vines. I worked for Mrs. . . . preparing meals for baptisms and weddings. Since everything took place on Sunday, sometimes I didn't get home until four in the morning by the time everything was cleaned up—then I had to get up to go out to the vines the same day.

Ms. Frader: Where you worked, were there certain tasks set aside for women and certain tasks for men?

Mrs. Vergnes: Yes, but the employers often asked the women to do the men's work, such as pruning, but did not pay them a men's wage.

III

Mrs. Rouaix, a vineyard worker for many of her eighty-five years, and Mrs. Cendrous, eighty-four (in 1979), also a vineyard worker, live in Coursan, Aude, in the heart of the Southern "industrial" vineyard. Mrs. Rouaix's husband, François, was head of the vineyard worker's union in Coursan in the 1930's. Both women saw changes in the nature of women's work in both the vines and in the home.

Ms. Frader: You both worked in the vines as children?

Mrs. Rouaix: We worked all the time—me, I worked on a vineyard called Céleyran (in the neighboring village of Salles d'Aude); there were twenty-eight of us, all women.

Mrs. Cendrous: We gathered branches on a day-rate basis.

Mrs. Rouaix: They kept us busy! And you know, when it's cold, it's no fun, gathering branches! [Even in good weather] one is always bent over; and your clothes always got caught in them. When children left school, the mother would have them follow her in the vines. Those who were good at school stayed. My child, he worked hard; he stayed in school until he got his certificate. But the others, who weren't doing well in school, went out to work. Children's work helped out the family; you know we weren't exactly poverty stricken. But I remember that at Céleyran, the proprietor took the children as they left school; he had them pick stones out of the vines to give them something to do. They were given 9 francs a week for this. It almost doesn't seem possible, the misery we went through. The women worked all day gathering branches, and with a spade, they had to make a hole around the [trunk of the vine] and put in fertilizer. We cut the grass and weeds in the vines, got rid of the lumps in the soil and all that. There was plenty of work for women!

Mrs. Cendrous: At that time [1920s] there was more work in the vines than now.

Mrs. Rouaix: Now there are machines, so the women stay at home, there are no longer the teams of women as there were earlier. Even for the harvest now they have machines. So the young people are unemployed—they are unemployed even before they have ever worked!
Neither Mrs. Rouaix nor Mrs. Cendrous romanticized their past experience; on the contrary.
Mrs. Rouaix: Those who work in the countryside have the most difficulty—and why? Those who work in offices have better retirement plans than those who work in the countryside. There's an injustice there. When it rains those who work in the vineyards can't come in out of the rain right away; the boss makes you wait, you get wet; while the office worker is sheltered and earns more! It's not right!

Ms. Frader: Was life much harder for women then, without washing machines, modern conveniences?

Mrs. Rouaix: Yes—you have to recognize things have changed now.

Mrs. Cendrous: Back then (pre-World War II) it took three days just to do the laundry!

Mrs. Rouaix: [We did the laundry] in large pots. There was running water in the village, but not everyone had it; I didn't have it; I had to go down to the canal. You'd put the washing in the pot, all nicely arranged. Then we made a big fire. We made cinders from the wood and scalded them in boiling water with the laundry. We scalded the laundry like that. Oh, it smelled good! I preferred that to washing machines. As for food, we couldn't buy meat very often, so we'd catch rabbits and we'd have enough for the entire week! We fed ourselves like that!

IV

In some wine-growing areas, women's contribution in the vineyard is still necessary. One woman worked along with her husband. The owners of a small vineyard, Mr. and Mrs. Serrurier, both in their fifties, live in the village of Venteuil, in the Marne. The Serrurier family represents a type of family labor which has all but disappeared in the twentieth century.

Mrs. Serrurier: I work in the vines with my husband and son, the vines demand a lot of manual labor, outside of what you can do mechanically; pruning, the *baissage de boles*, training the vines, all this is done by hand. Of course I also do the housework. Since we have been married, working conditions have changed a lot. In the old days, there were many operations which one did by hand and today are done with the tractor, especially for my husband, operations like sulphuring, cultivation. Formerly one cultivated with a horse and plow; now all that is done by tractor. [For women too] the working conditions have changed. Gathering of pruned branches was all done by hand. Everything had to be picked up by hand [and tied in bundles], but now, we put them in a wheelbarrow and burn them as we go. The branches are no longer used for heating or for cooking the way we used to; they're burned directly in the vines.

Mr. Serrurier: The latest advance is that now we have grinders which are attached to the tractor; people put the branches on the side of the road and then the tractor comes by, and the grinder picks up the branches, like a sort of thresher but it turns much faster. It crushes the wood and reduces it to dust; it's completely new.

Mr. Loubère: When your son was smaller, did you bring him with you?

Mrs. Serrurier: When he was very very small, since we were living with my parents-in-law, at that time, his grandmother took care of him. But those who had no one to care for their children were obliged to take them with them into the vineyards. Once they are two to two and a half years, there is a nursery school there in the village where one can take them. It has always been there.

Mr. Serrurier: It's paid for by the village.

V

Mr. Sabon, a proprietor and producer, described the effect of the family life cycle on his own wife's work and the double work of women. Mr. Valayer, another proprietor, accepts the limitations on women's wage labor and illustrates a traditional view of the place of women's work in the household.

Mr. Sabon: When we went out to rake up the weeds, my wife came with me every afternoon. Oh! Those first years of marriage! As long as there weren't any children. . . . As soon as there were little ones, then my wife took care of the house and the kids, and then she came with me. Only in those families which were much better off than we were, did the wife stay at home all the time until mechanization ended it. There are even a pair of women in Château-neuf who drive tractors. The fact that they were women didn't prevent them. I have a son thirty-five kilometers from here. His wife gets on a tractor, she goes with him; she works in the fields like a man! She does her house work and then she goes out to work with Bernard.

Mr. Valayer: Especially in viticulture, women have always worked in the vines. They gathered pruned branches, for example. They thinned out the leaves of the vines [to expose the grapes to the sun], they participated in the harvest, attached the vines to the stakes, and so on. But nowadays, women work very little in the vines; even during the harvest, because during the harvest there are teams which come in and take over the picking. Very few women partici-pate. Some still do. But in general, there are teams of ten to fifteen Spanish harvesters, men and women, or as yet some French, some students, who come. Women today take care of the house more, because the house provides her with a lot of work and satisfaction. After all, given all the comforts she has, all these machines, there is more furniture, she takes better care of the home, whereas earlier, it was neglected. Now, she grows flowers in front of it, she beautifies it and she beautifies herself—she goes to the hairdresser. In general, the wife of the vigneron has accepted the idea of staying in the country [rather than move to towns or cities as so many rural dwellers have]. It's in the viticultural regions that the countryside is the least depopulated. The coun-tryside is relatively more depopulated where there is livestock because the ani-mals have to eat every day, and be cared for every day. Those people who have cows have to milk them; for those who have sheep it's the same thing. In viticulture, on the other hand, especially with the means we have now, even if you have to perform a special [chemical] treatment, it's quickly done—in two or three days you can treat the vines, which means that Saturday and Sunday if madame wishes to go to the sea or even to the movies in Avignon, she is free to do so. In the past, it wasn't like that, because the work was slower; it took longer to do it.

VI

Unlike women in some other families, Mr. Valayer's mother did not have the double work of home and vineyard labor, in part because of her social class. Nonetheless, she was not exempt from hard work. Mr. Valayer suggests that women's lives are easier now as far as their household activities are concerned, although their time is now filled by other activities such as childrearing.

Mr. Valayer: [My mother] worked in the vines relatively little because I worked very early on and we employed workers [as well]. So, my mother attended to the care of the house and to taking care of the children. . . . Oh, yes, she had a lot to do in the house, because there was the farm yard. Now, in many homes, there is a dog or a cat, but no longer rabbits, or chickens or goats. In former times, as I said, people lived a little off the farm yard, even in viticulture, because they had a goat or two; some had a cow. Now, in many farms, these things are purchased. People devote themselves to the vine and nothing but the vine. This means that women no longer have to care for the farmyard as before, as my mother did, for example.

Mrs. Loubère: Did she make the children's clothes herself during the year?

Mr. Valayer: A little, yes. [But it was] mending, not exactly making the clothes. For making the clothes, there generally was someone in the village who knew tailoring, who knew how to make little dresses or clothing for children. Well, that doesn't exist any more, either. Now we buy everything all ready-made. Even for cooked food, women go to the market. If they don't have the time to make a meal, they go to the neighborhood specialty store, and buy everything, [even] cooked dishes. Earlier, that didn't exist. All this means that the woman is much freer; she had more time to take care of the children. The children require more attention now than earlier because now they're kept cleaner. Little children need their little cleaning up, while in the old days, the child sometimes had a little pair of pants and when he didn't that was OK, too. You see, it was not at all [like it is today].

As for progress, there are constraints which force you to give yourself to progress; you need to work, you need to produce more, but finally it's much more agreeable, I would say perhaps even better for women than for men. Women are relieved of much of the work they did earlier because their husbands, with their vineyards, manage to provide for their wives without their having to raise pigs or chickens.

VII

Mrs. Arnaud, wife of a large landowner in the Vaucluse, recalls her childhood and her initiation into vineyard work. Her account suggests that the daughter of a proprietor probably had a somewhat different experience from that of a worker, because her experience suggests a less rigorous sexual division of labor in the Vaucluse than in the Aude or Pyrénées-Orientales, and because of her role in account keeping; it also confirms the picture of women's importance in the family economy which emerges from the recollections of other vineyard women.

Mrs. Arnaud: I was the daughter of a vigneron and tradesman; my father made [and sold] grafts for vines, we were, first of all, people who worked a great deal. As young as we were, we began, on Thursdays (a day off from school) to go to the vineyards to gather the branches and afterwards, as soon as we were old enough, we began to prune the wood. With my older sister, we did my father's accounts from six to eight in the evening. It was real bookkeeping. Because he was a nurseryman, someone had to do the accounts every evening, so everyone worked. Around March, we would graft the stems which had been already pruned; then we re-pruned them in three parts. There were also other people who made the grafts which had been gathered. My father grafted and then there were women who grafted, also. They put the grafts in cases, they were watered, and then warmed; at that time we warmed them with charcoal in the middle of an enclosed room. After so many days the fire was put out, the cases were taken out and the grafts were planted—we called it putting them in the nursery. We were always busy! Even though we started to work very young—ten or twelve years of age—we also went to school which began in October. Before school started, all the children in the region came to harvest for their parents! If one had little friends of our age, they came to harvest with us; they were paid just as we were. In the country, the little ones—started work much earlier. There were always people who had very young children or very smart children. The boss did not always approve because even if their mother helped them, it slowed down the work a bit. [Still], they learned the trade. Let's say that when there were a lot of people doing something, the children would follow everyone else. They didn't find that unusual, you understand; they worked because a lot of people were doing the same.

VIII

Mr. and Mrs. André Doulet lived all their working lives in the Champagne village of Cumières, near Epernay, and their working lives were long, for they are now eighty-four and eighty-two. On March 17, 1983, they celebrated their sixtieth wedding anniversary. They are about as proletarian as one can find in Champagne vineyards; their land, just about half an hectare before they retired, could never provide them with even a subsistence livelihood, but only a small secondary income. Their main income was derived from the wages they both earned as agricultural laborers. The monetary contributions of Marcelline, however, were much more varied than what she earned as a vigneronne, for like most wives of rural workers she undertook many different tasks to help out her family. Since some of these jobs did not require high-level skills they were not high-paying, and although continually busy, the family was never more than slightly above the subsistence level. The family, despite the frequent absence of Marcelline out earning extra money, was close-knit, partly because the lack of transport impeded the geographic spread of family members; this, in turn, made the house into a home where parents and children clustered together before and after World War I. As Mr. Doulet put it, "We got on very well with our parents." In the past young people didn't frequently go out on their own; life was centered in the family.

Mrs. Doulet: There were houses to rent. Very often workers were lodged by their employers who had houses. The employer of my father had this house and three workers, so they were lodged here. In certain cases workers did the vines in exchange for housing. There were three rooms and the little bedroom above. Seven of us lived here. My father slept over there. Our room was the kitchen. It was like that everywhere. At our neighbors' there was hardly more than one room and they were fourteen living there. You know it wasn't as luxurious as the houses that people have now. Everybody had a little pile of manure in front of the door.

Workers like us, when we had been once a week to the butcher's, that was it. Well then, we had to raise a few rabbits, or a pig if you had a pigsty. Here we didn't have one. There was an oven so that my mother could make bread. We grew vegetables, beans. The owner gave us a bit of land for potatoes. Today if people are over thirty, they don't garden any more. Their gardens are the grocer's. Here we had chickens, some ducks. We went to the butcher's only on Sunday and we bought stew meat; that was the least expensive.

Mr. Loubère: Were these the conditions of all the workers?

Mrs. Doulet: Just about. There were also cellar workers *(cavistes)*. These were people who went to Epernay to work in the cellars of the big Champagne firms. They weren't rich either. Before the war they earned from 3 francs to 3.5 francs a day, that was all, for ten hours of work. Some of these cellarmen lived in the village and they went by foot like me, four kilometers each way. When I went on foot I went with several men.

Mr. Loubère: Was it after your marriage that you worked in the vines?

Mrs. Doulet: Oh yes. We got married in the month of March, and in the month of February next I found myself pregnant with my first daughter, and then two years later I had the second. Five years after I had the third, but I went pregnant to the vines. And I worked in the vegetable gardens also. I also did house work. I also went to the laundry stand—it was a drinking trough before and owners with cows had them led there to have them drink in the Marne. Afterward the commune bought a floating platform *(bateau-lavoir)*. We did heavy washing often; sometimes we washed twenty sheets at a time. I wasn't fat. I weighed about fifty kilos. One day, while launching my sheet, the board I had under me gave way and *houp!* there I was swept away in the Marne. I was belly-flat in the water. Happily there were women around me. There was one, young, who wasn't afraid to enter the water and who extended a tree-branch that I could catch hold of. Without that I'd have been gone. We didn't really have a good life; we worked for very little.

Mr. Loubère: Did you do your own cooking?

Mrs. Doulet: We cooked up a fricassee, vegetable stews, potatoes, green beans, lentils, peas. We had coal stoves. During summer we used charcoal burners. When my mother made bread we replaced the burner with an oven. I remember that on festive days my mother told her neighbors, "Bring your cakes, we'll put them in the oven." We made cherry tarts. There were many cherry trees here; now there aren't any because helicopters do the vine-spraying so we can't have any more trees. We lived on what we grew. We made preserves of fruit and vegetables. We had preserves for the whole year. We couldn't spend any money because we didn't have any. When you bought a pair of shoes for one kid, the other had to wait a month. There were no family allocations. You couldn't buy two or three pairs of shoes or two or three pairs of pants.

My daughter-in-law said to me, "You had a hard life, you went through all that." But in our old age, thanks to social laws, we're happier all the same. We've got a pension. My parents didn't have a pension, and as for me, I had had three children already but I still had to support my father. And nobody gave you anything. Among brothers and sisters, we did all that was needed: cared for them, nourished them until they died. Children had to provide for their parents.

Mr. Doulet: Our kids, out of four we've got only two still. They come see us every week, but we don't ask for anything to eat or for anything else. And then, we worked until we couldn't any more, so we stopped. I took my retirement at sixty, but I could still work and I went on working for ten years after my retirement. All the same we managed to get a little house. We don't owe anybody anything. My parents bought this little house and lived in it for fifteen years. We took it over because we told ourselves that we were going to get old. We won't be able to walk, nor climb stairs. Today, young people wouldn't be satisfied with this.

Mr. Loubère: Did your children go to the local schools?

Mr. Doulet: They went to the village school, not to high school. There's only my daughter who got a certificate of studies. The boys don't even have that. They left school and went to work in the vines, both of them. There's one at the firm of Moët and Chandon. He's the last, who I had at forty-three, and the other's an owner at Montereau. Both have vines and they each built a beautiful house. They're my only surviving children. They're good vignerons. They know the new ways.

Mr. Loubère: You said that your employer gave you a vineyard as a wedding present?

Mr. Doulet: Oh yes. A new law prevented them from expanding. It didn't amount to much but, *enfin*, it helped us to get a start.

Mr. Loubère: Did you get credit?

Mr. Doulet: That didn't exist for us, credit. There was the Agricultural Bank, but if you didn't have a backer, nor property, they didn't lend you anything.

Mr. Loubère: Didn't your sons have agricultural credits?

Mr. Doulet: Sure, to build a house, not to buy vines. We gave them close to fifty *ares* (an *are* is one hundredth of an hectare). Michel, our oldest son, he had some vines and when he died at forty-nine, they were divided among his brothers and that helped them. So in addition to their wages, they have their vines. As for us, we don't need anything. With my pension we can live. We don't go out, we don't travel, we don't go anywhere. We never knew what a vacation was. Today we could, but that's another matter; we can't walk very well anymore.

IX

For many young children and for young vignerons, the real school was the family. That was where young men and women learned the art of vine dressing. Well into the twentieth century, the family continued (as it had in the nineteenth) to determine the kinds of work children would do or whether they would work at all. But formal schooling and the potential it offered for socio-economic advancement was powerfully enticing to some and it rivaled the family in providing training for future professional and work skills. Mr. Centène, a small proprietor at Banyuls, Mr. Sabon, and Mr. Coca, a worker and trade union leader from Coursan, experienced this in their own lives.

Mr. Centène: We were three brothers; my father made me go to school until I was sixteen, but I didn't want to go to school; I wanted to stay at home and work on the land. My father wouldn't hear of it; at that time we almost had a falling out, because he wanted me to take some kind of job. One of my brothers worked in the post office; the other did his military service, he also stayed in school but he didn't want to stay on the land. My father was eventually happy that I stayed, but at first, he didn't want it. So from sixteen

(1911) I worked with my father until 1914, the declaration of war, and then after 1914, from 1919 to 1922 when I got married. I spent four or five years at home to help out the family. My father gave me 20 francs every Sunday. After the war, an agricultural worker made 10 francs a day and he gave me 10 or 20 francs for myself. My parents naturally taught me to be a vigneron. We didn't need to do an apprenticeship, you know. From age eight or ten, on days when there was no school, off we went to the vines to do petty jobs. We were initiated into the care of vines by just watching our parents or the workers who would point out to us what we should do. The first year I worked in the vines, my father had a worker and he put me to work with him and it was the worker who taught me. And I knew the work from having seen it done throughout my youth. I knew how it was done, but you have to be used to doing it; you have to have naturally, how shall I say, a sense of the work. So at that time, you learned either with the workers, or with our parents who showed us.

Mr. Loubère: Your son, will he become a vigneron?

Mr. Centène: Yes, he's going to continue. But, you see, I've a son and a daughter. My daughter married a policeman. He took his retirement and I shared the property with him. My son remains. There are three children, but not one will remain on the land. My daughter has three girls, not one will stay on the land. Well, I told them, "Now, when I die, your vines, what'll you do with them?" I've a granddaughter who is a teacher near Paris, in the Seine-et-Marne, and her husband is also a teacher. And I have a grandson who is a master geologist, he won't remain on the land. I've got another one who goes to school at Corneilla. He's nearly twenty-one years old. He wants to start his law studies, so he won't remain on the land either.

On my daughter's side, the oldest granddaughter is twenty-nine years old and she's a teacher in Paris. Her husband is a cook. And the other granddaughter is a teacher in Montpellier and also married to a teacher in Montpellier. I've another who married an Englishman. She's an English teacher, and went to work in England and married there. Well, they won't remain with the vines either. Now all the patrimony that has been preserved for 200 years up to now, where will it all go?

It's the same on my mother's side; all the land has disappeared; it's all been sold. There was only one uncle who had children; two girls and a boy. He made his career in Africa and his children stayed there. They were in Morocco but they've come back now. One of his daughters is at Pau; the other, the son, is a teacher at Carcassonne; there's another daughter who's also married; her husband has retired. They're all old by now.

X

Early in the twentieth century in some regions it was rare for peasant children to remain in school beyond the age of twelve, and many remained that long only because the law required it. *After 1918, many peasant fathers encountered previously unknown mores and values during the war, and their indifference to education diminished, but they still felt little need to educate their children above the elementary level. Mr. Sabon, a proprietor and producer, suggests that children themselves were often more inclined toward the land than towards school.*

Mr. Sabon: It was my father who taught me to cultivate vines. One was born to it. My father had a passion for horses and he inculcated that in me too; automatically I had a passion for horses. Being young kids, we used to go to pat the horses. As soon as you could, you put on the horsecollar in order to harness them. On Thursday (a day off from school) I was happy. My father said to me: "I'm going to plow down there, want to come? " and I traced out several furrows with the horse. When I left school, my father asked, "You don't want to go to school; you want to quit? Alright, you'll harness the mule and you'll go plow." I mean that's the way it was, and I trained myself.

I left school in 1922; I was twelve and a half. I earned my certificate when I was eleven and a half. I went a year longer in the upper level. I was the only one. I asked my father: "Why do you want me to go to school? " Then there was no age limit. My father said to the teacher, "What did you expect, he won't go to school anymore." "And if he won't go to school, what are you planning to make of him? " "I'm going to make a peasant of him," my father said. That's how it happened, I left just like that; I left to go to work with the mule. That was a fine time, it was finer than now.

XII

Mr. Coca saw vineyard work not only from the standpoint of education but also in economic terms, with the needs of the family economy occasionally taking precedence over the needs of individual family members.

Mr. Coca: For the majority of young people education took place in the vines. The majority of young people went into the vines, given that there wasn't the opportunity for training that now exists. Now things are better, there are two types of training in school: those who have the intellectual possibility of continuing their studies do so; then there are apprenticeship centers, for example, the technical centers where one can get special certificates, the B.E.T. *(Brevet d'Etudes Techniques)*, technical diplomas. That didn't exist in the past. There was, after primary school, what we called "practical school," business school. It was a minor training course which was completely different from present-day education. When I was a boy, there were thirty or thirty-five of us in school; out of the whole class, only three or four went either to the practical school or on to higher education. The majority went to work in the vines. It was especially a function of the economic situation. Right now there is a severe economic crisis, but in fact, there has always been a crisis, with variations. In the past, you had to pay to go on to school; there were no scholarships like there are now. It was very difficult. But at that time, if a family was going through difficulties, if a child did not have the intellectual means to pursue his or her studies or even the monetary means, the child would go to work in the vines. It was one of the consequences of the economic circumstances of the time. At that time families were larger than they are now; there were families with five or six children. It was hard to raise five children when there were no family allowances (instituted by the Popular Front government in 1936). The family lived with what resources it could. Well, sometimes, there were just the resources of the father and mother but really, a mother who had five or six children at home, didn't have much time to work, you understand. For supplementary resources, the children would go work to bring something home, and it was much better then than now, because now with young people, they may work, but they bring nothing in to the home, or at least not very much; they keep the money they earn. That's evolution. Formerly, one felt a family responsibility more; it was a bit of an honor for a child to bring some money home on Saturday (payday) when he was old enough to work. It was a question of personal responsibility which doesn't exist now. So in this area, from the point of view of the family, from the point of view of the home, it was better in the old days. One felt the spirit of helpfulness, of support for the needs of the home, whereas now it's complete negligence.

XIII

The more modern vineyard, with its demands for faster, more efficient labor, has altered the extent to which children can participate in the work process, as Mr. Coca suggests.

Mr. Coca: Let's take the harvest period for example, where, in the past, one took the work more slowly. During the day, there was time to amuse one's self in the vines, while working at the same time. Now, the work rhythm is accelerated since they try to get the maximum amount of work from the workers, and the working conditions have become much more difficult than they used to be. Earlier, a woman could have her ten or twelve year old follow her, and begin to harvest. Now, it's almost impossible—I won't say impossible because that's not a French word, [but it's] very difficult. Even without that, the kids are in school, that's true, but the young kids wouldn't be able to keep up the pace now. Well, it's more difficult [for families] from the economic standpoint, too, because the family which needed a supplementary income would say, "O.K., I'm sending my son or daughter to harvest." And you know, going back to classes is extremely costly, so [a mother] would say "If my daughter harvests fifteen or twenty days, that makes so much per day and that will bring in enough money to prepare her to return to classes." Whereas now, it has become very difficult to do that.

XIV

In some cases, apprenticeship within the family system of labor could lead to a partnership between father and son, as Mr. Arnaud recounts.

Mr. Loubère: You have followed in your father's footsteps. Can you tell me about your relations with him. Did he teach you how to cultivate grapes?

Mr. Arnaud: Ah yes, yes. Well, I'm going to explain to you my case, during the time I wasn't married. Well now I worked with my father, under orders. On the day I married, we made an agreement with my father. I became his cropsharer, that is, we shared the grape harvests.

I have a sister but it was I who worked and we shared the harvest. On my father's death, we shared the property. Only, my sister didn't marry a grape grower, so up to now I've worked the vines of my sister as a cropsharer, and I had the succession of my father-in-law. My father-in-law was a viticulturist. Also, so I had the share that came to my wife. That means that at present I have a holding of about twenty-five hectares of vines. And to let you know that we are viticulturists from father to son, next year I'm going to cede that holding to my son-in-law, because I have only one daughter; my son-in-law is a grower. At present I'm seventy years old, so next year I'm going to cede the control of the property to my son-in-law.

He'll give me a percentage of the harvest to live normally. My son-in-law learned on the job, his father was a viticulturist also. When I tell you that at Sainte Cécile we live on vines only, you see how it is. My son-in-law is a son of a grower, he worked with his father before marrying, then he did just like me with mine, he worked the vines of his father on halves. And at present, given that I've only a daughter, he's going to take on the totality of my land. That will make for him a property of some importance; he'll have forty hectares. He won't have it entirely for his own; his father and we must live from it. At least these are family arrangements.

That's going to be, if you wish, when I've given everything to my son-in-law, that'll be the association of two middle-sized properties, because all the same, the holding of forty-odd hectares that he'll have, that begins to make a piece, that begins to be rather important.

XV

Mr. Guerre, native of Venteuil in Champagne, vividly remembers his family's origins and its vicissitudes over several generations. Family life, he feels, used to have a more intimate character, with firmer generational ties; and the culture of the vines brought father and son into closer contact and mutual respect. The riots of 1911 which he mentions resulted from the violent opposition of vignerons toward champagne merchants selling fraudulent beverages, that is, sparkling wine made wholy or partly from grape juices imported from other wine districts and yet labeled as "champagne." Mr. Guerre is proud of his family history and his roots in the soil. His thirty-four acres of vines form a large holding.

Mr. Guerre: I am fifty-six years old and have been a vigneron as long as I can remember. I succeeded my parents and grandparents. I've Champenois roots through my mother and Limousin through my father. My [paternal] grandfather was a mason; he went up to Paris after the Commune of 1871, and the fortune of his trade brought him to Champagne where he settled down. But my father wasn't drawn to masonry; he became a vigneron. Little by little my grandparents bought land, parcel by parcel. At present I work fourteen hectares with my children; my brother has seven hectares. We have wine presses together and a building that we bought where we work on the harvest and make our wine together.

I learned the trade as anyone did at the time. That's to say, it was my parents who were the masters of my apprenticeship. Parents, grandparents, because grandparents had a little more authority than parents. There were some books also. And lots of observation. And now, I've got to admit, there's been such an evolution over thirty years, that the training you could have received then is now out-of-date, because there are so many new ways, new techniques, and new products.

My father was a vigneron, full-time, and he's still alive. He's eighty-six years old. He also began making wine shortly before the war of 1940, after the economic war of '34.

Mr. Loubère: Your family settled here in the village. Are all your familial memories anchored here, in this village?

Mr. Guerre: My maternal grandfather's family lived in a village lying several kilometers from here, and his parents were the successors. Their parents had not been prosperous in business and they sold everything, so that my maternal grandfather, at eleven years old, was [penniless]. He was taken in by an uncle, and aunt, and when thirteen years old he arrived here in the house of another uncle for whom he worked for a whole year, all year for 50 francs. And that continued until he was old enough for military service. At that time, service lasted three years. Before his military service, he married my grandmother.

This uncle had given them to believe, and had even promised, that they would succeed him in as much as he had no children. There were several nephews in the same condition; he used them all in turn, such that these young men— when they were twenty-three or twenty-four years old—had practically nothing. So they married in the village; my maternal grandmother was a native of the village.

I remember when he told me about his first acquisition of a vineyard of three *ares* (.074 acres). He put all his savings in the *Caisse d'Epargne* because he didn't want to borrow at that time. Those who borrowed, had to take out a mortgage, not only on the property, but even on themselves. They began like that. And then they went through the phylloxera invasion which destroyed the vines in Champagne, as everywhere else. They were helpless to deal with mildew and other maladies of the vine. They knew nothing about either the products for treatment or about the means to carry out treatment. That life was difficult, very hard.

They took part in the riots of 1911. My grandfather was sent to prison for three weeks. At that time there were no loud-speakers. To be heard, you had to impose silence; there were no other means. Well, my grandfather, having been three years in the cavalry, returned a corporal bugler. He was very well known; I remember that he was first-rate. Since the leaders were from Venteuil, our village, quite naturally they asked him to remain with them. Well, it was he who sounded the call for attention, to get people together, to get them to listen. He was so good that he was always at the side of the leaders, each time a photograph was made. So when the leaders were arrested, inevitably my grandfather was put in jail with them.

Mr. Loubère: What kinds of relations were there between parents and children? Were there relations of both love and friendship and of authority?

Mr. Guerre: Ah yes, both. That was natural; authority was natural. Parents were authoritarian and back then, that was perfectly normal. There were few revolts, but basically it was accepted. No question of contesting, of rebelling; that was unthinkable. But parents were not at all authoritarian in the bad sense of the word. One had relations with one's parents that showed repsect. I don't mean that today there is no more respect toward parents; but there are not the signs of respect that you found in past times. Today you become real friends *(copains)*. What can you expect, in the vines, you talked together.

My grandfather used to relate how things were when vines were grown haphazardly (not in rows). He began as a worker, then a very small vigneron a little later. And the, well, all the difficulties they had, the hardships they had in the crisis [of 1911]. You listened. You didn't have a transistor like today when it is nearly at the bedstead. Today, when you come home from work there is no more conversation at the table because there's the television running in the corner. In the old days there was conversation and reading, and people listened. I find that it was all the more profitable than what you can see today, from what goes on today.

I remember that families came together more easily in the past. There were village festivals, for example. Venteuil is our town, with a hamlet on each side. I lived in the hamlet over there; grandfather was in the town, and we had an uncle farther away. Every year there was the holiday of the patron saint, which lasted two days, each of us in turn [served as host to the others]. In as much as everybody played an instrument, there were other occasions to meet, without mentioning anniversaries and marriages. So much so that seven or eight times a year there was a family reunion. And you listened. I find that I am very happy to have heard all the recollections of those people. These were their experiences but I profited a little all the same from their experiences.

Mr. Loubère: And you, like your father, you taught the trade to your children?

Mr. Guerre: Yes, but at present you know, they take risks more easily; they are perhaps more open because they don't have the impression of taking risks. They use their imaginations. But that's normal, it's the advantage of youth to move ahead.

XVI

Mr. Serruier provides a brief but significant view of the youth of today. It is clear that, like so many parents, he is not quite sure of the moral basis of his judgement; he is mildly critical of young people, but like Mr. Guerre he admires their adventurous spirit.

Mr. Loubère: In what terms would you compare your relations with your parents when you were young, and your relations with your son today? Is there a difference?

Mr. Serrurier: A big difference, yes, a big one. I think that children are not as attached to the family today. What do I mean by attached? Let's say that in some sense they don't care a fig for their parents. Perhaps that's not the term to use. They don't care fully for their parents as we did, as one did in the past, you see.

As for work, the younger generation has much more time off. Nowadays they begin Friday, like many, and go out Friday evening. Saturday morning [my son] still works a little with me but Saturday afternoon there's no way to make him work; all the young people do that, or at least most of them. They don't work on Saturday afternoon, they get together as pals, I think, because, you know, they don't tell me much, these kids. Well, on Sunday there's no work and on Monday we've got to call him several times. I mean each time he takes off he comes home on the stroke of four or five in the morning.

I'm not against that, all the same, but let's say that these are abuses, without being abuses; these aren't the same ways as ours. When we went out as kids, we didn't have the same habits.

Mr. Loubère: Has the changing means of transportation played a role?

Mr. Serrurier: Well, I think so, there is transportation and then there's money that accounts for a lot, because at the time when I went out I didn't spend the money that my son spends now. When I began to go out there was the bicycle. Well, you couldn't go very far, you know. Now there's the automobile, they're even beyond the stage of motorbikes.

Mr. Loubère: Have the bonds between generations weakened considerably?

Mr. Serrurier: Oh that depends on the family. Long ago, there was much more intimacy. There was only Sunday to go out and yet, when there was work to be done on Sunday and parents asked you to help, you worked with them. Things are no longer the same.

XVII

Family life in the past was usually marked by strong paternal presence. Mr. Centène recalls the power of his father in the family.

Mr. Centène: In 1910, there was a candidate for deputy from here—from Banyuls, itself. He was a writer who had a certain renown at the time; and since he was from Banyuls, naturally everyone voted for him. He was a social-ist, while at that time, everyone was a radical, moderate, etc. The socialists won and that kicked up an enormous reaction. There were even protests here in Banyuls—they had to bring in fifty or so police to control the population— each side resisted. I remember because I was young and my father didn't want anything to do with it. He forbade us to get involved in politics in any way— to such a point that, I remember, that year, 1910, I took the elementary school leaving certificate and during the exam a professor asked who my father had voted for—you see how far they went—and I told him "I don't know anything about that." Because if I had asked my father who he had voted for, he would have given me a good hiding. I wouldn't have wanted to come back. Because the old man was severe, I tell you. When I was in school, you couldn't even go out on Sunday or on holidays. "You will go out at such a time and at eight o'clock you will be at home, eh!" And that was that. Now—my mother was mistress of the house—that was her domain; there was no question about that; he didn't poke his nose into it. But as for discipline and the children and the rest, it was he who ruled—until I married. Even when I was married, I had to listen to him.

The family was always important. My father had three brothers who spent a
lot of time together. Holidays were family reunions and I remember, for the
holiday of the patron saint—which falls on August 29 at Banyuls—we were
sometimes fifty at the table, the whole family, from my mother's side as well
as from my father's side; everyone came together. In winter, when we killed a
pig, for example, the whole family would get together—one day at one person's house, the next day at another person's house. It was a time of festivity.

XVIII

If parents and especially the father were a powerful influence in the viticultural
family, they did not, however, generally exercise much control over marriage,
although this could vary across social classes. Mr. Centène recalls the character
of marriage when he was younger. His account suggests that duties such as
military service could sometimes be more important than economic considerations
in delaying marriage.

Mr. Centène: Well, long ago, parents arranged marriages. But in my era, no;
that had disappeared. Some arranged marriages, even so, up to a certain point.
One had a certain amount of freedom. Only if the daughter-in-law one brought
home did not please your parents, you understand, then sparks flew, but in the
end it was not obligatory [that the parents approve]. Ordinarily matches were
made between people from the same village. Here, the daughters of sailors
obviously married sailors; the daughters of landowners married the sons of landowners; it was rare that the daughter of a landowner married the son of a
sailor, and yet the sailors also had land and also had vines. I'm talking now
about the period before the war, before 1900. That was the custom. As for
the landowners, it was rare that boys courted girls from other villages, since
there was not as much communication [between villages] as at the present
time. So what simply happened was that families from here had relatives who
had settled in a neighboring village and during the village festival, the people
from over there would come here, or the people would go there and make
acquaintances. It happened that someone married a young person who was not
from Banyuls, but it was rather rare and after 1920, that changed completely.
And people married in church. It was rare to see a civil marriage. The priest
had a certain importance in the village, even for those who were not churchgo-
ing.

Mr. Loubère: Did couples marry young here?

Mr. Centène: That depended. Long ago, people married rather late, because
after 1910, young men who enrolled in the army did seven years of military
service [because of the war]. So, when they returned, you understand, they
were already twenty-seven years old. So they married rather late. But those

who drew a good number as a result of the lottery system and remained here, and who didn't do military service, married younger, at twenty-two, twenty-three, or twenty-five years maximum. To get married, you know, didn't take a lot of money, there were not many expenses. Families at times organized a family reception—that depended on whether people were well-off or not. Otherwise, you know, money didn't grow on trees. As I recollect, my father was twenty-seven or twenty-eight when he married; he was born in 1864. He had worked since the age of fourteen. He worked at home with his father, for the family, and when he was married, my grandfather never gave him a penny: for his pocket money, he did a bit of smuggling; he went to Spain to get alcohol which he brought here. On the day of his wedding, that day or the evening before, my grandfather made a big thing of giving him five 20 franc pieces—these were gold at that time. [My father] took the pieces and threw them on the table. He wouldn't take them.

Here it was not the custom for girls to bring a dowry. There were always parents on one side or another who gave them some money, but for a regular dowry as it were, like they have in some places, no.

Mr. Loubère: And did the girls begin to work early on?

Mr. Centène: Of course girls had always worked, just like the boys. That is, they worked as housekeepers. They worked at the home with their parents, or in the vines, but not much; they learned a trade or they learned the work of the house: to drive the animals, care for the animals, work in the kitchen, washing, ironing, all that. They gathered olives, they worked during the harvest, and then in winter as well, to gather branches in the vines; that was all the work they did outside the home. Some worked as seamstresses. If not, the girls did not really work. That has also changed. Now, women work like the men.

XIX

A worker, Mr. Coca, recalls marriage in his youth and the changes in attitudes towards marriage. His account differs subtly from Mr. Centène's and reflects the class differences between these men. Mr. Coca grew up on a vineyard estate, where his father was an overseer (ramonet). His reflections on marriage are also suggestive of the important ties between family members in working class households.

Ms. Frader: When people married in the old days, did they marry earlier or later than they do now?

Mr. Coca: I think that on the average we married somewhere around twenty years of age. While, it's pretty variable, it's difficult to know. I think the situation isn't the same. They don't marry now; they live together for two or three years, and either it works out or it doesn't work out. . . . To my way of thinking, it's not better. That's evolution, perhaps; young people want it like that. But earlier, when they married, they saw each other, they learned to know each other, which is normal and a girl did not marry before twenty. I'm speaking generally; there were perhaps younger marriages—that happens. In general it happened like that; one waited to become mature and then, especially, one thought about having job security to be able to live, to be able to have a peaceful household. When there was no security, obviously it forced people to wait. It's no longer comparable to [the situation] now; it's just not the same.

Ms. Frader: Did the young people of Coursan have many occasions to meet people from other villages? Did they tend to marry Coursannais or people from "outside?"

Mr. Coca: That's hard to say. I think that the majority married within the village. Certainly, because there were not the means of transportation which there are now. So it was hard to meet a girl or a boy from other places. Whereas now, one frequently sees a boy from Coursan who marries a girl from Narbonne or even farther away or vice versa. Now people have the opportunity to move around; they have the means of transportation which we didn't have. In my day there was only the bicycle. Well, to go out on a bicycle wasn't much fun. Whereas now, in moving around, they have the opportunity to make the acquaintance of a boy or girl and it often ends in marriage. Long ago, the means weren't available to be able to marry "outside."

Ms. Frader: There were, even so, people who came to the village for the grape harvest, who came from other regions?

Mr. Coca: From the Ariège for example. Sometimes, there were also some who eventually married [here]. I have a friend who married a girl from Bordeaux; she had come for the harvest, then they got to know each other and they were married. But that was an unusual situation at that time.

Ms. Frader: And did parents get involved in the choice of a husband or wife? Do you think they exercised much control?

Mr. Coca: No, that happened a lot in bourgeois families who would not permit, for example, a bourgeois son or daughter to marry the son or daughter of a worker. That has always been the case, perhaps less now, but in the old days, that existed. But in our milieu, I don't think so, with some exceptions.

Ms. Frader: Once married, how did young people arrange their family life? That is, did the newlyweds live with their parents for a certain time?

Mr. Coca: At the beginning [of the marriage], it was common enough, in our milieu. When a couple married, they commonly lived with one or the other set of parents at the beginning. Sometimes they alternated, a month here, a month there; all that, for the parents, was a way of starting off the young couple. . . . At the beginning [parents] helped them out, if you see what I mean. That, too, was a consequence of the economic situation. In the beginning, young people who got married, didn't have much or even had nothing. Now it's not the same. They marry; they have everything, while in the old days, they had nothing. So the parents would keep them a month or two months. After a certain while, they moved out; the young lived with the young, the old lived with the old. The young people would leave, look for lodging, make their own home and lead their family life as they wished, because they had no constraints; they felt independent, which is logical.

Ms. Frader: And as for people who lived on the large vineyards as you did, what did they do? Did they continue to live on the vineyard with the parents, too?

Mr. Coca: Yes. When I married, I lived for a while in my parents' house; my parents had a house given to them by their employers; it was big enough and had enough room for one more household; that's pretty common.

Ms. Frader: When young couples separated from their parents, did they maintain contacts, a sort of exchange network?

Mr. Coca: Yes, that has not changed. The fact of leaving their parents and becoming independent did not suggest an intended break between young and old; only I think it created a more limited relationship and one which, as a result, went much better. Because you know very well that a young person cannot get used to [living with parents]; for example, son-in-law, with his mother-in-law, his father-in-law, sometimes things would get heated between them, you see. I've seen situations in young households where parents and children lived together and the sparks flew a bit, but once they separated, they lived much better than previously. However, one mustn't say that the links have been broken; no, on the contrary, I think that relations were even better. What gave the parents pleasure was to invite the son to eat at their home, especially on Sunday. One day it would be at the husband's parents' home; the next Sunday it would be at the wife's parents' home. Later on, on holidays like Easter or Christmas, it would be one big reunion; this proves that relations were not cut. On the contrary, they improved. This has stayed in the tradition; it has not changed much.

Ms. Frader: In a village like Coursan, which is not very big, did the fact that people live close together facilitate the contacts between parents and children?

Mr. Coca: Yes—exactly, because often, although a couple could not live with the parents, they could arrange to live in close proximity. For example, parents here, have the children across the street; that happens often enough. But relations were very good. I think that there was a spirit of solidarity between parents and children in the family, which was much greater than what we have now. Even outside of the family household, the solidarity between neighbors and friends, in my opinion, was more important than now. Right now, I think that there is a spirit of egoism, you see. It's perhaps a consequence of the present circumstances. On the other hand, in the old days, the spirit of solidarity was striking, even very poignant. When there was a neighbor who had difficulties, or was sick, as soon as one could, one did the maximum to help him out.

XX

Another working-class couple reflected on the economic constraints of marriage and family life. Mr. and Mrs. Casadamont have been vineyard workers since their early teens, when they left school. They briefly explain the economic requirements of the marriage ceremony, and the role of the bride afterward. For working class couples, the need for two incomes was pressing.

Mr. Loubère: What did you need first to get married, a little money, some savings?

Mr. Casadamont: That depended. You know, in general, the fellow who was to get married, the future husband, it was he who paid the betrothal expenses. Then the parents [of the girl] paid for the wedding ring and whatever the engaged girl wanted.

Mrs. Casadamont: At that time you had to dress up, all the family dressed up, the bride, brother, sister, everybody. Well it was always after the grape harvest, in October, November, you see because you earned a little money from having picked grapes. Well, most marriages took place in October, November, December.

  And automatically we went back to work [after the wedding]. As for me I think that two months afterward I worked every day. I needed to, because we said, "We'll buy that, we're going to buy this." Very well, we were happy to be able to buy things and pay for them you see. If the wife could work that really helped the household as long as there were no kids on the way. After children came, you had to stop.

Mr. Casadamont: When we got married, both of us worked; that permitted us to live a little better, to put some coins aside each week, not a lot, but we succeeded in always putting some aside.

Mrs. Casadamont: Yes, we were happy to see that there remained something all the same.

XXI

A similar view of changing family values comes from Mr. Sabon, from Châteauneuf-du-Pape, who married in the 1930's. Mr. Sabon had to go outside of the village to meet young women. This was a phenomenon of the depression that must have been fairly common in small communities. His account suggests a different element of parental control over daughters than for sons.

Mr. Loubère: Did one try to expand land by marrying?

Mr. Sabon: Ah, certainly yes. But you see, there weren't many girls in Châteauneuf-du-Pape. Well, if there had been one who owned land, one would have said, "That one, she's rich," and one would have tried to take her over in order to expand the land, that's human. When I wanted to get married, there were no unmarried girls in Châteauneuf; there were none at all. I had to go find one nearby if I wanted to marry.

That's really true. There had been the war of '14–18, there were few births; and there weren't many girls. The girls who were of our age married young men who were four or five years older than we were; and we moved into the lean years.

There was Boiron who married a girl from Courtheson, Michel a girl from Sorgues; as for me, I married a girl from Tête-Rousse; Barot married a girl from Sorgues. We were too young for the girls of our age; we weren't developed enough for them. For example, Mrs. Brote, who's my age, married Brote who's ten years older than she. Paul Amouroux's wife was younger than we are and he's ten years older than us. We used to say, "Christ, they're taking them all from us, the girls, we won't have any more for us." But that's exact, believe me, that's how it happened. Well, we were obliged to go elsewhere. On Sundays we rode off on bicycles; we went to drink an aperitif, we went strolling in villages nearby. There were dances and that's how we met girls. When you had friends, you know how it is, you went to the café and you spoke to other young guys. As for me, that's how I met my wife, by means of a friend. One day I said, "Oh, she's charming that one there." She pleased me and I began courting her and I made her my wife; that's how it all came about. There are two cases here in Châteauneuf of persons who arranged marriages, where someone acted as an intermediary to arrange a marriage between a girl of Châteauneuf and a gentleman who was not from Châteauneuf. That happened twice.

Of course, parents had a lot of influence over the choice of marriage partners at that time; it wasn't like it is now. Nowadays girls are left on their own; they go out in the evening; while formerly. . . . Years ago, the mother, a girl's mother came to the dance with her and you couldn't lead the girl around too much at all. Believe me, it wasn't like now. Parents had more control over their daughters then.

XXII

The variations and frequent crises to which French wine economy has been subject since the end of the nineteenth century often meant that a vigneron was not always considered a good match. Mr. Guerre, the proprietor from the Champagne, remembers how the hard times experienced by wine growers in the 1930s influenced attitudes about marriage.

Mr. Guerre: I knew [misery] in '34; I was 11 years old then, and I'm not ashamed; I know about it thanks to my parents. I often say to my children that they don't understand. I remember once, my mother bought two steaks; there was one for me and the other one she cut in half. In '34 I saw wine selling for 200 francs a *pièce*. It was difficult then, from '32 to '34; 37 families left Venteuil; the town was emptied of its youth. These were people who were very, very badly off, really. And I remember at the time, hearing mothers who had daughters say, "My daughter will never marry a vigneron. Never, never!" That wasn't good. Everyone was out to hook the schoolteacher. He was a rare one. A good woman, a neighbor, told me some years ago, "You're lucky; you have nothing more to do; you have money." I said "Listen, you remember the time when you said 'My daughter will never marry a vigneron?" I liked your daughter a lot; if she'd married me, well, today she would be profiting from the prosperity of the vineyards and the vignerons." And what do you think she replied, she said, "You remember that?!" Well of course, I certainly do remember!

XXIII

Mr. and Mrs. Guillemard, proprietors—producers in their late seventies live in Pommard, the Côte d'Or, one of the regions which produce the more aristrocratic wines of France. Although their view of parental influence in marriage differs from some of the preceding accounts, they are in agreement with the view that the meaning of "family" has changed in recent times.

Mr. Loubère: Who arranged the marriages? Was it the parents or you, yourselves?

Mrs. Guillemard: The parents, yes, they arranged them a bit, but in general the young people chose together.

Mr. Guillemard: And then, in the old days, even so, there were marriages of interest.

Mr. Loubère: The proprietor ['s son] who marries the proprietor ['s daughter] ?

Mrs. Guillemard: Even so, the young people have been choosing on their own for a long time.

Mr. Guillemard: The young people take care of it now. But there is less and less a sense of family. In the old days, we were cousins with everyone; we called ourselves cousins, although we really weren't. Now there is brother and sister, then next first cousin and then after that, that's all.

Mrs. Guillemard: Now it's not at all the same. It depends on the people. Occasionally there are [cousins], but [more often] one makes friends; one has friends.

Mr. Guillemard: No, there is no longer the family spirit there was earlier. It's because we move more, because the young people go out more.

XXIV

In most agricultural societies, in the past, the distinction between work and leisure was more difficult to make than in our own time. Even in rural areas today, work and sociability are intimately connected, and leisure and amusement often derive from or spill over into work. The harvest is a good example of the link between the two, where long, backbreaking days of grape-picking were relieved by equally energetic eating, drinking, and carousing. But the life of the vigneron over the first half of the twentieth century was hard and the memory sometimes has more room for work than for leisure. Of course, social class differences are evident in the description of leisure activities. For workers, the variety of amusement which entered family life was more limited than for the small proprietor. And leisure did not have the same meaning for women as for men. Changing times and leisure activities have also eroded the sociability of an earlier age, as some of the following people suggest.

Mr. Guerre, the proprietor from Venteuil, in Champagne, remembers the amusements of his youth.

There were, in many villages, a music society, sports clubs. As for me, I played soccer when I was young and I played lacrosse. And then, work in the vines was a lot more difficult than it is today. We worked every day of the week. Now, on Saturday, it's normal that one rests, but since there are no workers on Saturday, we would reserve the least difficult work for that day— work in the wine cellar, looking over the equipment and then, gradually we worked it out so that we did that during the week and then took Saturday off. But I can still remember that [before that], until midday on Sunday, we worked and often didn't finish, because we had to do all the [chemical] treatments, spread sulfur, carrying the containers on our backs, plow, weed, and gather hay for the horses. Now there are no more horses. But it was difficult, really very difficult.

XXV

Mr. and Mrs. Casadamont suggest that for workers, old forms of village sociability are disappearing and that modern technology and rising prices may be making some viticultural families more private in their leisure activities. Leisure for men and women is quite different. If men's leisure has succeeded in detaching itself from work, it is not clear that women's leisure has done so. Some of the views of Mrs. Casadamont of this subject are echoed by Mr. Coca, the worker from Coursan.

Mr. Loubère: I've been told that people used to drink more heavily than they do now.

Mr. Casadamont: Earlier, one drank more because now, someone who has a wedding party [for example] restrains himself from drinking because he knows that if there's an accident, after you're stopped, there's the alcohol test and you risk paying a fine. In the old days, that didn't happen. You drank and you left [the party]. First of all, there weren't so many cars; you left on bicycle or you got a ride or took a bus. So you could drink more; whereas now, one drinks almost not at all, especially here in the Midi. I see it when I go to the café with friends. Two or three times a week, on Saturday, or Sunday, we go to the café to play cards, I'm almost the only one who drinks. I have a muscat. My other friends who are proprietors, they drink a Vichy (mineral water). I say it's not possible that as proprietors, they drink Vichy and I drink wine!

Mr. Loubère: The cafés, do they play a pretty important role in collective life?

Mr. Casadamont: Yes, because there was no mail in the old days. So every day, the café was full. Here, in a village of 700–750 inhabitants, there were four cafés before the World War II. Now there is one. We also have a community center, but the young people don't go there now.

Mr. Loubère: Has television changed things a lot?

Mr. Casadamont: It's the television, all that.

Mrs. Casadamont: But I don't know—perhaps we read more. In summertime we'd go out just like that, four or five people, we'd sit in front of the door, we'd stay there until nine or ten o'clock. We've lost some of what used to animate the village from the human point of view.

Mr. Casadamont: Now, we meet on the public square. We meet, we talk, we laugh. In the old days, when drinks were less expensive in the cafés, we went to the café, we played cards, we spent the evening like that. Now, we go to the café or to the community center. You have a drink, one day one person pays, another day it's another who pays, but each time it's almost 3 or 5 francs out the door.

Mr. Loubère: As for the women, you don't go to the café?

Mr. Casadamont: Yes, on Sunday there are some.

Mrs. Casadamont: But its rare.

Mr. Casadamont: The girls, they go; the girls now, they're there every day. Customs have changed.

Mr. Loubère: What do you do to amuse yourself when the men are at the café?

Mrs. Casadamont: You know, I like to read a lot; sometimes I'd hurry to get my work done, I'd read a little bit, but the next day I'd have to get back to work. After supper, there was ironing to do and sometimes sewing. Sometimes in summer, the women go out into the street to take the fresh air and they talk. But it's nothing like what we knew thirty, thirty-five years ago. Even though I like to read a lot, I won't read if I have to knit or sew. You see for me, that's leisure, but I find that it's beneficial leisure. Now, with television, the majority of people stay home. My situation is not unique.

XVI

Mr. Coca has also seen the older form of sociability pass.

Mr. Coca: In the past, in the evening, after eating, if the weather was good, everyone would come outside in front of their doors to take the fresh air. There were groups you'd pass in the village streets, groups of eight or ten all around, who talked, they'd spend the evening like that until ten at night. While now, you don't see that any more, or you see it less and less. Everyone is in his corner. Now, look at the people in front of their doors, maybe you find two or three, that's all. While in the old days, I'll tell you, one could still find corners where there were seven or eight who sat and talked. . . . Today it's not the same.

XVII

For some workers leisure times were few and far between; this was especially true for working class women, for whom double work was the routine (and, as Mrs. Casadamont suggests, still is). Once women returned home after a day of wage work, the demands of domestic tasks did not leave much free time. Mrs. Rouaix, of Coursan, Aude, remembers her leisure time with difficulty.

Ms. Frader: What did you do for amusement in the old days?

Mrs. Rouaix: There was usually a dance on Sunday. Every Sunday, we danced in a café. That was all there was. [It was just] the young people from the village. There were no cars, like now so we stayed in the village and danced.

Ms. Frader: And in the family, in the evenings, what did you do for fun? Did someone tell stories?

Mrs. Rouaix: Oh, no! You know, in the evening we worked. There was the housework to do, you had to prepare the food for the next day, so we didn't think about having fun; it was hard.

Ms. Frader: And were there popular holidays at the time? What about the 14th of July and May First?

Mrs. Rouaix: On the 14th of July, we danced, with music, we danced around the whole village, that was all. [On May First] there would be a demonstration. We had a big meeting, all the people would come together and afterwards we marched around the village with the coronet and drum. In the evening there was a dance. Later, when we had movies, we'd see a film in the evening. We all loved to dance. But I wouldn't want to relive what we went through because in those days, we suffered too much. We don't want to see any of it again.

XVIII

But for Mr. Coca, leader of the vineyard worker's union in Cousan, the May First holiday had a special significance.

May First, long ago, was celebrated every year by a gathering of workers. There was a large meeting which took place in the town hall and I remember well that the room was too small. Too small, why? Because there were masses of people. To spruce up the evening, the union showed a film for free— everything was free. And the evening ended with a demonstration throughout the streets of the village, with music and flags. . . . it's one of the memories which will stay with me my whole life. I experienced those evenings, I experienced them as a kid, in my adolescence and as a union militant. Now that really had an impact on me. As one who lived all these May Firsts and remember them, I'm sorry now that the situation is not the same, because on May First now, [the union] is practically not followed and is supported very little. And that makes me a little heartsick since I was a part of that period where every year, the union celebrated May First, with its traditions. When I organized them, the May First celebration began with a concert; then there were speeches, and finally singing the "Internationale." You had 500 people standing, singing the "Internationale." That was really remarkable. I'll never forget it. In my personal opinion, people now shirk it because it has become a regular, paid work holiday. In the old days, when a guy took May First off, he was afraid of being fired. The day before, he had to go tell his employer, "Tomorrow, I won't be working." Often people were fired [because of it], but the guy became aware of the struggle in which he was engaged.

Chapter Five
Cooperative Wineries and Vignerons

IN ITS SIMPLEST terms a cooperative winery *(cave coopérative vinicole)* is a facility owned by an association of grape growers. It is managed by an elected administrative council which hires one or more professional wine-makers to vinify the grapes brought in by all the affiliated growers. Each member enjoys a proprietary right over the finished wine, his share being measured by the weight and sugar content of his grapes at the time of entry. Some cooperatives return the wine to members who sell it themselves, but this practice has nearly come to an end because large scale marketing carried out by the cooperative is more profitable. The cooperative is neither a profit-sharing nor a capitalist enterprise; nor is it a truly socialist experiment although such was the intention of early social reformers.

The idea of cooperative production as a way of freeing workers from their capitalist employers—or exploiters, if you wish—appeared in the early nineteenth century, and was a basic ideal of early socialist thought. Its greatest success, however, was not in manufacturing but in distribution at the retail level. Cooperative stores spread widely, managing to eliminate middle men and provide urban workers with products, especially food, that were less costly and free of dangerous additives: no sand in sugar, no water in wine and milk.

Cooperation in viti-viniculture did not appear until the twentieth century, and it too, was socialist in its early phase. During 1901–3 growers in the small commune of Marausson (Hérault) established the first one. They were socialists; they pooled their lands and resources, and prospered. By this time democratic as well as revolutionary socialist politicians began to moderate previous demands for the collective ownership of land, pointing out to their peasant followers that their small holdings, the result of their sweat and labor, were sacrosanct; only large estates were to become public property. This trend fit well with growers' preferences. As we noted in chapter one, the vigneron was at heart a peasant and the full ownership of his plot was historically an element in his sense of being rooted. In consequence there was little desire among other growers to imitate the pioneers of Marausson, and it was not until the end of World War I that cooperatives spread at an almost revolutionary rate. From 1919 to 1939 their number grew

Fig. 18   The cooperative winery "Free Vignerons" of Maraussan (Hérault) that successfully
initiated socialist penetration of wine production in 1901–3. Interior, the great
maturing casks and a hand-driven pump.

from eighty-two to 827 and from 1939 to 1973 rose to 1,195. In the latter
year they made fully half of the table wine of France and about one-third of her
fine wines, that is, wines labeled according to their geographic origins *(appellation
d'origine controllée)*.[1] In this rapid growth, cooperators lost sight of their socialist
origins.

There were several reasons for this remarkable growth. Some of them will be
explained in the interviews so we shall be brief and general here. The chief reason
for setting up cooperatives of any kind was to save family-size holdings (one to
seven hectares) and this was especially true among little vignerons. The landless
worker could not participate and has never benefitted from them. Rather the small
grape grower created them to improve his income and to survive the ever worsening
economic crises that periodically struck him: 1903–8, 1920–23, 1934–39, 1950–56.
Only by rationalizing the making of wine could small growers compete with larger
growers whose costs were lower per hectare and whose bargaining power vis-a-vis
wholesale merchants was greater. The rising costs of transforming grapes into wine
undermined the small producer who was forced to accept the ridiculously inferior
prices that large distributors offered them for their grapes or newly fermented
wine. In addition, ideally, cooperatives managed by skilled enologists offered the
prospect of wines of better quality, as contrasted with those of small growers
deficient in technical knowledge and equipment. Again, by concentrating wine
production in a large cooperative, the bargaining power of small vignerons collectively
could be enhanced, with a resulting rise of prices. Not only could cooperatives

Fig. 19 Vignerons Libres cooperative, exterior view, with casks attached to railroad cars for transport to market.

Fig. 20 Comportes loaded on a wagon for the transport of grapes to the winery.

make better wine, they could more effectively market it.[2] Cooperatives grew most extensively in Languedoc and Roussillon where the production of ordinary wine assumed its largest dimension. There, on the Mediterranean coast, about 560 cooperatives have enrolled 79 percent of grapegrowers and turn out 60 percent of the region's table wines, as well as 25 percent of all ordinary wine in France.

In other areas, such as Côtes-du-Rhône, where early-maturing wine is a staple, cooperation has made rapid headway.

Fig. 21 The cooperative winery *L'Esperance* ("Hope") in Coursan, Aude, in the late 1930's, with horse-drawn carts for transporting grapes and wine.

Fig. 22 A medium size cooperative winery in the Côtes-du-Rhône. The large outdoor tanks have controlled temperature for fermentation and storage of wine.

In fact, not all the high hopes for cooperatives have been fulfilled. Traditionally these wineries have accepted all the grapes of member-growers, regardless of quality and type. The results have often been nondescript, mediocre beverages selling at low prices, and hardly capable of permanently relieving the financial weakness of small growers. For this reason many individual vignerons have refused to join. They, like Mr. Feschet among our interviewees, take a special pride in creating estate wines from their own grapes. In their eyes, the blending of grapes of various qualities and types is a form of vinicultural miscegenation from which nothing good emerges. To avoid this, cooperatives in regions well known for fine wines insist that members meet certain standards of production, follow prescribed methods of cultivation, and replant their vineyards with better vines. The interviews in this and other chapters will also make clear that cooperation has not saved all viticultural families: many have left the land, and if not the entire family, then its younger members have found it necessary or preferable to move into more secure professions. The young have often refused the precarious existence of grape growing with its alternating phases of feast and famine.

Despite their drawbacks however, cooperatives have become the most important means of making small vineyards into viable enterprises and have saved them and their owners from extinction. Particularly in areas of mass production, too many small vignerons are still limited in their resources, without sufficient capital to furnish a cellar, and without storage capacity to mature and sell wine during periods of lucrative prices. Not only are they unable, as simple grape growers, to compete with large owners who enjoy the advantage of size, they are unable to bargain effectively with large *négociants*, that is, with the men who make and mature wine which they eventually distribute to market centers in Paris and other cities. And not only the small grower, but the worker-owner, as Mr. Raspaud explains, has also survived, thanks to the cooperative, but less and less as a worker imbued with class consciousness and collective ownership as his goal, a point taken by Mr. Darricade. The old style individualism of Mr. Feschet, while still active in some areas of fine wine, has been disappearing, indeed has already ceased to exist as a fact of life. Every aspect of the wine industry is now controlled by decrees, regulations, and regulatory commissions; in response cooperatives are growing in number and membership as even medium growers are entering them because, like the smaller growers, they cannot otherwise comply with many regulations, and also to avoid the high costs of equipment. Increasingly viticulturists are concentrating on one activity, grape culture, and leaving the perils of wine making to highly trained experts and the sale of wine to marketing professionals. So far, this evolution in the south has not eliminated the continuous crises resulting from overproduction and lagging sales of low-grade table wines. Elsewhere there is no crisis and no rush to join cooperatives, unless they can turn out a superior product to attract the more sophisticated drinkers of today's post-industrial society.

In this society many of the smaller cooperatives have proved ineffective as marketing agents. Those confined to one or several villages simply do not have the personnel and contacts to discover and exploit new markets; moreover they often do not turn out sufficient volume to attract the interest of wholesalers and importers. To overcome this weak link in the chain through which grapes became wine that must eventually repose on the shelves of retailers, village groups have begun to federate out of economic necessity. Particularly in the Rhône Valley and the lower south over the past decade they have built common bottling facilities and set up marketing organizations that have become dynamic enough to prospect market potential within and outside of France. Formerly cooperatives sold most of their wine in bulk, that is, in barrels, carboys or other large containers. Wholesale merchants purchased it to blend with Algerian, Spanish, and, recently, Italian wine because cooperatives often produced beverages low in alcohol and weak in body. These *bibines* are now a drag on the market. With the steady decline of consumption in France, and a rising preference for better wine, the more progressive co-operative federations have responded to these changes in several ways. Their managers have, with the aid of state subsidies, modernized equipment and urged the membership to plant superior grape varieties by offering bonuses for healthy fruit. With better grapes they can turn out beverages to satisfy a more demanding domestic market and attempt, with a certain success so far, to penetrate foreign markets. Of course, this aim requires dealing in bottled wine, that is, wine labeled as V.D.Q.S. *(Vin Délimité de Qualité Supérieure)*, or even as A.O.C. in regions with an already acquired reputation such as Bordeaux, Burgundy, and Champagne. Elsewhere cooperatives have obtained backing from their Chambers of Agriculture, and set out to inform the general public about their regions and their appellations. There is indeed a viti-vinicultural revolution—a permanent revolution—taking place in France. Most small growers have little choice about joining a cooperative if they wish to become part of it.

---

1. La Confédération Nationale des Coopératives Vinicoles, *Annuaire national des caves et distilleries coopératives*, Ed. 1974, pp. 9–10, 133 ff.

2. D. Boulet and J.-P. Laporte, *Contribution à une analyse économique de l'organisation coopérative* (Montpellier, 1975), pp. 1 ff.

I

It is not difficult to understand why cooperatives arose earliest in the lower south, where ordinary wines were the chief item of trade. Small growers were often cheated by local commission agents who procured wines for large whole-salers. Mrs. Rachou, née Faure, recalls an unpleasant encounter between her father and such an agent in the village of Quarante (Hérault). Of course, such personal memories could show bias, revealing only one side of the real situation. There were undoubtedly many small producers who did not know how to make drinkable wine, who used rotten grapes or infected barrels, and whose final product was defective. Vinicultural cooperatives, nearly everyone agrees, raised the level of quality for small growers, and, as Mrs. Rachou notes, even large growers have begun to join them.

Mrs. Rachou: After the year ended we sold the wine from the bottom of the barrel, because you can't keep it and there are always lees, you understand. [It is distilled into cheap alcohol].

The brokers profit from it. Then later, let me tell you what happened at our place. At our place we have a press and all that. Well, a broker came from Cruzy, and he took away some samples [of wine]. Then he came and said to my father:

"You know, your wine is good but has an odd taste."

My father asked him: "But what taste has it? "

He said: "It has a copper taste. It has a copper taste."

"It has a taste of copper," my father said, "since one sprayed with copper to save the grape crop from rot."

And he said, "And the other cask, it also has a taste."

"It has a taste? That's the first time anyone said that to me. I've got other clients, they buy wine from me; it's not for that that I gave you samples. They buy my wine without seeing it. They said to me: 'You want to sell wine, Paul, well it's worth such a price and I'll give you so much'; if you're a seller, you'll inform me."

The broker said, "That astonishes me. It's got a taste of earth, so I can't give you a price. . . ."

My father said to him: "Listen, friends we have been, friends we shall be, but go back to Cruzy, this wine's not for you."

That's what happened in the past, the little producer, they took him in like that. It's for that, rather, that the cooperative was set up; it was set up only by the little people. Now there are all the big producers, there are those with 2000 hectos [who have been joining].

II

Mr. Raspaud is a worker-owner in the village of Tautavel, where most growers work their small vineyards either with their immediate relatives or a few hired hands. They are all actively involved in the cooperative. Byrrh is a huge buyer of grapes to make cocktail or aperitif wines that it sells under its own label.

Mr. Loubère: Have cooperatives had an influence on the life of workers?

Mr. Raspaud: Yes and no. [Yes] because it's simple, if there were no cooperative, we could not be owners. We don't have the means to have a personal cellar, as that was done in the past. And it's the creation of the cooperative cellar that led the workers to buy several parcels of land, little by little, and to be able to have their grapes vinified at the cooperative winery. But if the cooperative made that possible, you must admit that at the beginning of the cooperative, there were many owners who refused (look what it's come to, that class struggle), they refused to mix their grapes with grapes of workers.

Here, the pioneers of the cooperative cellar, they were above all the owners, because workers, they hardly had a bit of land, they made little wine, at first for family consumption; then they pushed forward, they had the owners lend them barrels or they bought used barrels, and made a little wine. But they had the problem of merchandising it. You understand very well that the negociant, he was not going to buy, he was not going to mature a batch of 10 hectoliters from the agricultural workers, if there was a cooperative cellar.

What also pushed toward the creation of the cooperative cellar of Tautavel, that was created in 1927, it was the firm of J . . . . Because it had a policy of scorn for the farmer. It was a monopolist at the time in the wine market. So it had cellars outside and over the whole world. And the vine owners, then they had worked all year on their crop, they had worked with love, even for the period they went to extremes as during harvest when they had a cutter passing behind the gang to pick up the clusters that the gang had missed, a single grape that fell to earth, it was gathered up like the ball of one's eye. Very well, they arrived at the loading dock, and the firm refused [to buy their grapes]. They had no vats, where were they going to put the grapes? All year they had counted on the harvest and it refused their crop.

We studied this later on; it came a little from the mental state of the manager of the cellar of Tautavel. He was a zealot for the firm, but his intelligence was mediocre. If he tried that today he'd be lynched. But since he was the only buyer in our market, he imposed his prices, he had you. You sold by the kilo all the same, so the grapes of Tautavel, they were paid like those of the plain.

So when the owners learned all these problems and they saw that Byrrh made enormous profits from their sweat, several already had started, saying: "We have to come together, we have to set up a cooperative." And they set one up. Now, 95 percent of the harvest is vinified by the cooperative cellar.

III

Mr. Emilien Soulié was also a vineyard worker and small owner who somewhat lyrically expresses his views on cooperative viniculture in Languedoc, where it was born before World War I.

Mr. Soulié: The cooperative cellar for the vigneron, it's the temple, if you're Protestant; it's the cathedral of wine [if you're Catholic]. It's the strong box of vignerons. These are images that represent it well.

In our present conditions, if there were no cooperative winery in our region, 40 percent of the viticulturists would have given up, would no longer be viticulturists.

Mr. Sagnes: Did it permit agricultural workers to become owners?

Mr. Soulié: When my father came, he was an agricultural laborer. But he began to buy. My mother said to me: "There is the vineyard that we bought," and she explained to me: To the proprietor from whom they bought land they didn't pay at once; he gave them five years to pay and he imposed a rate [interest] that was surely usurious. Well, the first year they harvested and they paid. When they paid it off, they began to buy another, then another.

But there were problems in the trade union. They arose because the agricultural worker doesn't want to take into account the income he earns from the vine, and we have explained his situation in a scientific way. It's that the agricultural worker who does his seven hours for his employer, who goes to work one or two hours on his own vines after his work day, he succeeds a little in demobilizing his consciousness. The agricultural worker knows that his wage will never permit him to live well; his preoccupation is to work his vines, to have his vines, and to abandon a little the class position of the agricultural laborer.

And me, I've gone even farther in my analysis. Me, I considered that it was a surplus value that the worker, when he worked his own vines, brought to his employer. So, I'm going to tell you why. Because to the extent that he abandoned in part his defense [of class], he made no defense of his wage, his principal thing, thus, he demobilized in part or in total or for three-fourths his struggle to snatch from his employer the social value of his labor power.

IV

A quite different point of view can be found among cooperators who own larger vineyards. Mr. Centène was a medium owner before retiring, and is the elected president of the cooperative l'Étoile in Banyuls-sur-Mer where the excellent muscat grape produces sweet wines that enjoy an international reputation. Banyuls lies in the foothills of the Pyrénées, where they rise out of the Mediterranean. He also gives us a glimpse of economic conditions that left many growers with little choice but to join a cooperative or face ruin.

Mr. Centène: Cooperatives, up to a certain point, have regularized so to speak the commerce of wine. Many cooperatives like ours or others have launched themselves into commerce, you understand. That has given a surplus value, if you wish, to the harvest, to the wine.

Cultivation was very profitable until 1920. After 1920 there was a crisis of two or three years after the war. Naturally things picked up afterward. And in

1935 again, we had to pass through a crisis, a big crisis equally of lack of sales, when all the great growths of France nearly caved in. And it was at this moment that they created the I.N.O. *(Institut National d'Origine)*, and an appellation of origin which raised our prices a little until 1960. In 1960, already, once again, the price level became stable at a certain moment. Despite the rise of the cost of cultivation, despite the rise of the cost of living, prices did not change. That led up to a huge crisis in 1969 when three-fourths of the vineyards, here, had been abandoned, so to speak, and that was the reason why so many young people quit their holdings. In 1969, forty agricultural workers' families left Banyuls. No one wanted to grow vines. And that crisis lasted four years.

Mr. Loubère: Did cooperatives bring about changes in the way of making wine?

Mr. Centène: Yes, yes. That created a drama because it was an artisanal wine, if you wish, while now, with the present methods of vinification, the quality of wine has been much improved. What is good for cooperatives is that merchants who buy from cooperatives have wine that's always the same quality. While when one bought from a [lone] producer, who made, let's say, 200 hectos of wine, it was a certain quality of wine; at another [producer], the quality changed, it wasn't the same wine anymore. It might have been the same in quality, if you wish, but either in the color, or the bouquet, there was a difference. Now you know that the consumer who buys a wine he likes always wants the identical wine. Well, the merchant who was obliged to buy from Jean, Pierre, Paul, and Baptiste had to go over to blending, if you wish, in order to deliver the same quality of wine to his clientele. While now, with cooperatives, merchants who arrive here know: "At this cooperative, I'll have one type of wine, but at the other I'll have exactly the same type, or very little different."

This means that commercializing is much more simple, which was not the case when the owner himself made his wine. So then, cooperatives have naturally brought about great progress in merchandising wines.

Mr. Loubère: The persons who are managers of cooperatives, do they have much experience?

Mr. Centènne: Yes yes. That's to say that when the cooperatives were founded, exactly, vinification was carried out by old cooperators like me, for example, who had the habit, when still young, to see how to make wine. In the beginning, vinification in the cooperatives too, was made in a disordered way, however, since many years, since 1950 or '55, so to speak, in each cooperative there's an enologist to make wine. As here, we have an enologist who is responsible, from the harvest on, for making wine and maturing it. Moreover, there's a director who is concerned with selling it.

You see, the director, who commercializes, he's in contact with the communal consumers' representative and that's his job. As for vinification, treating the wines, it's the enologist who's in charge. Me, I'm here to supervise, as president, to try to supervise, that's all. I hardly have to work at all, so to speak.

The cooperative has another advantage in the sale of wine. It's followed more the taste of consumers than could the little isolated owner who makes his own wine. This isolated owner makes his wine, good, but he makes it in his own way. While in the cooperative with its commerce and its production, we are obliged to take into account the person who buys wine; it's he who orders. If the wine doesn't please him, he says no.

V

Mr. Paul Arnaud is a grower at Ste. Cécile in the Côtes-du-Rhône, and the president of the vinicultural cooperative there. He describes the success and growth of the organization as vineyards expanded and new markets opened, both of which came about after 1918. The growth was such that the village appropriately lengthened its name to Ste. Cécile-les-Vignes.

Mr. Arnaud: There were very few viticulturists here who made their own wine. My father had his little cellar, he had his vats, he had his barrels. There were many viticulturists who sold their grapes. Well, you had in the area three or four wineries who bought these grapes, paying whatever they wished, but the people had no other outlet for their harvests. At the end of 1926–27, there was a huge harvest; grapes sold badly, and they decided to set up a cooperative cellar. So it was set up in 1927 and started business in 1928. My father was one of the founders and administrators. Well, this cellar had a modest capacity, because there were many fellows who didn't want to join it. You know, they hesitated. They said, "What's that thing going to turn out? " *Enfin*, let me tell you, it was built for a volume of 15,000 hectoliters, and at present it's eight times larger. In the first year it vinified 8,000 hectos more or less.

Now this I'll tell you, this cooperative enables the people of Ste. Cécile to grow more vines because they no longer had the problem of selling their grapes. They carried their grapes to the cooperative winery; an administrative council or a commission for sales took on the job of selling the wine. This was one less problem, and moreover, it became so much less costly to equip a cooperative cellar than for each grower to equip his own individual cellar.

Bon, this winery went through several enlargements. There was at this time at Ste. Cécile, the founding president, Mr. Farjon, who was a man both energetic and far-seeing, and he was one of those who helped create the controlled appellation Côtes-du-Rhône. Before, we had only ordinary wines, wines without a name; our wines were good, but they had no noble title. Well, a little before the war, I mean the second war, we got the controlled appellation Côtes-du-Rhône. That was a real incentive for the vineyards.

My father was an administrator in the cooperative winery, and after the war (1945) I succeeded him. I was for several years its administrator; that was my schooling. And then for twelve years I was president of the winery. Under my presidency, we had two very important expansions: we renewed all the equipment for handling grapes when they were received; in 1970, here in Ste. Cécile, we installed ultramodern receiving equipment.

The Crédit Agricole financed all this at low interest rates. When the winery was set up, rates were 3 or 4 percent. At present [1978] they are 8 or 9 percent. Rates have climbed only since 1970–1971. Before and after the war they were 3 and 4 percent, depending on the duration of the loan, and its size. This varied a little each year.

What I want to say is that after the Second World War, viticulture in Ste. Cécile undertook a great extension and another cooperative was created. We now have two cooperative wineries, which are very important moreover. Ste. Cécile is the village that produces the most Côtes-du-Rhône. Yes, that's rather strange because the appellation Côtes-du-Rhône extends over the whole valley of the Rhône. I mean it begins a little south of Lyon and it comes up to Avignon, about 150 kilometers. And I believe that there are 120 communes that have right to the appellation Côtes-du-Rhône. Now, Ste. Cécile alone produces 10 percent of the total. That's why we have two fine cooperative wineries. And it's true that at Ste. Cécile we live exclusively off of wine. We don't have cows, we don't have horses; we're viticulturists.

The cooperative had an enormous influence on the life of the vignerons. Those who were obliged to sell their grapes could not discuss prices. Grapes are a harvest that is so fragile that once they are picked they must be brought at once to the vats. Well, people grew fewer vines as a result. Now, I think that even the cooperative is a little responsible for an excess of wine, because it's so facilitated the work of the vigneron. He's free of all commercial cares. He picks his grapes, he carries them to the winery, and that's all. [So he plants more vines.]

The administrative council and the sales commission do the rest of the work. Each meet once a week. Then, all the cooperators are convoked two times a year in a general assembly. They attend in large numbers here in Ste. Cécile. The general assembly is most important; the financial situation is made known. Some time before the harvest an information meeting is called, when the date of the harvest is fixed. The president also gives information on the sales realized up to then, on the outlook of the crop. These meetings are well attended.

Then, there exists a *syndicat* (union) of vignerons which unites the cooperators and persons who don't belong to the cooperative, because not everybody is a cooperator.

Chiefly little vignerons belong. There are some large ones also, for Ste. Cécile is a very, very cooperative village.

What's lacking is a sales organization because cooperatives sell only whole-sale, by tankloads. We've tried bottling a little of our wine, but we can only sell bottles retail. You see, when I was president of the winery, my dream was to expand direct sales [to customers] as much as possible, because otherwise we're subject to the will of wholesalers. Only, to undertake direct commerciali-zation, to organize a commercial service, we need heavy investment and coop-erators are reticent.

Well, since we spoke of Mr. Valayer, in setting up the *Cellier des Dau-phins* at Tulette, he did a sensational thing. (The *Cellier des Dauphins* is a bottling and sales center for several village cooperative wineries). Perhaps at a given moment we could have joined it, but the majority of our general assem-bly did not want to. It carries out direct sales, it groups cooperatives, it sells wine all over the world. While we other cooperatives, we're still at the artis-anal stage, I would say. We bottle a little, but *enfin*, we're still under the thumb of merchants.

VI

Cooperatives have never been as widespread in Médoc as in Languedoc-Roussillon or in Côtes-du-Rhône. Bordeaux and particularly Médoc have such a reputation in the international world of wine that wholesale merchants have managed to control the local markets and sell wine of all categories. Cooperatives have not managed to attract large numbers of small growers in regions renowned for their fine wines, Médoc, Côte d'Or, Châteauneuf, and Champagne, even though most of the wine produced in these regions is ordinary. Producers of the latter attempt to ride the coattails of the fine producers and can, with some success, command higher prices. Hence they feel less need for cooperatives. The 1930s were, however, exceptionally bad, and the impulse toward organi-zation began then. Mr. Darricade, president of the cooperative winery at St-Yzans-en-Médoc, recalls these conditions.

Mr. Darricade: Cooperatives began here in 1934, that terrible period of 1934. In the region, the Bordeaux merchants profited from our poverty, it must be admitted, to buy wine at low prices. The harvest of 1934 was a great vintage, abundant and of high quality, which doesn't often happen. They offered little peasants 600 francs per *tonneau* (900 liters) for a good wine like that. And then, when we formed a cooperative the next year, although '35 was not a good vintage, the merchants realized at once that we were going surely to defend ourselves because we didn't sell off the wine at once. Oh some sold off a little, but less so because cooperators received advance payments [from the new winery]. Then wine rapidly rose to 800 francs, that's all. Let's say that if they created cooperatives, it was above all to try to keep prices up. And also viticulturists, burdened by having to make wine, could now leave that to the cooperative.

Mr. Sagnes: Has anyone ever challenged the wine classification in the Bordeaux region? (In 1855 Bordeaux wines were classified for an International Exposition in Paris. Since then changes in the classification have been rare.)

Mr. Darricade: No, but as far as I'm concerned, it's unjust. Cooperatives are hurt by it, and they are hurt also, which is very important, by the château appellation. There exist in Médoc an *appellation château* and a generic appellation, that is simply Médoc. Well, the individual, whoever he is, if he makes only ten barrels of wine, he can get his classed as a château growth. But the cooperative can't sell its wine as chateau grown. For the past fifteen years we've struggled for this and we can sell some as château. Out of 10,000 hectos that a cooperative produces, about 2,500 hectos can be sold as château, all the rest is simply "Médoc," period. And to label a wine Médoc is to cause it to lose some value relative to the château label. There's value in price but not in quality. So that's an injustice; very, very, serious.

The cooperatives have taken action against this, but too modestly in my view. That's the results of cooperative directors.

Mr. Sagnes: Aren't the vignerons combative enough regarding such problems?

Mr. Darricade: Not enough, not enough. There's no tradition of struggle in the region.

Mr. Sagnes: Perhaps they suffer less from crises than in Languedoc.

Mr. Darricade: Because the appellation Médoc sells higher than the wine of Languedoc, which improves somewhat the means of living here perhaps. But they haven't got rid of that injustice in classification. It's all so stupid because they're not combative.

The majority of cooperators are little owners, two or three hectares, because they have another job, they don't only grow grapes. There are little and some medium owners, not real big ones. [Because there are few members in each village,] the cooperative is intercommunal, grouping five communes.

VII

Mr. Feschet, owner of a sizeable vineyard near Suze-la-Rousse in Côtes-du-Rhône, once belonged to a cooperative winery but withdrew. Like all the independent growers we have met, he does not want to blend his grapes with those of other members, and he is convinced that he makes a superior wine on his own and for less cost. He also points out that the independent producer is not isolated in his ignorance; he has extensive consultative and advisory services available, at minimum expense, sometimes even free. He effectively sums up the outlook of most grape and wine makers. Mr. Payon is a local

*bookkeeper with some vigneron accounts, and Mrs. Payon, his wife, is employed
at the Université du Vin, a center of wine education and of laboratory analysis.*

Mr. Feschet: I left the cooperative in 1976. It was to improve the revenue of
my property. Being in a cooperative is all very well, but the costs were higher
than in my own cellar because here we do the work, we don't always watch
the clock. On some days we put in fifteen hours in the cellar. The costs of
vinification are much lower. *Bon*, cooperatives are commercial, they attract
growers who harvest grapes, who bring them to the cooperative, who no longer
are concerned, save to wait until the cooperative gives them money. On the
other hand, when you start from the beginning, grow the grapes, and go to
the end and sell the wine, well you have to care for the wine, you have to be
concerned.

There are members who go to the [cooperative] cellar, they carry dirt, and
who knows what else, to say the least, and they don't give a damn once
they've brought in their grapes. After, the cellar master, he has to do the best
he can to do something with that, to make wine of it.

Mr. Loubère: You have a solid knowledge of wine-making?

Mr. Feschet: Ah, yes, first because my father always made it, and then all the
same I have the aid of an enologist who advises me, who analyzes the grapes,
and the wine afterward.

To buy equipment, well you have to borrow. My father had a hand crusher
and a hand press, a little hand pump, that's all the material you need to make
wine, along with wooden vats, yes. Before refurnishing my cellar I looked at
others, at the material of cooperatives. I decided against installing a stemmer
[to remove stems from grape clusters]. We have automatic equipment, press,
pump, that's all you need. And vats.

Mr. Payon: And then there are a good many technical reviews.

Mr. Feschet: These aided me in the choice of material.

Mrs. Payon: And then, you have to point out that the companies that do the
installing, they're very careful. They keep the vigneron informed, show the
utility of one vat, or of another, work out costs. They're well informed of the
vigneron's needs and do everything to make him aware of all material.

Mr. Feschet: Because, for the same cellar, you can spend thirty million francs
or you can spend a hundred million if you put in ultramodern equipment, all
automatic.

Mr. Loubère: With all that and with all the regulations that you must obey, do
you really feel that you are master of yourself?

Mr. Feschet: Ah, very certainly, I try to remain so as much as possible. I'm
more so than the cooperators; I'm more of an individualist.

Mrs. Payon: He feels more like a viticulturist than a cooperator who depends on the cooperative. If the cooperative, by misfortune, produces bad wine or sells it badly, even if it had good grapes, there won't be any profit.

Mr. Feschet: We, if we act stupidly, we have only ourselves to blame. While if a cooperator brings good grapes to the cooperative, and it places wine in a contest, and medals are won, they don't belong to anyone in particular. Me, I always brought my good grapes but I've never had the satisfaction of the good grapes I brought. But since I've set up my own winery, last year (1978) I won two medals, and well, there's nothing that's brought me more pleasure than that; I know it for sure. This year I won only one but that's a satisfaction no cooperator can have.

It's the artisan spirit that encourages you to always do your best, to try to do better.

That's what urged me to set up a winery. Because over years and years that I brought my good grapes to the cooperative, I've never received satisfaction as a result of the quality of my merchandise.

Chapter Six
Vines and Wines

IN ORDER TO COMPLETE the picture of the life and work of vignerons, we have assembled some of their recollections about their own profession. The quality of their life, their family patterns, their leisure activities, are all the reflections of their activity as vignerons.

As a professional the vigneron is an artisan as well as a technician: he must know his job, must understand the value of quality, must know how to use his hands, his body, must do physical labor. He must also understand the techniques and tools of the trade, must keep himself advised of new techniques, and must be ready to invest capital in his "enterprise." Increasingly even the small grower must acquire a risk-taking mentality, borrow capital, balance his books, and purchase or rent machinery. Cooperatives have relieved him of only a part of these managerial functions; the growing of good grapes is still almost exclusively the main task of the vigneron as an individual, and his skill as a grower is a determining factor in the quality of his product. In regions known for their fine wines, cooperatives will often not accept immature or defective fruit from their members. To survive, a vigneron must be or must become a professional.

This has required an open mind, a knowledge of tradition and a willingness to experiment wisely. Some growers, seeking to cut the cost of tillage, have resorted to *non-culture*, that is nontillage: the use of herbicides to kill weeds between vine rows rather than plowing or hoeing, or the spreading of plastic sheets between vines to prevent weed seeds from germinating. On this particular method, winemen have divided opinions. But any observer has only to look at most vineyards, their "manicured" surfaces, the near absence of weeds, to recognize that they are the creations of the true grape professionals of the world.

This perfection of the craft is the result of a long evolution, some would say a revolution. Until the phylloxera invasion of the 1870s vines were grown *en foule*, that is, randomly, in disorderly bunches. The planting of new vines, however, allowed growers to lay out vineyards in neat rows with sufficient space between them for the passage of an animal, a plow and a man. This was the first step in the process that has led to the increasing use of machines: the animals have nearly all been replaced by tractors, either narrow gauge to fit between closely

Fig. 23 Turn-of-century vigneron using a hand sprayer to cover vines with copper sulphate.

spaced vinerows, or set high on an inverted U-shaped frame with widely separated wheels that enable the driver and motor to pass above one or more rows (the *enjambeur* or straddler). More recently have come mechanical pruners and harvesters to the mass-production vineyards of the south. Most vignerons accept some of these innovations, and have gone heavily into debt to purchase them. But, as several of our interviewees reveal, they have misgivings because of the high costs as well as the rare usage of certain machines. This is particularly true of wine-making equipment, such as crushers and presses—the first to break the skins of grapes, the second to squeeze juice out of the pulp. With this consideration in mind, many small growers have joined cooperatives precisely to be relieved of

Fig. 24 These vines will never be harvested mechanically. Courtesy of Photothèque ITV-
M. Mackiewicz.

the burden of wine-making. In the vineyard, however, machines have many
advantages; tractors, although more expensive than animals, do not require hours
of feeding, nor do they need daily attention. Vignerons now enjoy more leisure,
can take long vacations without having to worry about who will feed the horse.
Machines have generally provided relief from heavy labor, as we noted in the
chapter on work; they have also brought greater efficiency and speed in routine
tasks. On the other hand, they have raised costs enormously for small and medium
growers, and have created pressures that disquiet several of our interviewees.

Pressures upon them result from the need to augment revenues in order to
amortize debts, and to buy even more machines. Mechanical devices may not
have a sex, but they are fertile all the same: machines beget machines, hence
the pressure to go more heavily into debt to acquire the very latest model.

This brings us to the human side of the profession. Many vignerons reveal the
symptoms of stress. Their only source of income is derived from grapes and wine,
and the sale of these nonessential products has been precarious in a complex
world. Their market, especially the outlets for rather cheap ordinary wine, has
always been unstable, and recently it has become even more so with the competition
that has arisen from Italian, Spanish, and Portuguese producers. The instability,
both of the quality of fruit resulting from seasonal weather conditions, and of
prices resulting from varying annual yields, have adversely affected growers of
ordinary wines, less so growers of fine wines.[1] The former therefore have turned
increasingly to the national government for aid in the form of subsidies, controls
of production, and prevention of fraud, and protection from foreign competition.

Fig. 25   Narrow-gage tractor plowing close to vine rows. Courtesy of Photothèque ITV-
M. Mackiewicz.

Fig. 26   An *enjambeur* or straddle tractor.

Generally, most growers resort to parliamentary pressure groups to achieve their
major goal: stabilization of production and prices. When peaceful persuasion does
not work, however, many of them turn to demonstrations in the street. Sometimes

orderly demonstrations turn into violent riots, as occurred in the south in 1907, in Champagne in 1911–1912, and more recently again in the south.

The wine industry—grape as well as wine growing—has increasingly called upon governmental intervention; the advocates of ordinary wines have put through, since the 1930s, several versions of laws designed to limit production, space out sales of wine in accordance with market demand, and prevent the sale of false or fraudulent wine. These laws are now generally referred to as the Code du Vin, and the repetition of their passage has, even while improving them, also shown their failure to stabilize the market.[2]

More successful has been the official classification of wines according to characteristics, as a means of offering wine buyers some assurances regarding the origin of the wine and the grapes used to make it. The growers of quality fruit and beverages were the innovators of this legislation. Its aim was to bring into accord the contents of the bottle and the claims on the label. If on the label the producer inscribed Châteauneuf-du-Pape, the buyer must be assured that the wine came from there, that it was not a blend of wine from elsewhere and some Châteauneuf. The term *appellation d'origine controlée* (AOC) is such an assurance. It means that producers have conformed to official requirements regarding grape varieties, yield, and geographic location of vineyard. It does not guarantee quality; an AOC wine can be mediocre, but it is authentic, it conforms to the label. That is the only guarantee that can be offered by the government agency charged with enforcing AOC regulations. In this the French were pioneers and innovators; what is notable is the distance that winemen have put between their traditional indi-

Fig. 27 Champagne bottles stored in *pupitres*, neck down so that sediment will settle on the corks. Courtesy of Photothèque ITV-M. Mackiewicz.

vidualism, their former repugnance of government regulation, and their present embrace of a truly regulatory politics. It would seem from what we describe above that greater change has come about in the organization of the profession than in its technology and entrepreneurship. In fact, one has not and probably can not take place without the other. Mechanization and scientific know-how, both in the vineyard and in the winery, have overcome many of the misfortunes that once reduced crops, which partly explains the steady increase of yields since 1900. Mechanical sprayers, even aerial dusting as well as spraying, have given a high level of protection against insects and fungi in the vineyard. Late spring hail, a most ancient enemy of vines in cooler climates, has been partially overcome by either seeding clouds or causing explosions among them by means of high-altitude rockets. This latter device is not to be confused with turn-of-the-century anti-hail cannons whose ground level bursts were useless and soon abandoned. In large wineries, computer controls have replaced the once hand-operated machines, and indicate the time to rack (change wine from one container to another), to filter, and to bottle, plus numerous other operations, as well as examine the chemistry and quality of the wine. Certainly it is easy, when observing the array of machines that now carry out many operations, to forget the human factor. The truth is that all aspects of the wine industry lead one back to the human factor: human choice, human action. Regardless of the machine, grape growing and wine making are very personal acts even if the grower's personality expresses itself only by pushing a switch. Such a simple act can never be more than the last step in a long process of decision-making that begins with the grape harvest and primary fermentation, and ends only when the wine is sent to a wholesaler or directly to a customer. Advanced technology has lessened some of the unknowns and risks in grape and wine growing; it has not eliminated intelligence. On the contrary, the traditional knowledge and wisdom that fathers once imparted to their sons no longer suffices for survival in a highly competitive industry. In ever growing numbers the heirs—and a few heiresses—of vineyards are attending or have completed courses in technical schools at the secondary level. When they graduate they can begin the education of their fathers.

This turn about of generations is more than an interesting assertion; it is indicative of the true change that has taken place in France: the disappearance of the peasantry.[3] Vignerons are "peasants no more." One must ask whether they ever were peasants, and the response depends on one's interpretation of the term "peasant." The term has generally referred to self-sufficient dirt farmers with a small holding, isolated, traditional, and generally dependent on a large landowner. This kind of grower has not existed in significant numbers in France since World War II. Given their market outlet, French growers never fit perfectly the definition, drawn up with cereal growers in mind. Given their technical education, their capital investments, their market economy—vignerons could not under any circumstances be considered peasants. They have become independent growers. To use an adaptation of David Riesman's terminology, they are other-directed by the economy and government, and inner-directed by their traditional way of life. The

Fig. 28 An *enjambeur* equipped for foliage spraying against insects and fungi.

Fig. 29 Wine maturing in a Bordeaux cellar. Courtesy of Photothèque ITV-M. Mackiewicz.

tension between the two has sometimes produced violence, as they struggle to survive in an increasingly complex world.

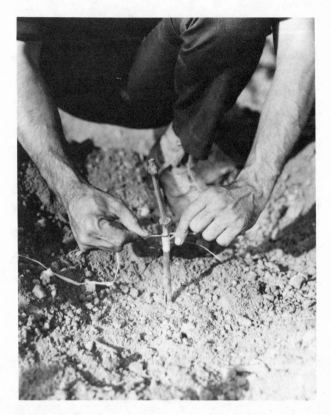

Fig. 30 Grafting a French vine to American root stock. Courtesy of Phototheque ITV-
M. Mackiewicz.

1. For the influence of yield on price see Jules Milhau, *Etude économétrique du prix
de vin* (Montpellier, 1935).

2. For the government's policies see Charles Warner, *The Wine Growers of France
and the Government since 1875* (New York, 1960).

3. Henri Mendras, *The Vanishing Peasant, Innovation and Change in French Agriculture*, Tr. Jean Lerner (Cambridge, Mass., 1970).

I

*Mr. Valayer is a vigneron with many facets of expertise. Here he confronts
the enormous problem of selling high-priced French wine within the new
European Economic Community and the competition posed by Italy in the
present and Spain in the future. He attempts to explain why the role of
government has expanded so markedly in the wine trade and describes the
image of wine in the public mind.*

Mr. Valayer: Very well, life is like that. As soon as something doesn't go right, the alarm is sounded. You've got to do this; you've got to do that. As for me I think it's best to organize. Evidently there are several measures that the government ought to take, for example, as regards foreign importation of wine. What is certain is that here [in France] we have social legislation that's costly. The French profit from it and that's fine. But we're sometimes not in a good position as regards costs of production, you see. This means that we need, sometimes, for the government to slightly apply the brakes on imports from countries who've got a better position regarding costs of cultivation, for example, or costs of labor, and so on.

Mr. Loubère: The vignerons of Languedoc strongly oppose imports of Italian wine. Do you in the Côtes-du-Rhône feel the same?

Mr. Valayer: I'd say that here, maybe we're less affected. But it's certain all the same that, in that regard, the competition, if not illicit, it's not completely loyal. This isn't the fault of Italians, but you understand, Italy has not had a viticultural survey; they plant as they wish; they don't have any regulations. And moreover, they don't have the same costs of cultivation; their labor is less expensive; they have fewer taxes than us; so they can sell wines cheaper in the French market than we can sell ours.

And now if Spain or Portugal enter the Common Market, we risk strong competition from those wines, maybe more than from Italian wines.

Mr. Loubère: Has the Common Market opened foreign countries to your wine?

Mr. Valayer: I don't think the Common Market has been favorable to viticulture. It's favored stock rearing more. We sell more wine in Germany and Belgium, but whether there's a Common Market or not, the Germans and Belgians want to drink wine so they'll buy it since they produce little or none. This is excellent for us, but there also, we still feel the competition of Italian wines. But, *enfin*, let's admit that for the controlled appellation wines, things aren't bad at all. For certain wines, everything is very good, even too good, because Burgundies are at exorbitant prices, Bordeaux also. For the moment there aren't any great problems, no crises for controlled appellations.

What disquiets us is that in France, you know that in France they're making—we don't understand we vignerons—they're heaping on wine all the evils, under the name of alcoholism, often wine is accused of causing it. Now, it's proven that it's not in areas producing wine that there are alcoholics, but where people drink [distilled] alcohol. And even I'd say, at this time, when certain young people get in accidents, people say they drank. But what did they drink? Certainly it was not wine or very little. They drank whiskey, they drank *pastis*, and so on.

II

Mr. Gardère reminds us that not even the great growths of Bordeaux are immune from crises. He explains that his is a profession making a luxury

162

The Vine Remembers

product, suffering from limited technical change and excessively high labor costs. Even the manager of Château Latour cannot take his market for granted and the weather does not always favor the great.

Mr. Gardère: We're in the Bordeaux region; it's a region with great potential for production, you know, but which has always tended, for many reasons, either to overproduce or underproduce. There's never been equilibrium of production, because nobody can, in my humble opinion, organize grape production. Then, we're in a country where each does what he wants, we live in our own way. But, in truth, there are two machines that absorb the excess: they are war and famine. After the war of 1914, there was a grand economic boom until about 1926. At that time, the first growths like Latour, Lafite, Mouton and others sold for 40,000 francs a *tonneau* [900 liters]. At that moment, with a *tonneau* of first growth wine, you could pay a worker over nearly six or seven years. Two years later this same wine was worth 12,500 francs a *tonneau*. Poincaré had arrived. (Poincaré as premier devalued the franc, checking inflation.)

Between '26-29, it was the great collapse; the wine companies of Bordeaux crashed down; there were bankruptcies; it was the great overturn. But with or without Poincaré the market would have gotten a bloody face, because everything was too expensive quite simply. Then it was Wall Street, 1929, prohibition in the United States, the dollar crisis, etc. And there we are between 1930-40; it was the great crossing of the desert, the great poverty. Can you imagine that in 1935 you were paid to uproot vines? You signed a contract to uproot your vines and not to replant for thirty years. That's 1935.

1939, came the war. We had three to four vintages in the cellar unsold, no money. That was real poverty. 1940 the Germans came; with our money they drank our wine, they absorbed the stock. 1944, they departed. 1945, prices of the controlled appellations were freed, because the Germans had fixed the prices. A *tonneau* was worth 18,000 francs. Prices were freed and in a few months rose to 100,000 francs and 120,000 francs. I'm using old francs because I'm used to old francs and also because they were in use at the time [100,000 old francs equals 1,000 new francs]. That was euphoria, we took off again, all was well.

And Blum arrives in 1946 [Léon Blum, socialist premier briefly] and imposed arbitrarily a decline of 5 to 10 percent. But with or without Blum, we'd have gotten a bloody face, because everything was too costly. And we declined in a catastrophic way. There we were with prices between 35 and 40,000 francs several months later. We were at that moment cheaper than the wine of the Midi. Our foreign markets had not yet reopened, we relied on internal consumption. Means of transport were still too limited, you know, after the war, time was needed to get things going.

Large quantities of wine were declassed; all that Médoc, the Bordeaux region, Saint Emilion and others could produce as controlled appellation, all were

declassed to make ordinary table wine for Paris. In Médoc, these were wines
of the good years '47–48–49–50. Vines were impoverished after the war because there were no fertilizers or dung during the war. Our yield was ridicu-
lous, merely on the order of twenty hectos per hectare in very good years,
wines with 12° and 12°5 alcohol. There was no need to chaptalize (add sugar
to raise alcohol). Had we gotten sugar we'd have used it in coffee because
we'd not even gotten enough for the winery; that's simple. Well there, we're
again in great confusion. Once more vines are uprooted and in 1955 compensation begins for uprooting. There are 2 francs per vine to uproot.

Alright, in 1956 there was a shortage resulting from lower production so
automatically there arose the notion of rarity, of penury, and we tripled prices
in a few months. And there we are, once more in a state of euphoria, a
certain well-being, all is well and continued until the crisis that gripped us in
1972. But it was less severe than those of the past.

Which meant that from 1960, especially 1964–65, we began to attract
multinationals, which penetrated in two ways: 1) investment in the lands of
estates, which is a good investment; 2) investment in distribution companies.

As regards production they regenerated the value of large properties; that is
very good. You know, we are poor people. When dollars, pounds sterling, yen,
all that you want arrives, we think, 'Come unto me little children,' as the Bible
says.

Well, they also took an interest in commercial companies, and that's dangerous; that's dangerous because those people, multinationals, they are financial
empires, inside of which you find everything, as in a shark. You find peanuts,
petrol, automobile factories, porcelain, everything. There are divisions, departments. At the summit of the pyramid there is a financier, he knows nothing
about all the products that he sells but he knows finance well. All the firms of
Bordeaux are passing under foreign control. Production is reduced and prices
rise so much that to sell one bottle requires even more investment. One day,
these people earning much money took note that prices no longer rise—we're
approaching 1972—and whether there has been concerted action or merely
hazard, all those big houses that are under foreign control begin to resell their
stock.

There is here an invasion, there is submersion of wine in bottles which
represent, perhaps, at lest two vintages that come back on our heads in public
sales at Cristy's in London, at Chautebise in Belgium, a little everywhere. Foreign owners sell hundreds of thousands of cases of wine because prices are no
longer rising, because they believe that money is immobilized, earns nothing
and they sell. And that's the great crisis, the big depression of 1972, which
began in 1972 and lasted three years.

Mr. Sagnes: Are crises here as serious as those affecting Languedoc?

Mr. Gardère: No, much less serious. They are perhaps more brutal because
we're in a region where one has become accustomed to a certain standard of
living. In spite of the fluctuations of the market, I believe that products of

quality are more and more secure. Normally appellation wines of good quality, which have escaped the anonymity of lesser wines, like those of Languedoc, normally they should have a good future before them. On condition that viticulturists and distributors are serious people, which is not always the case on one side or the other.

[As regards viticulture] I'll tell you about the growing of grapes. First, what does one seek in the cultivation of vines? It's to have the maximum yield consonant with the best quality. The notion of yield is an economic necessity.

It's certain that production per hectare has seriously developed. As for me, I knew that period between the two wars. After the first war, taking into account the impoverishment of the land, you produced 20 to 25 hectos per hectare. That was very little, but costs were very little also. You understand, we worked with a horse, a cart and a plow. When the horse stopped, we let him *paquager* (graze) to use a Gascon term; he didn't cost anything. Today a tractor, whether it works or doesn't work, it's very costly. It's all the more expensive because it's a special tractor, an *enjambeur* that's manufactured by artisanal methods. At present, a straddle tractor costs 9 million francs with its material. Why? Because instead of thousands being made, only a few hundred come out, and it's used infrequently. Today we're overequipped with mechanical devices that we use only in certain seasons.

The same type of overequipment results from the vat: as soon as we draw off the fermented wine into barrels, the vat serves only one month out of a year. Keep in mind also that viticulturists do not always use common sense, the wisdom to equip themselves modestly. Everybody wanted a tractor, even if you had only 20,000 vines to work; you were contented to be riding high. There's always a childish aspect in our comportment; man will never be an adult. At the cooperative, a friend tried to set up a CUMA (cooperative to use agricultural material in common). He got two replies: "When the weather is fine the tractor will go to you; when it rains I'll get to use it." The other, "How much commission do you make on material? " The project fell through. That's it, man is like that.

Formerly there were the agronomic research station of Bordeaux, and the INRA (National Institute for Agronomic Research), but their information did not circulate; in general people worked in isolation, unaware of scientific findings, or even rejecting them a little. Finally there was a change of generations. The generation before the [second] war, to which I belonged, in a certain measure absorbed this information; it was obliged to adapt itself. These children were better educated, traveled more, and then there were the radio, journals, *enfin*, an ensemble of things that surrounded us, that had not existed before, so that information spread better. The war also improved conditions of production: we produced more per hectare while making as good wines [as in the past].

You know, we are 100 percent conditioned by our profession: respect nature, observe nature, let nature inspire you and you can't go wrong. Nature is in such equilibrium, it's perfect.

I knew the period between 1930 and 34, that period of catastrophic crisis. The baker refused you bread, he wasn't paid for three years. Then we ate the produce of the farm; we ate only ducks, chicken, pork because the butcher refused us meat for the harvest. And they paid us in wine or *piquette* (second wine made of water and grapeskins), we had a little more *piquette* than wine. Well we took the *piquette* and in the evenings we rolled the barrel along the side of the road, for two reasons: first, it didn't make any noise on the grass, and second, the roads were not yet asphalted and the stones would have caved in the barrel, so old it was. When I relate that to my children they have the impression that I'm speaking of the Middle Ages; that's amusing.

We've seen our village lose population because, in fact, we can now work more surface area with fewer laborers. Formerly when I entered Château Latour with Henri Martin there were oxen, mules and horses. We sold all that and bought tractors. When we arrived in 1963, workers with spraying machines on their backs took ten days to sulphate the forty-five hectares of vines we have; now we do it in two days with a tractor. We sold the oxen fifteen years ago. In fact there's a mutation in this region, engendered by the economic boom, which has come in fifteen or twenty years, when it should have taken, to be digested more easily, a period of fifty years.

Mr. Sagnes: All the same, to have horses and oxen in 1963, that's rather late.

Mr. Gardère: Yes, but there are still a certain number in the region. Why? Mechanization penetrated slowly for two reasons. First, because people here are distrustful, especially in viticulture, because if you destroy a vineyard you have to replant it and while it will produce in five or six years, it will produce fine wine only in fifteen or twenty years. The first *enjambeur* I saw demonstrated in Médoc about twenty years ago, it tore out every other vineroot. The *enjambeur* was not yet perfected, and then, research to create these machines was at first not undertaken save by artisans. At first there were only small firms. Renault, International, Ferguson were not interested because how many *enjambeurs* could they sell in Burgundy, Champagne, and here? 400 to 500. So it developed slowly, there were many trials and errors, and even now it's not perfected, and never will be. So there's an ensemble of obstacles, you see.

III

Mr. Sabon recalls the necessity for and the rise of AOC (Appellation d'Origine Controlée) in Châteauneuf-du-Pape where it arrived early. The French were the first to work out such a system, designed to prevent fraud in wine labeling and vigorously resisted by less than scrupulous merchants. AOC came into existence because of need to prove the quality and integrity of wine during the crisis years of the late 1920s and 1930s.

Mr. Sabon: When my father returned from the war in 1919, I was eight or nine years old. My father now worked the vines and the vines began to provide a revenue. Well, he made friends during the war, being an officer, he knew doctors, politicians, his fellow officers, and they told him: "After the war you'll send us some Châteauneuf, we want to drink it." And that's how, after the war, my father began as a retailer, sending wine in carboys and cases. Me, I began to work, I took up tending the vines, and my father took up selling by correspondence because wine was selling badly otherwise.

It was at this time, 1926–27, that the grandfather of Paul Avril, who was named like him Paul Avril, and my father, went to solicit the aid of Baron Leroy de Boiseaumarie, newly married in Châteauneuf-du-Pape. They wanted him to become president of the *syndicat*, because they wanted to form one to defend Châteauneuf, because the local merchants, they were three or four, every year at the time of the *vendange*, they brought in raisins from outside and sold the wine as Châteauneuf. The baron explained that he was ignorant of these matters; he would study them, however, and give a reply in six months: "I'll tell you yes or I'll tell you no."

Eh bien, wines were selling badly; the most we sold were in Burgundy; there were only Burgundians coming to buy our wines.

Mr. Loubère: For blending purposes?

Mr. Sabon: Ah, that, *monsieur*, I can't tell you what they did with it; I didn't see it. They came to buy wines or they transformed them or . . . .

Well that's why the *syndicat* was formed: to prevent merchants bringing outside grapes into Châteauneuf, so there wouldn't be too much wine, then we could sell it easier. Baron LeRoy, at the end of six months, when Mr. Paul Avril and my father returned to see him, said to them: "I accept for a year. If I do well you will keep me, if I don't you will kick me out the door." And Baron LeRoy remained president for all his life. And after he created the [appellation] Côtes-du-Rhône, he created all the other controlled appellations and you know, we owe him a lot, we owe him a big candle. I mean, I spoke often with Baron LeRoy because he came often, the meetings were held in the house where I was born. He came by, he said to my father: "Meeting of the Commission [of the syndicate] at two o'clock," or at ten o'clock or at eleven o'clock, and you know, he was on time and if there was someone late he said, "Oh, *monsieur*, say there, you're a little late; next time try to be on time." He wanted to reform the *syndicat*.

There was a *syndicat*, but the former president didn't do anything, so we had to recreate it. But the viticulturists of Châteauneuf-du-Pape, when we asked them to pay dues, no longer wanted to belong. Well, my father had to implore his friends. So he went to find his viticultural friends and these viticultural friends, who were reticent, demanded of my father: "We really want to be part of the *syndicat*, but since we have vines outside the territory of Châteauneuf-du-Pape, well, we'd like for the vines to be included in the appellation of Châteauneuf-du-Pape." Since this was the first of limitations in France, when my father put the question to Baron LeRoy, the Baron said: "Mr. Sabon, don't worry yourself; we'll act so that the experts who are going to come, who'll be designated by the court, include these lands and like that we'll all be in accord." That's what came about.

That was in '26–27. And well, there were lawsuits, because the local merchants attacked the *syndicat*, did not want it set up—you understand, we were attacking their interests—that was normal. These trials lasted I can't remember how long. I attended them in Nîmes in 1929, when my father had a car. There were suits because, when one established a delimitation, those who were left out wanted to be included, the experts passed them by.

That was the juridical machine. And even then, there were wine crises. Wines did not sell too well; wines sold, I don't know, I recall in '35–36, for 500 francs a barrel. What complaints then! And it's then that some viticulturists, among them Mr. Paul Avril, went to Burgundy to see what the Burgundians were doing. And we began bottling and little by little, viticulturists like us began to put wine in bottles.

As for our direct sales, the merchants complained at first, but yes! But what can you do? Say, we wanted to live too. If only the merchants had been honest. You know *monsieur*, when wine is aged in wood it improves; the merchants knew that, those in the village. So with a barrel of Châteauneuf and two barrels of another wine they made three barrels of "Châteauneuf." That's how that happened, to be sure.

IV

Mr. and Mrs. Guillemard of Pommard in Côte-d'Or describe the sacrifices that a young couple had to make to get ahead in the profession after World War I. They note that vignerons often had to cultivate other crops, either to make ends meet or to acquire capital to buy land; Mrs. Guillemard worked alongside her husband in their common effort; tilling the soil has always been a couple's work and, when the children became adolescents, the whole family's work. We also glimpse the changes that came about in the methods used, and the effort required to form a clientele of buyers. They also attempt to answer a difficult question: is there a vigneron mentality? They are much clearer in telling us about some of the moments of catastrophe that befell them in Pommard, their efforts to insure themselves against excess losses, and how they took up life once more after each catastrophe.

Mr. Loubère: How did you learn to cultivate vines?

Mr. Guillemard: On the job. As soon as you finished the communal school you went into the vines, you did what you could, you did women's work, and as

you grew you continued to learn. There was no agricultural high school as
now. You learned on the job, it was the old men who taught the young how
to work. They were good vignerons. But for making wine there weren't many
who could do it. In the large wineries there were men much more skillful than
our grandfathers. There were maladies; they didn't even know about them. And
then, they didn't have the chemical products and so they harvested when the
good Lord wanted them to harvest. But at times the grapes were destroyed by
mildew; they got nothing and they didn't know what it was all about.

Mrs. Guillemard: Explain how it came about that they found the use of copper
sulphate.

Mr. Guillemard: Oh sure, when the vine was supported by stakes, you attached
it with strips of straw covered with copper sulphate and the stakes were dipped
in copper sulphate to extend their life. And then, they noticed without much
effort that the vines attached by straw covered with copper sulphate, that they
didn't have mildew. They could overcome mildew.

Now such maladies have almost completely disappeared save for several pests
that they can't guarantee against. There was a system of defense against hail
(firing explosives among clouds and requiring mutual sharing of costs). But that
didn't work, for a good reason, because there were recalcitrants who wouldn't
pay their share. Now we'd be nearly guaranteed if only there was a defense
against hail. Frost comes, but not much.

Mrs. Guillemard: We're aided a great deal by the agricultural services that
instruct us about treatments. We subscribe to the protection of plants and they
tell us to sulphate from such a date to such a date. Until now that's how it
works.

Mr. Guillemard: The poor old man (grandfather) he worked from sun up to
sun down. He worked 200 meters from the village; he didn't even come to
lunch at the house. He had his lunch in the vines.

Mrs. Guillemard: And then, people weren't rich, you know.

Mr. Guillemard: And that [work] wore you out. They had just enough not to
die.

That was around 1910, all that. After the war of '14, things were already a
little better. Me, I began work during the war; there was no one else. There
were only the kids and the women. Well, it was necessary to keep up the
work. You had to begin nearly as soon as you could walk. At twelve-thirteen
years I was already behind a plow.

Mrs. Guillemard: Me, I went to school, they sent me. I obtained my certificate,
it wasn't much, but even so, I was at school until sixteen years old. I wanted
to do something else, so I came home. Then I worked in the vines from
sixteen on. I worked in the vines, I liked that. We had to do something, to
work well. Then, depending on when you earned a little, on advancing, if you

found something to buy, you bought a vineyard. At that time (c. 1910) there was no question of credit. You bought when you had money. For a vineyard, you sometimes deprived yourself to buy a vineyard. You had to.

Mr. Guillemard: Because nearly all the vines that we have, save those that came from my father-in-law; we two bought them.

Mrs. Guillemard: We pulled ourselves up like that, slowly. Sometimes at the end of the year there wasn't much left, but all the same we had managed to buy something. We rose very slowly. After, we got tractors. We already had for sulphating that hand-driven apparatus you put on the back; that was heavy on the back. But it was better than what there was before, a broom dipped in the product and shaken over vines. Later, we had the thing for a horse, a big drum on the horse, and we sprayed on either side. That was easy, less fatiguing. After that we had the horse-drawn cart, a cart for sulphating. There were several nozzles; you did big vines all at once; that was quicker. Then we used the tractor. Then, after a season of hail, it was impossible to penetrate the vines. We hired a helicopter, and since then we sulphate vines that are difficult to get to by helicopter. Now there are new products, which are much more practical.

Today, there's still manual work that you're obliged to do. Pruning, you won't find anything to replace that; or attaching branches to metal wires.

Mr. Guillemard: At first, all vines were supported by stakes, you had to attach them cane by cane.

Mrs. Guillemard: You couldn't do many in a day. That's evolved for us. It's less hard now.

Mr. Guillemard: Women worked as much as men. My mother, she went into the vines as much as my father.

Mrs. Guillemard: And then, women used a spade to turn soil. Now you can still see some of them spading all the same.

The big changes came after each of the two wars. Wine rose in value at once when the soldiers returned home from war in 1919.

Before the war they cultivated other crops, they always had some cows. They raised chickens or a pig to be butchered for the household. You see that helped out a little.

Mr. Guillemard: While now, there's not a single cow in Pommard, and no more horses, not one horse. We buy all our food. We've exclusively viticulturists. Oh, we've a little garden: we grow potatoes and a few vegetables.

Mrs. Guillemard: In about 1960 we really began to bottle our wine.

Mr. Guillemard: Me, I began to put a lot of wine in bottles and began to export it. I traveled in the United States, in Belgium, in Switzerland, in England.

Mrs. Guillemard: We found French clients who came on their own like that. They came a first time, and then, without our doing anything, they were clients. Our French clientele have evolved considerably, more and more. They seek wine from the vigneron in place of going to wine merchants.

Mr. Guillemard: We sell nearly all our wine like that. Formerly we sold both grapes and red wine to brokers, sometimes when it was coming from the press. We sold it in barrels.

We began to enjoy a certain well-being after the first war, above all at the initiation of the law on appellations of origin, towards 1931–32.

Mrs. Guillemard: In 1931 my father was president of the commission of the agricultural *syndicat*. He was president at the time the law on origin was promulgated. There was a lot of debate at the time. With this appellation, sales are regulated, that's all. Now, more and more, they try to make quality wine.

Mr. Loubère: Is there such a thing as a viticultural mentality?

Mr. Guillemard: Ah, sure there is!

Mrs. Guillemard: It is entirely different from the mentality of farmers.

Mr. Guillemard: It's a spirit that welcomes you; it loves fun, but it is the honor of the village, of wine, of the reputation of great growths. Now the work is less well done, they weed; they do no more. Work is no longer as carefully done as in the past. Since there are tractors, everything, good Lord, it's done quickly. Work's not as well done.

Now, workers are so expensive, with social charges, you've got to get all you can out of your employees, they cost so much.

Mrs. Guillemard: In a year when there's wine and wine sells well, everything's all right. But in a year when it hails and freezes. . . . As in Côtes de Nuits. [In 1979 hail destroyed the grape crop in Côtes de Nuits.]

Mr. Guillemard: Some of us are insured. We insure a part of our crop or our costs of production. We can't insure all the crop.

Mrs. Guillemard: In 1945 there was nothing left [after a deluge]. You should have seen how the earth was carried down the slope. Then we had to go find this earth and carry it back up. All the topsoil was washed down. How to carry it back? In a basket on our backs.

Mr. Guillemard: On the back, imagine! It's a basketful of earth, back up the slope. I guarantee you that that pulls your vertebrae.

Mrs. Guillemard: What does that represent a basketful of earth when emptied?

Mr. Guillemard: A teaspoon. Look, you have to carry up many basketfuls of earth. Well the old folk, they passed their time carrying up soil and making walls. Then we demolished the walls, blocked the drainage ditches. Then we took note that this was wrong.

Mrs. Guillemard: We pulled down the walls because it was easier to use tractors without them, to turn. Then when rain came like that, we became aware that we should have left the walls, because they stop the force of the water.

Mr. Guillemard: We had even found, when demolishing, some culverts that were made so water would pass underground and not wash soil away. We demolished them and suffered the consequences.

In the first years when we began working with tractors when water came down the slope it arrived like a veritable torrent at the bottom. It carried everything away, the roads, all.

V

With Mr. Soulié we see another side to the vigneron's character—the nervousness and excitability of the southerner; but such emotion is not confined to the Midi and appears elsewhere in times of crisis. Demonstrations, protest marches, road blockages have become almost routine along the Mediterranean coast where crises of overproduction follow crises of falling prices with dismal fatality. Like ardent southerners of the United States who cannot forget the Civil War or forgive defeat, the southerners of viticultural France recall their riots of 1907 and persist in the myth that overproduction is the result of fraud, dishonest merchants, and politicians in their pay. This belief was the cause of the 1907 riots.

Vignerons today are highly politicized. Below is a list of some of the organizations that play a part in their life and work.

    C.G.V.M.:   Confédération Générale des Vignerons du Midi (pressure group of vignerons, with some police power to hunt out fraud.)

    MODEF: Mouvement de Défense des Exploitants Familiaux (organization to defend small family farms)

    C.G.A.: Confédération Générale de l'Agriculture (professional organization)

    C.G.T.: Confédération Générale des Travailleurs (the major labor union confederation)

    C.F.D.T.: Confédération Française Démocratique du Travail (a large labor union confederation)

    F.E.N.: Fédération de l'Education Nationale (a national union of teachers)

    F.O.: Force Ouvrière (third largest labor union confederation)

    CIDUNATI: (confederation of small retailers and artisans)

This list should be kept in mind when Mr. Soulié gives his definition of the viticultural mentality: it is clearly not an individualistic one in the south, nor in most other areas. Even the opponents of cooperative wineries accept regulations as regards yield, cultivation, grape varieties and production; they have indeed imposed these regulations on themselves.

Mr. Sagnes: We have begun to take up the problem of defending viticulture. Since the Liberation [1944] there have been a whole series of viticultural movements to defend the profession. I believe that the first dates from 1953. Can you tell me about their evolution?

Mr. Soulié: Yes. Well, as for me, I believe that you have to go back to 1907 and the organization of the C.G.V.M. just after 1907. As a result of that they made a kind of viticultural survey in which they took a census of land. And the declaration of each grower's quantity of wine from each harvest.

We took up the League of Small and Medium Viticulturists, which was created in 1932. That had been the first organization and there was the Federation of *Syndicats* of Cultivators, which was also born of the Liberation, from the C.G.A. These were the first movements until 1950–51. Vineyards needed to be reconstituted. We passed several years with a kind of surplus value, surpluses that we sold. And in 1953 appeared the first viticultural crisis and from it came the first decrees that anticipated the uprooting of vines. On 30 December 1953 there was a decree which began to classify viticultural territories [according to their suitability for grape growing]. It had no effect and was opposed. But it's still referred to.

The crises were born from lack of sales. In 1953 the price of wine fell because of an abundant harvest. There were demonstrations by cooperative wineries, the Federation of *Syndicats* of Cultivators, the League of Little and Medium Viticulturists, and then the first Viticultural Action Committee was born. I was president of it.

This was the first time we took to the roads. That was the first demonstration at Béziers; we put wagons across the road. We didn't have an encounter with the police. The Gendarmerie came and cleared the way. This was only the first demonstration. Well then, really, the most important were in '62. In '62 we spent two or three nights on the railway tracks at Béziers. We began to burn, to throw stones. This was widespread, always with the Action Committee, called the Coordination Committee. This Action Committee was born in '62 with the same members [as the former one].

In '62, in the early demonstrations, the big owners didn't demonstrate, their conditions of production allowed them a [profit]. After 1962 all that expanded, '62, '66, '69, *enfin*, '71, then '73, '76, that was the big demonstration. Because the situation grew worse as soon as viticulture entered the Common Market. That's to say, the agricultural common market began in 1957, and it's in 1962 that viticulture got its common regulations, and we got the Common Market with the free circulation of produce. And from 1970, we began to receive imports of Italian wines, that, it's clear, began to weigh on prices. [Here follows a very confusing statement which, in sum, argues that Italians have advantages denied to the French, chiefly lower costs of production, and less expensive vinification by large companies]. Italy was at the stage that we were in during 1907. So much so that, at that moment there, there emerged an image which said, and still says, that each time that a hectoliter of Italian wine arrives, it represents the depth of poverty of Italian viticulturists, notably those of southern Italy.

[In opposition to this] we exhausted all the means that viticulturists used to defend their demands. We don't need anyone else and workers should beware [of losing their jobs]. We sensed, by round-about means, that the leaders refused the support of workers. We led the fight inside. . . .

Mr. Sagnes: Who is "we" ?

Mr. Soulié: The MODEF, the cooperative wineries were won over; finally the Communist Party proclaimed, "We support the struggle of the viticulturists."

The Communist Party played an important role in this matter; and the C.G.T., C.F.D.T. and the F.E.N. The F.O. didn't want to participate. But we went beyond them; we sought the retailers of the CIDUNATI.

I'm the one who proposed to the regional action committee the occupation of the [Montpellier] cathedral, and in effect Maffre (Emmanuel Maffre-Baugé, a southern vigneron leader) said to me, "You, Emilien, you're going to occupy the cathedral? That doesn't seem possible." We were at Pézenas when we decided on it. Me, I led 150 viticulturists and we went up to the cathedral. There was an abbot, Abbot Laurène, who was very close to us and who was pleased to welcome us. We stayed for ten days. The first evening the bishop arrived. I went up to him and said to him, "Monseigneur, you don't know me, I'm Emilien Soulié, mayor of Montblanc." He said, "Yes," and I said, "I welcomed you with much pleasure in the mayor's office of Montblanc; I'm happy to greet you again." He responded, "At Montblanc, very good, it was perfect, but here I am at home." *Bon*, every evening he came to see us and in between time, we sang the song of the 17th [regiment. It mutinied in 1907 rather than move against rioting vignerons in Béziers because it was composed chiefly of natives of this area]. We left the evening before Palm Sunday, Thursday to Friday. From there we went with the fishermen of Sète, who had blocked the port.

After '76, it was over, with Montredon, and at Montredon (where there were riots and two deaths) really there was a massing of forces.

Apropos the strikes of September '57 during the *vendange*, we were well organized; we were powerful and we succeeded; we won the strike. Little vignerons, seeing the change there was in twenty years, we won them over; they said to the important proprietors, "You must sign [the collective contract]. And since, there's not been one strike, and with the departure of young people, already it became difficult for us. Viticultural management put a convention in place; it indexed salaries by category and in line with the S.M.I.C., (minimum guaranteed wage for industry) I mean the S.M.A.C. (minimum guaranteed wage for agriculture) at that time.

But the employers of Aude finally repudiated the contract. And now, there is not the human material to take up the battle. The trade union is dead. Not the Tunisians, Moroccans, not even the Spanish are unionized. We tried but they tell you, "What's the good of it? "

Me, I believe there's a civilization of the vine and wine. That means the viticulturist, in monoculture, is more open, more evolved than the polyculturist. We, the viticulturists, we work to produce and we're in search of improving that production. The polyculturist who grows three or four crops, there's always some disappointment; he can't advance his research, his reflection, as we can advance ours, to always do better, economize our time, produce better. Governmental projects want us to become polyculturists, because monoculture is quite dangerous in a system like ours where there's no guarantee, no minimum [income] to live, because in socialist countries the state intervenes. But here, when there's a bad harvest, it's explosive. So, on the political level, monoculture becomes an obstacle to the development of the capitalist system by developing so highly.

Well, I consider that the civilization of the vine is a reality; wine is a reality with what the production of wine evidently brings. In the production of wine, to produce wine that flows . . . *enfin*, Maffre sang of it very well in his book *[Vendanges amères]*. And there's another thing, it's that in the southern region which produces wine uniquely with its soil, its sun, its climate [and with the] intelligence . . . , the richness that the viticulturist possesses, which is handed from one generation to another with transformations, all that causes me to consider that there's a manner of living in viticultural regions like ours; we live in another fashion than regions like Creuse, Aveyron, or Corrèze.

This is the last point. The vine leaves time to viticulturists, they can do other things; they can occupy their leisure according to their tendencies, their philosophic and political convictions. I who am a vigneron, to make wine is really something. You don't make hay, you don't make potatoes. You assist at a transformation in which you participate.

VI

M. Darricade of St. Christoly in the Médoc notes an important transformation in the process of fermenting grape juice into wine over the past fifty-odd years. It is amusing to note that wine makers generally believe in the need to add sugar to fermenting must, to chaptalize, but believe that other regions—not their own—add an excess of sugar. He also reveals his fear that Spain's entry into the Common Market will benefit merchants who blend wines rather than growers who usually care for them through their first fermentation and sell them to merchants. So it is not only the Languedocians who are apprehensive about the future. In fact, until relatively recently, religion played a role in allaying the apprehensions of Médoc growers. We are also reminded that this great wine region also suffered its crises but has organized to defend its interests, more successfully than Languedoc.

Mr. Sagnes: What is your opinion of chaptalization?

Mr. Darricade: Oh well, I'm a partisan of sugaring when it's indispensable here, as in rainy years when you can't attain a minimum quality otherwise. But when the weather is friendly to the vigneron or if you can made an authentic appellation, I don't see the utility of chaptalization, absolutely not. Otherwise we couldn't sell a Médoc wine with the appellation Médoc if we didn't chaptalize. But really, let's say, we don't chaptalize excessively here. There are regions where they chaptalize a little more: Champagne, Burgundy, Alsace. As for us, all the same, it's rare that we don't pick grapes at 10.5°–11° in bad years, while there are regions where they harvest at 6°, 7° and 8°. [The sugar content of grapes determines the degree of alcohol in wine]. One must not cite them, one must not criticize other regions; that would not be proper of me.

Mr. Sagnes: What has been the evolution of wine-making since the 1920s?

Mr. Darricade: Very well, in my opinion, they were wrong to let the must ferment too long in the vat. They were not in a hurry to move grapes from vats. They said, "*Bon*, we'll draw it when it's cold." Then they went to do other things, then one day they said, "*Bon*, we must go draw the wine." What they did was to leave the wine a month, a month and a half [with the skins]. *Bon*, the vats were very deep, there was no risk as regards acidity. But that made wine too tannic, heavy. While now we ferment rapidly. In my opinion that doesn't remove the bouquet, on the contrary. That makes wine lighter in the stomach. As for me, I find that's better; it's indisputably better.

Médocs now are very digestible, very, very digestible, more than formerly. I remember my parents, they made old wine like everybody; everybody made old wine, but it was heavy, too tannic. There are years when it's wise to macerate a little more to give a little color, because there are years when there's a little rot. But if there's too much rot, you musn't let it macerate too long, that imparts a taste.

Mr. Sagnes: What is your view of the Common Market?

Mr. Darricade: In the period preceding the Common Market, they told us, "You know, we must enter the Common Market because you will see the free exchange of your produce, you won't have any more problems sending a case of wine to Belgium, England, and Germany." Then we discovered that it involved a lot of red tape, and that is very, very expensive.

It didn't bring any improvement for us. We still sell to our traditional customers. You know that Médoc is widely consumed in Belgium, a very little in Switzerland, in Holland, in England, a little also in America. But *enfin*, if only Belgium and Holland were large like France, for us that would mean good business. Well, they're little, otherwise they're big drinkers of Médoc, connoisseurs of wine.

Mr. Sagnes: Does the broadening of the Common Market pose problems for you?

Mr. Darricade: Viticulturists don't feel it or don't apprehend it because they're badly informed, in my opinion. When it came about, we were having good times here; wine was and is selling well. They have a temperament that is not disquieted when things go well; they forget that bad years can return. They forget that Spain makes some very good wine, vinified at present with modern means.

In the Rioja, there are French viticulturists installed there with French vines. Look out there! We're not on our guard enough there. As for me, I say it because there will be bad years which will benefit Bordeaux merchants who, with Spanish wines, will blend it [with Médoc]. So all the merchants favor the Common Market.

That's significant. I'll tell you, I'm worried, old viticulturist that I am, I'm worried because I know the trade well and how it works. Private' interest takes precedence over everything else, always with importers. For the viticulturists of Languedoc, don't you think the importers of Italian wine gain the most? They don't give a damn about French viticulturists; that's a shame that, it's a real scandal.

Mr. Sagnes: In regard to viticulturists' attitude toward natural phenomena, hail, drought, etc., can you describe them?

Mr. Darricade: Yes, well I mentioned processions a short while ago because here we had invasions, in the spring, of the *altise*, vulgarly called the vine louse. The *altise* is a little insect, on young shoots. These little lice change into caterpillars and gobble up the leaves. That used to be a bane at the time. They tried to catch them in traps; there were a pile of gadgets in the vines; none were effective. So they used to organize [religious] processions so there would be fewer lice. These processions began at sun up; very early the parish priest made processions in the fields.

That no longer exists, but it lasted until the Second World War. What struck me when I was young, because I was there, I was a choirboy, what struck me is that there were a lot of hamlets in each commune. Well, then they went in the fields, they ended up sometimes in a hamlet and there a temporary altar was set up; there was a basket in which there was a rabbit or a chicken for the priest. At all the altars there was something. These processions drew a large following. It was a custom for St. Marc's day, every year. At the head someone carried a cross and others carried little bells and as they walked they made ding, ding. They had that even if no lice invaded; it was preventative undoubtedly. That was typical all that. At present no one believes in it anymore; they prefer to spread insecticide, it's more effective.

Mr. Sagnes: As regards the agricultural crises of the 1930s and 1950s, what were their effects on the population?

Mr. Darricade: In the 1930s already, the sons of proprietors left, abandoning their vines, the family hearth, in order to become functionaries or find another trade. For that reason we've got sons of proprietors, now retired, who were policemen, soldiers, etc. That was less the case than in the 1950s; in the 1950s, it was terrible, the emigration was enormous. Wine sold very, very badly and since living was expensive, it had already risen, that became difficult. The cost of living was not in accord with our income. Then, you know, there were some who could not marry, they didn't even think of marrying because their father could not hire them when married. Here, the commune, let me cite, in 1930 we were 630, we've now no more than 380.

These two periods cut us down. The return from the war was very difficult. Fathers of families were prisoners; when they arrived they found their property untilled, wives could not do everything. It was necessary to reconstitute. With what? With what money? It was for this that here, in the region, there were some small owners who planted native vines directly [without grafting onto American roots], vines for table grapes, hybrids, in order to make a little money quickly. After, they reconverted to the traditional Médoc varieties. That was a terrible period.

VII

Mr. Hudelot is a young enologist who, with other owners, is seeking to recreate a vineyard that had earlier existed and flourished in the highlands overlooking the Côtes-d'Or, and are called the Pays Hauts or Hautes Côtes. We reproduce his interview extensively for it is full of information about the many initiatives that must be pooled to carry out this enormous task. This vine area, of secondary value when compared to the golden slopes, had been destroyed by the phylloxera and there was little incentive to restore it until the recent upsurge in demand for good quality table wine from Burgundy.

Mr. Hudelot: I'm a native of the region here, and I knew the difficult life of the region in the 1950s. That's not a long time ago but in fact, let's say that the life of the region between 1925 and 1950, it didn't change much. It evolved very little, a little with the beginning of mechanization on its way in. But let's say, really, that the first tractor arrived here—it's my father who bought it in 1954—and that was, truly, a first beginning of modernization of the life of our villages.

This region, here, has been viticultural for a very long time. This region is the *Hautes Côtes* [upper slopes] and it was planted in vines in the last century, with an extensive surface of vines. And then the phylloxera caused the vineyards to disappear entirely. The region had to reconvert to polyculture, with many difficulties.

The people who lived here survived in extremely limited conditions; that's to say by using the horse and by using old procedures. They grew cereals, of course; they grew beets, potatoes, some fruit, fruit that was sold by some directly to consumers. And they tended vines also.

There was an embryo of a vineyard that remained, but these were vines that were not always well tended. Some Pinot was planted, but very little. There were especially what they called productive hybrids.

What are these hybrids? They are American hybrids which were hybridized to obtain varieties that needed no treatment and resisted phylloxera. That more or less ended in a total economic failure for this method, and brought economic defeat for the region because the wine of the hybrids was of poor quality. So how did people live here in the early century?

With a few vines and a polyculture, with the aid of a horse for some, and for others labor, as always, with hand tools. I've seen, myself, vines hung on a stake and worked by hand. Other vines were on palisades and worked with a horsedrawn plow. The first tractor used to cultivate vines, it was in 1960. It was my brother who bought it in 1960.

We were three children in the family. My father continued the system of polyculture. My sister, she saw that there was no means of livelihood, she left; she's a school teacher, she left to work in town. My brother, he loved to work on the land, he wanted to stay and work with our father, hoping already to modernize. And me, I became a student. I left, I had no vocational bent to become a viticulturist. It was only after forming an association with my father that I came back to the land. So my brother tried to modernize and in 1960 he bought the first *enjambeur*.

The vines were those planted by my father in 1954 when he realized that my brother wanted to stay on the land. He had already, in 1957, begun to plant Pinot vines to try to obtain wines similar to the great wines of Nuit Saint Georges, Chambertin. But since the wines here were not known among the merchants and the public, the market was very difficult. So we had already begun to think of bottling the wine and selling it directly to consumers. That was the initial idea.

But in order to live after all, my brother was obliged to sharecrop, that is, to take over the vines of an owner at Nuits Saint Georges and to work them, sharing the income by halves. He had 2.5 hectares in a first growth, and these vines brought him a worthwhile revenue. That allowed him to live and to begin planting vines here in our own village [Villers-Fontaine]. You see the evolution of these things, and it's only from 1960 that you can say that the region began to budge. And the same thing happened in other villages nearby. In our village there are only two, perhaps three growers who've felt the necessity to modify tradition. Otherwise this viticultural tradition of the early century, it would have perpetuated itself, and the people here with new economic needs could not have continued to face it; they would have been obliged to quit, to abandon their land to go work in town.

Mr. Loubère: Was there any influence from outside that encouraged the planting of Pinot?

Mr. Hudelot: None, none. In the region of the Hautes Côtes, there was no such influence because, if you wish, the people who inhabited the Grande Côte, the great wines, these people had succeeded in forming a *syndicat*. And after the war they created a monopoly of the great wines.

But even the people here, when we told them of our plans, they did not believe us. People said, "No, they're dreaming, they're young, they'll never succeed." So no one from outside aided us, not even the banks. Bankers lend only if they believe the business is sound; if it's not, in their thinking, they don't lend. We had enormous difficulties. We had no money. We had great difficulty putting aside a small sum to start off.

We financed ourselves in part. We began by buying the land. Then we brought in the SAFER (land purchase society for rural expansion) a semi-public organism, to facilitate land purchase. Its purpose was to buy all the scattered parcels it could, [to regroup them], and to resell [concentrated holdings] for new farms. So we had state aid from this angle. But the SAFER had many difficulties; it was active at least eight years here but it succeeded only in part. It failed to acquire land that owners refused to sell.

Land wasn't expensive here, 1,000 francs per hectare more or less, because no one believed in it. Well, each one of us tried to find money, first to live, then to begin a savings account for investing. We'd begin by buying land, then material. We began very gently, a snowball, you see, what you can call an economic snowball. Well my brother, he had his vines at Nuits which brought him in a little; my wife was teaching, which made it possible to support the family, and me, I opened a technical office at Dijon which earned a fair amount which permitted me to invest.

I bought land, ten hectares; then I went to the bank and I told them: "*Voilà*, I've ten hectares, that's already capital." Meanwhile the land began to rise a little in value. From the fact that someone began to do something, others took an interest and the land began to increase in value. That happened rapidly; there was a constant progression in the years 1970–73, and land rose five or six times in value, and after, even more. Well now the bank took an interest in it, loaned us a small sum, and said: "You're going to work." We now began to plant and when we had no more money, we went back to the bank for a little more. Well, our procedure was like that.

And then during the 1970s this movement which began for us in our village, it spread to other villages. And then people began to meet. They created a *Comité d'Aménagement* [organizing or fitting-out committee] once more under state regulation. And this Comité was patronized by a viticulturist of another village nearby, who had already shown a certain evolution, and who succeeded in finding some subsidies for the region from the Ministry of Agriculture. These subsidies were used, by priority, for the creation of vineyards, and notably to concentrate holdings, an ideal operation to complete the work of the SAFER. The SAFER owned 80 percent of the land. The other 20 percent was rearranged in an arbitrary way—with the owners' accord of course, they were placed in another sector—and that's how we completely restructured the villages and notably ours. With the land that my brother and I had bought, and our parents', we had about twenty-five hectares almost all in one holding,

which is enormous, which is a step ahead that reverses the viticultural traditions of the Côte and which is practically unknown, even in Clos Vougeot.

Only we had land that was totally uncultivated, with woods and with stones
that our ancestors had gathered. They had worked vines, and had made small
terraces to plant vines. By hand they had gathered thousands and thousands of
small stones to build, as they're called here, *murjets* or *murets*, patois for
small wall. These stones, we had to remove them, clear the land, and bring
back up the slopes soil that had been washed down by erosion. This meant
hauling thousands of cubic meters of soil, and putting stones in place to form
a contour road on which machines could turn. For all that we bought bulldozers; we had up to three at the house, old ones that we bought cheap and so
we had to do a lot of mechanical work on them. But that was our heroic
period when each tried, with old machines, to restore value to the soil. We
had to remake the profile of the terrain, because we were sure that the surface was not properly inclined: there had been terraces, there had been
ditches, there were holes in places. We had to remove the topsoil, put it aside,
remodel the profile of the subsoil and then put the topsoil back in order to
reconstitute a perfect slope. So we worked like that, we completed one or two
hectares a year. The bank, seeing that we labored so much, encouraged us.
We mortgaged the domain, and in consequence of its increase in value, the
bank gave us each year a little more money. Well after that things were
easier.

Well, another important revolution in the creation of new vineyards here,
consisted of the fact that people from here who had the idea of recreating the
vineyards, were interested in a new Austrian technique of planting, by a gentleman called Lens-Moser. Already before the war he had perfected, in his vineyard in Austria, a technique better adapted to mechanization. This technique is
already used in the United States, but not used in our vineyards with their old
traditions. It's the technique of low density planting and wide spacing. Well, all
our vines that we've planted here have been planted with a density three times
less than normal, with a spacing three times wider, three meters between each
row, one meter between each root.

Well, of course, this method is not officially authorized, and we obtained
permission to plant several hectares. I think that over the years about 300 to
450 hectares were planted in this new way. After twenty years of experiments
that began in 1959, they began to perfect this new method of training vines.
The advantages of it were clear. It was possible to use ordinary tractors that
could also be used in polyculture, because some growers continued polyculture
while they began planting vines. Each person did as he could in order to live
during the years a vineyard was being created. They had to wait [five to seven
years] until grapes gave wine, and they got an income from their investment.
Well, the use of classic material, with the lowered risk of frost, lowered their
costs by 40 to 50 percent. This was enormous because if you succeeded in
producing grapes at a cost 40 percent lower than traditional costs, that would

allow you to produce a cheaper wine, thus a wine, if it's good, that's going to attract buyers.

Our aim was to attract a clientele with quality wines. The quality was proven to us because all the same we had some Pinot grapes, my father planted then in 1957. So in the 1960s we began to get some wine, 1960-'61-'62. '62 produced an excellent wine and we were convinced of it. We compared a Nuits Saint Georges and the wine produced here in 1962; we didn't taste much difference, sometimes ours was better, but we never said so because all the big specialists of viticulture would have howled. That's what induced us to plant here and to buy a maximum of land: with inferior costs of production we could sell our wine two times cheaper while earning as much. That was the wager, and I suppose that after twenty years of experiments we won the wager: our region is replanted, and from 300 hectares we've grown to 1,000 hectares. There are many private holdings of quality appellations that are extremely profitable and extremely viable.

After all that came an interesting phase, that of commercialization. The vines were planted and the wine was in the cellar. Of course we had to create cellars. We didn't have enough cellar space; we had only those of our grand-fathers but they were tiny, badly arranged. We used them to store bottled wine because they had excellent temperature and humidity. But we had to build vat rooms for vinification and each of us made them with his own means. We built our own, working on weekends, days off, whenever we had time and were not among the vines.

As for sales, we envisioned a system of bottling and direct sales given that the wine of this region was not widely known, and that the merchants were not interested and the foreign market even less, ignoring the existence of our wines.

Well, there were two options open to viticulturists:

1. Those with a sizable vineyard, and who possessed a house, building and material to make and mature wine themselves and could bottle it. These persons sometimes formed into groups, either as a family as we did here, or among friends to create a group for production in common, a GAEC; it's a French juridical formula.

2. Those with too small holdings, about two hectares, could combine to set up a cooperative. Well, there is here the Cooperative des Hautes Côtes, made up of about 50 percent of the viticulturists, which is working very well, makes an excellent wine and hasn't stopped growing since the day it was constructed.

The growers who produce their own wine have also formed a group for selling it and have constructed a tasting cellar called the House of the Upper Slopes. It's a building in our regional style, erected by all of us. Its purpose is to make known and make available our wine to tourists and friends, everybody who wants to taste our wine in its wide variety. They can go to this *Maison* where they will be welcomed, served, and even provided with rustic meals.

This building is a center of publicity. It's also a place for us to meet, to get to know one another better, to unite for common action, to make known different techniques and results. We believe that "Union gives force" and that has been one of the factors of our success.

VIII

Mr. Garbail, a small viticulturist of St. Germain d'Esteuil, was one of the founders of the cooperative winery of Prigmac (Gironde) and presided over it from 1950 until 1976. In this time the cooperative served growers in twelve communes. Mr. Garbail here explains the particular problems connected with the sale of Bordeaux wines by cooperatives and individuals.

Mr. Sagnes: How do you go about selling wine?

Mr. Garbail: We sell to a wholesale merchant with the local broker acting as intermediary. It's the broker who gathers samples and who presents them to the wholesaler; he sends in a dozen, as many as he can. The merchant consults his cellar master who tastes them, and then buys the ones that suit him. But I'll tell you this, in general, for cooperative wineries, nearly all the wines are analogous; they're sound and don't run the risk of being refused.

Mr. Sagnes: Can you age this wine indefinitely, or does it become bad?

Mr. Garbail: It never becomes bad; simply it is no longer the same wine; it loses some of its youth, but it's very good. I must tell you that during a tasting, the mayor of a neighboring town who had invited us, gave us a wine of 1897. I assure you that it was good.

Mr. Sagnes: Well then, the longer you conserve Bordeaux wine, the better it is?

Mr. Garbail: But there are limits. First, it depends on the year. You have a good year; when it's a good year, that means that the wine is full, it has body, it has all the qualities to age in the bottle. Well then, it needs up to ten years before it's good to drink. That's in a good year, not every year.

Mr. Sagnes: For example, is 1975 a good year, must it be kept for ten years?

Mr. Garbail: To do it justice, yes. The error made today, with the accelerated vinification that we presently see, is to drink it too young. No one waits long enough; the longer you wait, the better it is. Now you've got the wines of other years, which are less full-bodied, which are acceptable, and after three years are good to drink.

   Not all years are good to produce fully matured bottles. Moreover, for example, among the châteaux there were the years 1953 and 1963, I'm thinking principally of 1963, when they didn't even sell anything. They removed their wines from the market. They preferred to sacrifice the wine rather than down-grade their reputation. Well then, at times, the châteaux sell a secondary appellation, at whatever price they can get [using a different label]. They don't sell, for example, a bottle of Château Bechevelle if it does not truly have the quality of a Bechevelle.

Sometimes they exceed the grape yield allowed them. [Wines of AOC status are the produce of vineyards with limited yields per hectare. The higher the wine's status the lower the allowable yield]. Some may be allowed to produce only thirty-eight hectoliters per hectare. When they surpass that yield they are obliged to give their wine a secondary appellation.

Mr. Sagnes: How can one know whether a particular grower has exceeded his legal yield, given that he makes his own wine?

Mr. Garbail: That's not difficult. If he wants to commercialize his wine he's obliged to declare it [state the quantity produced to local officials who know his normal yield]. If he doesn't declare it, he must not sell it. On that one is very strict, the Fraud Service oversees this, and there is a controller in each canton. It's very strict that, and for cooperative wineries also. In Médoc, in general, we're held to 45 hectoliters per hectare. Sometimes we get 60 hectoliters. Then, if you have a [classified] label, you're accorded 5 hectoliters over the limit; the rest must be sold off as ordinary wine. In general we try not to surpass the limit because an excess quantity yields less quality. That's always been the case. We manage to keep to our norm of 45 hectoliters by planting 6,000 vines rather than 8,000 vines per hectare. That means the vine rows are more widely spaced.

IX

Mr. Fernand Marisy, grape grower at Cumières (Champagne), is splendidly representative of the self-made man; he truly sums up the vigneron who has seen the worst of times and is now basking in the best of times. We can not state that he progressed from rags to riches; his living odyssey has rather been a hard struggle from wage worker to independent owner. His keen sense of pride lies in his sense of accomplishment; he has made it on his own by dint of sacrifice and determination. His dogged individualism still lingers as a trace of an older culture, gradually mitigated by the economic necessity of forming part of a collective group, the cooperative, to transform his grapes into wine. One can visualize him standing, as a grower, alone against the elements: and yet one must see him as a willing cog in the collective machinery of the winery.

Mr. Marisy: As for my family background, my parents were natives of a farm community about thirty-five kilometers from here. It was a place where there

were not vines, only farming. I became a viticulturist after the end of the war.
I took part in the resistance and joined the Leclerc Division. Military life
helped me to mature, and I got the idea of leaving this farm country where
you hardly earned a living at that time.

So I arrived here on a bicycle, like that, by chance. I saw a large estate. I
asked the owner if there was a job open. He said yes, driving a truck. I had
a military driver's license so he hired me on the spot. I worked for many
years on a large estate here in Cumières, for a big viticulturist who taught me
the profession. And gradually I bought small bits of land. I spent twenty-five
years building my small holding, little by little. I worked twenty-two years as a
laborer, team boss, got responsibilities. Finally I set up on my own, and I've
always been on good terms with my former employer. I got some good advice
and very good training in an enterprise that was highly disciplined. I and my
wife worked hard, to be sure. We had six children and I've succeeded in
finding positions for all my children. Now, having reached sixty, we've started
thinking about retiring. My living conditions were rather hard in the beginning,
housing conditions especially after the war because in this area destruction
came to 80 percent. In 1940 the Germans burned it out, and as a young
couple our living conditions were somewhat precarious, but in those days you
couldn't demand too much.

We lived in one room only, my wife and I, and when we had the first baby
there wasn't even water, only electricity. It was rudimentary; you had to pass
through the attic to get in the large room. Afterward, we had a second room
that my employer had made for us. Then our housing improved over a long
time, with water and a toilet in the courtyard. There was no bathroom. But
when you're young you can accept all that.

There were other workers because it was a big domain with both vines and
farmland. Then there were lots of fruit trees because at that time the wine of
Champagne wasn't selling widely. Before 1950 living conditions were harsh, and
large growers had to grow grapes, cereals, and fruit so they could fall back on
grains and potatoes if champagne didn't sell well. For example, there were a
lot of peach trees here.

Mr. Loubère: Were the other workers married and housed like you?

Mr. Marisy: Most were married and everybody lived in the village. Two of
them lived three kilometers from here, at Damery. As for me I was housed for
eight years by my employer. After that I found a house with some vines for
rent. While working for my employer I cultivated the vines that came with the
house. That permitted me, in addition to my wage, to get ahead, to buy other
land. My wage served exclusively to pay for household needs, and what I
earned outside the usual hours of work for my boss, I put toward buying a
piece of land. At that time land was not so expensive; it was still accessible.
As I told you, on the slopes there were many fruit trees because before the
war (1939) growers sold little wine and few grapes and they planted fruit trees
in place of vines. After the war there was an extension of the vineyard and

the possibility of selling a little more wine, grapes and champagne. Naturally they began to rip out the trees and, as for me, I benefitted from the low price of this land. So I began to plant vines on it, which came out much cheaper than buying a planted vineyard. We planted ourselves. What's more, with my brother-in-law who lived in Cumières, we did our own grafting. We had learned how to graft and everything there was about vinegrowing. We planted our own vines to earn more rather than buy them. We sold the surplus to make a little gain.

We had a nursery. All that required a good deal of labor. We worked on holidays, on Sundays, and then in the evenings until eleven o'clock or midnight to prepare the grafts. We worked hard; we even worked in the vines of other owners to spray them in the evening or very early in the morning. After the war we still had the traditional fifteen days of paid vacation, and during these fifteen days, we went to work for another employer. It was easy for us to work for others; we got along well with them, and we had lots of offers. We couldn't satisfy all the offers because we were always in demand. We selected the best offers.

Mr. Loubère: What were the working conditions like?

Mr. Marisy: That was still the time of horse-drawn plows, and hand-machine sulfuring. The horse-drawn sprayer made its appearance about 1950. This phase lasted several years until the arrival of the first *enjambeurs*, which brought about a veritable revolution in Champagne. That was in 1955–56. It was at Cumières that there was the first straddle-tractor and it was I who drove it with my employer, Mr. Lucien Leclerc. At that time the change was astounding because our methods of work were completely changed. For example, when spraying vines with the tractor, we could cover six rows of vines at one time, twelve going and coming, whereas with a hand sprayer we covered only two. Then there was another revolution, the use of herbicides so that we no longer had to plow the vines, to pile up soil over the roots and then even it out. Doing this by hand was very hard work, and it was hard on the vines because it destroyed some roots. We've been using herbicides for about fifteen years. We tried it out tentatively at first. That was not a spontaneous leap because the vigneron is distrustful by nature. It must be the large grower who experiments first, and the others say, "Ah, since it worked for him, now we're going to try it!" We prefer that our neighbor be the fall guy *(essuie les plâtres)* as we say in our jargon.

Mechanization in general improved improved the living conditions of workers. It's also decreased their number, since there where you needed ten persons, now you only need three, for example. What's more, mechanization also penetrated the cellars where the personnel has declined. Workers who retired were not replaced. Rarely were they fired. Sometimes vine laborers left voluntarily; they found better jobs in the big champagne firms. Work conditions and pay in the big firms are better than in the vineyards. In general, workers of a certain age were kept on by their employers.

There was a retirement system, social security, before the war, and it was improved after. Whoever worked continuously until the age of sixty received a decent pension that allowed him to live, with a little vegetable garden and a bit of vineyard that he kept to get his personal bottle of champagne. Pensions are even better now.

The size of holdings have increased over time. For example, in 1950, with not even a hectare of vines, a family lived, if it had a vegetable garden and some animals. Now you need two and a half hectares. That's evolved with progress and needs because everything is enormously expensive: chemicals, sprays, material, so you need more land to survive. A viticulturist with two and a half hectares can now live easily.

Mr. Loubère: When you were a worker did the trade union attract many villagers?

Mr. Marisy: No. At that time unions existed more in the towns than in the countryside. In the countryside they grew especially on the large estates. On small estates they had a hard time to grow. As for me I never belonged to any union. I always worked things out personally with my employer. I never had any problems with my employer, never, never.

Some workers looked to the union for certain problems. There were those who wanted big wages while not being sufficiently productive. As for me I never had any problem. I was apt at doing my job: plowing, cellar work, vine training, supervision. When I wanted a raise I told my boss to give me one or I would quit. He recognized my work and was grateful to me. I don't see why I should join a union. Moreover, they were in politics and that I've never liked. I never asked to be protected by anyone; I've always defended myself.

Mr. Loubère: Have cooperatives helped the vignerons?

Mr. Marisy: Yes, enormously. That's to say that each individual doesn't have to invest in cellar equipment that's very expensive. Now we can work as a collective which benefits a lot of us. Also, the quality of our wine is raised because we can centralize production over a wide area. Since tasting and technical committees supervise our wine very closely, we're protected against accidents. The viticulturist who works alone, on his own, has heavy investments, and he's at the mercy of accidents, such as wine that won't sparkle, while we're fully guaranteed against that.

We worked very hard in the past. now we're happy; we're satisfied.

Conclusion

THIS BROAD VIEW of the life and work of the vigneron has shown that there are remarkable similarities among the major vineyard regions of France, in areas such as women's work, patterns of leisure and festivity, customs surrounding family life and generational relations. We emphasize similarity and not identity because numerous and subtle differences exist as well. Class relations, for example, in an area of mass production such as the Mediterranean south have taken on a different color from class relations in Burgundy and Champagne, where vineyard workers (as distinct from property owners) were far fewer in number and less likely to think along class lines as opposed to professional alignments.

In many cases, social class has influenced the experience of vignerons to a larger extent than have specific regional characteristics. Workers and small growers in the lower south, for example, have had a tradition of militancy going back to the early 20th century which is not very different from that of their Champenois counterparts. Social class has also lent a similarity to women's lives and work in regions whose vineyard economies are as different as those of Mme Douley in Champagne and Mme Rouaix in Languedoc. Women in the vines have continued to work the double day as have women in the workforce almost everywhere. As vigneronnes they labored actively in the vines with men, but were also engaged in a multiplicity of jobs apart from men, including the raising of their own children and caring for their households, as well as the households of their middle class counterparts. The wives of small, independent growers, regardless of region, performed a multiplicity of tasks, although they may have remained more confined within the boundaries of family and village for work and sociability, than men.

If class has been an important determinant of mentality and behavior, there have clearly been those from region to region, who have struggled to leave the constraints of class. Workers in all winegrowing areas have begun to be landowners— a process which began before World War II, but which has since accelerated with the availability of agricultural credit banks and the desire for independence. For some, the acquisition of property has meant the demise of class consciousness; for others it has been the fulfillment of a dream of autonomy.

Most vignerons agree that the material conditions of grape growers and wine producers have improved considerably since the early 1900s. Indeed, where better conditions could not be achieved, there has been rural depopulation; not as a

187

solution but as an escape from the harsh lot of past generations. No matter where we look—housing, work, transportation, diet, hygiene and health—growers and workers have seen their living standards improve since the beginning of the century. They live and work more comfortably. Do they live more comfortably, however, with the other changes that improvements have brought? Social scientists often repeat that the major discovery of modern society is change itself, the acceptance of, indeed the demand for, innovation; the "invention of invention." There is much validity in this statement. However, many older vignerons often express misgivings about technological change, as well as about the transformation of personal relations, the weakening of family ties, and the isolation of individuals from the larger community. Although in some cases, their memories may idealize past conditions, the elderly vignerons, with their roots in another time, are often the least certain about the benefits of technological and social change.

Patterns of leisure and festivity also show a remarkable similarity among viticultural regions, ranging from those confined to the immediate family to those of a more public nature within a village or rural town. Here, conviviality, which the French call *sociabilité*, was as common in the cold north as in the torrid south, on the broad coastal plains of the west as in the valley slopes of the east. Everywhere, the mixed *veillée* was a common event up to about the 1940's, as was a sexual division of sociability, seen for example, in male gatherings at the local café, at times in accordance with political alliances, always in accordance with class identities. Not even rising standards of living have changed this age-old cleavage in rural society.

Apart from these similarities, there are still important differences among viticultural populations. Material well-being as a permanent achievement is an assumption more common among the producers of fine wines, whose incomes have continued to rise over the years, than among those who produce more common wines. The vignerons of the lower south are less trusting of the durability of prosperity and they display a keen anxiety about the future. Most of them have managed to survive, yet they have witnessed the failures of comrades who had to sell or even abandon their vineyards. The emigration of these men and women has left many villages too small to survive as viable centers of life. Southern growers have combined their economic grievances caused by low prices and the lack of sales of their wine with a militant sense of regional loyalty that is equally menaced by outsiders (that is, northerners). Defense is their watchword.

The independent artisanal mentality which has characterized vignerons for centuries has been strong enough to prevent some from joining labor unions, but not so strong that those of the less aristocratic wine-making regions such as Languedoc-Roussillon, do not see the benefits of cooperative wineries. Indeed, growers in the lower south and in the Rhône valley in particular, have turned massively to cooperatives in an effort to survive on the land they love. And they have not been entirely disappointed. If contemporary cooperatives are somewhat removed from their initially socialist or collectivist inspiration, they have nonetheless created a sense of solidarity for the small independent growers who belong to them. Grower-owned wineries have brought many of the material gains and security that characterize many grape growers today and have mitigated the anxiety normally experienced by independent vignerons in these regions. These cooperatives have imposed greater discipline on viticulturalists by refusing to accept inferior fruit and also by using the latest equipment in the wine-making process. The old belief that cooperatives could never turn out good wine has been proved false. On the contrary, their future is relatively secure. Cooperatives however, have not attracted all those vignerons whose individualism and artisanal sense of pride have survived the recent tendency towards concentration and large scale operations. In areas of fine wine production such as Burgundy and Champagne, the notion that small is beautiful and profitable persists. Still, these growers share something important with the cooperators: a love of the land. Very few landowners, however small their holding, would willingly give it up.

On the other hand, many have been more willing to give up the task of wine making to trained specialists. And this sector of the industry, viniculture, has also evolved along lines that were already apparent in the later nineteenth century. The chemistry of wine has become less and less of a mystery, and the maker's control of the process, from the vineyard to the bottle, is now well established. Mechanization has accompanied this change, from the initial crushing of the grapes to the application of labels on the bottles. The mechanization of viticulture has had an even more direct effect on rural life because most growers have continued to cultivate their own vineyards. Specialized tractors have replaced animals to pull plows and large chemical sprayers. This change has certainly relieved the vigneron of the physically exhausting work of tilling the soil by hand to remove weeds. Even pruning's physical effort has been eased by the introduction of pneumatic shears. A system approaching full mechanization has appeared since the 1940s chiefly in the lower south and in the Bordelais where the first mechanized harvesters have appeared in the large vineyards that can benefit from their use. The use of machines does not differentiate one region from another, but the extent of their use varies considerably; mechanization has also had a varied effect on those who have been touched by it. A boon to the large and small grower alike, machines have usually meant unemployment for the worker.

All of these innovations have come together to provide vignerons with more leisure than their grandparents ever dreamed of. Most of our older interviewees tend to miss not the hard labor of the past, but the uses of leisure. Communal gatherings for conversation, singing, dancing, game-playing, courting and festivity have very nearly come to an end, at least as regular events. Entertainment designed to fill the longer hours of leisure has become increasingly commercialized, provided by professionals via the cinema, television and spectator sports. The village, it is widely felt, survives as a place to sleep, eat and watch television, with little life and character of its own. Although there are numerous exceptions to this view, some astute observers of village and small town life question whether greater leisure has had entirely beneficial effects. It has not, for example, prevented younger people from leaving the village.

Much has been written about the rural exodus in France—an exodus in evidence since the end of the 19th century and which accelerated rapidly after World

War II. Indeed, the "vanishing peasant" identified by Henri Mendras and others was responding to the very real and pressing conditions of rural life: repeated market crises, the relatively harsh conditions of existence, the higher wages and greater creature comforts of urban life. These conditions have affected vignerons just as they have affected other rural dwellers, and although many of these conditions are now changing and some have found the means to survive the periodic instability of the market, others, especially youths, continue to make their way from the vineyard to the town. Neither the increasing leisure time or the relatively easy working conditions which have been the main benefits of mechanization have succeeded in holding the younger generation since World War II. Who, our interviewees ask, quite legitimately, will be left to train the vines in the future?

Index